Judaism in America

The Columbia Contemporary American Religion Series

Columbia Contemporary American Religion Series

The spiritual landscape of contemporary America is as varied and complex as that of any country in the world. The books in this new series, written by leading scholars for students and general readers alike, fall into two categories: some titles are portraits of the country's major religious groups. They describe and explain particular religious practices and rituals, beliefs, and major challenges facing a given community today. Others explore current themes and topics in American religion that cut across denominational lines. The texts are supplemented with carefully selected photographs and artwork and annotated bibliographies.

—

Roman Catholicism in America
CHESTER GILLIS

Islam in America
JANE I. SMITH

Buddhism in America
RICHARD HUGHES SEAGER

Protestantism in America
RANDALL BALMER AND LAUREN F. WINNER

JUDAISM

in America

Marc Lee Raphael

COLUMBIA UNIVERSITY PRESS

NEW YORK

COLUMBIA UNIVERSITY PRESS
Publishers Since 1893
New York   Chichester, West Sussex

Copyright © 2003 Columbia University Press
All rights reserved

Library of Congress Cataloging-in-Publication Data
Raphael, Marc Lee.
    Judaism in America / Marc Lee Raphael.
        p.   cm. — (Columbia contemporary American religion series)
    Includes bibliographical references and index.
    ISBN 0–231–12060–5 (alk. paper)
        1. Judaism—United States—History. 2. Jews—United States—
    Identity. 3. United States—Religion. I. Title. II. Series.

BM205.R37 2003
296'.0973—dc21
                                                    2003041010

Designed by Brady McNamara

♾

Casebound editions of Columbia University Press books
are printed on permanent and durable acid-free paper.

Printed in the United States of America
c 10 9 8 7 6 5 4 3 2 1
p 10 9 8 7 6 5 4 3 2 1

CONTENTS

ACKNOWLEDGMENTS

My research for this book has included attending a full worship service (and, as the reader will note frequently, listening to conversations at the food table afterward) at more than one hundred Conservative, Orthodox, Reconstructionist, and Reform synagogues all over the United States. In addition, I have frequently used the archives of these congregations and conducted interviews (usually informal) with the rabbis and (less frequently) other professionals who served these institutions. On rare occasions I have recorded the sermons I heard during worship services and the conversations I participated in after worship.

This is therefore both a history of Judaism in America and a participant-observer description of Judaism in contemporary America. Printed and manuscript records provide the main sources for the historical sections; interviews and participation are the primary sources for the descriptive parts of the book. Since I identified more than two thousand synagogues and more than two thousand rabbis before making my choices of where to visit, my "sources" are but a sample of the variety of Judaic life in this country, but I hope they are representative.

A few individuals played important roles in the gestation, evolution, and conclusions of this book. James Warren, executive editor at Columbia University Press, invited me to write the volume and provided regular suggestions and critiques as well as support when I encountered a serious obstacle. He has made the final product much better than it would have been without him. Jeffrey S. Gurock, Lily Klaperman Professor of Jewish History at Yeshiva University, has been an uninterrupted source of information, strength, and encouragement. Nobody knows more about the history of Jews and Judaism in America than he does, and I have learned much from him, while being endlessly grateful for his friendship.

The congenial interlibrary loan librarians at the College of William and Mary have provided sustained support, made more difficult by my living 150 miles from the library. My carpool mate and colleague, Julie Galambush, endured six hours each week for two years listening to my ideas about Judaism in America. Her questioning and reflections clarified much and her encouragement affirmed much. I am appreciative of her immense patience and friendship. The manuscript was largely crafted at Harris-Manchester College of the University of Oxford. I am grateful to the late Donald Tranter and his wife Joan for lodging arrangements and gracious hospitality, and to Ralph Waller, principal of the college, for arranging an environment conducive to scholarly writing. I continue to write books with a pen and sheets of paper, but the press found this medium unacceptable. Tamara Cooper cheerfully helped me transform my text to a computer-readable format. And my wife, Linda Schermer Raphael, has taken considerable time from her own teaching, research, and writing to accompany me to worship services and to reflect on what we saw and heard. She has been a continual blessing.

Judaism in America

CHAPTER ONE

What is American Judaism?

There are about six million Jews in the United States today, and the population projections by most demographers are for an "expected long-term decline in numbers."[1] Three commonly discussed reasons for this projection are lack of new immigrants, low reproduction, and high intermarriage rates. There does not seem to be any likelihood of large-scale Jewish immigration to the United States in the near future. Jews have been notorious, at least since the 1950s, for residing in the lowest ecological fertility category, or being unable to even reproduce the parental generation. And, Jewish intermarriage rates are high, with a concomitant dilution of each generation.[2] Thus their absolute numbers have continually declined, and, since the American population has continually increased, they are a steadily declining percentage of the general population. When the author began his academic career, Jews were 3 percent of the American population; in 2000 they were 2 percent.

And these Jews live overwhelmingly in the suburbs of the largest American cities, and (secondarily) in those same cities. They are, by every measure, among the highest socioeconomic groupings in the United States, and they tend (no matter to which of the four branches of American Judaism they belong) to share many of the characteristics of upper-middle-class urban Americans. Whether Orthodox or Reform, their wedding receptions and bar mitzvah parties, the clothing they wear on special occasions at the synagogue, and their occupations, are quite similar to those of non-Jewish Americans at the same socioeconomic level. When the author interviewed hotel personnel who cater wedding receptions, they repeatedly told him that the only significant difference between a Jewish wedding reception and a non-Jewish wedding reception is that the Jews eat more food and drink less liquor than the non-Jews.

This sociological discussion of American Jews does not presume to know precisely how to define Jews. Jews often joke about how the definition of a Jew in modern times is anyone who asks the question "What is the definition of a Jew in modern times?" Indeed, the joke has much truth, for American Jews are preoccupied with trying to define who is a Jew. Synagogue leaders must define a Jew before they can decide who to admit and, even if they admit as members most anyone who knocks on the door and pays their dues, they must ponder how "Jewish" must one be to be called to the Torah for a bat mitzvah or to serve as an officer of a congregation.[3] If this quandary is left unresolved, so congregational leaders explain, the synagogue could become a place where there are no boundaries (often citing Judaism in the first and second centuries of this era), and soon Christians (or, minimally, non-Jews) might be participating in the most sacred rites of Judaism and/or selecting the rabbi who will lead the congregation.

Thus, is someone with one Jewish and one non-Jewish parent a Jew? What if the non-Jewish parent has converted, for a Jewish convert is, legally speaking, just as "Jewish" as someone born of two Jewish parents? But are all conversions equally valid, e.g., does each wing of American Judaism recognize conversions of the other wings? Does it matter whether the Jewish parent is the mother or the father? And in how much investigation should the synagogue leaders, or "Membership Committee," engage? Ought the policy to be "Don't ask," or should the membership application have sufficient questions for the congregation to determine how Jewish the applicant might be? These, and other questions about Jewish identity, must necessarily occupy the Judaic community, lest it ignore all boundaries and surrender any distinction between someone who is Jewish and someone who is not.

Early in American history Jews mastered the challenge of acculturation and became active in politics and culture on America's own terms. But we are not chronicling the (largely) secular story of Jewish blockade-runners, civilian contractors, and financiers in the Revolution, or Jews who served important political, judicial, entrepreneurial, and (especially) cultural roles in the late nineteenth and throughout the subsequent century.

President Theodore Roosevelt, in October 1906, appointed Oscar Straus of the Macy's department store family secretary of commerce and labor, and he became the first Jewish cabinet member. Numerous Jews early in the twentieth century—among them Eddie Cantor, Irving Berlin, and Al Jolson—and late in the same century—including Steven Sondheim, Bob Dylan, and Barbara Streisand—were deeply committed to American mass culture. But their stories have been told, repeatedly;[4] our task is to explore the history of Judaism, the religious tradition, in the setting of America. This remains to be told by historians.

If we generally define the subjects of this book as those who participate in the religion of Judaism, whether in the synagogue, the home, or both, as opposed to those Jews who deny any interest in the religion of Judaism, it only leaves us with about half of those six million American Jews. No more than half the Jews in the United States consider themselves "religious," and less than half the Jews in America are affiliated with a synagogue. True, many affiliate during the years they have children at home, so that they will be eligible to participate in the holidays, life-cycle events, and schooling that affect their children, and then drop their affiliation (i.e., stop paying annual dues), but many of these Jews consider themselves "religious" (Judaic), even without synagogue membership, and attend worship services on Yom Kippur, celebrate Passover with a seder or liturgical meal, and hire a rabbi to officiate at the wedding of their daughter.

Although synagogue membership alone, therefore, does not reveal all those Jews who consider themselves religious and are part of this study, it is the main arena for expressions of Judaism in America. While the number of Orthodox synagogues remains a mystery (the national organization does not reveal figures and estimates thus vary widely),[5] there are about 875 Reform congregations, 850 Conservative congregations, and 100 Reconstructionist synagogues in the United States. Orthodox totals are less than either Reform or Conservative, as fewer than 10 percent of American Jews affiliate with an Orthodox congregation. The best and most frequently cited estimate is that of those Jews affiliating with synagogues about 45 percent are Reform, 42 percent are Conservative, 9 percent Orthodox, and 4 percent Reconstructionist. Despite the small percentage of

affiliates, Orthodox Jews are often given one-third representation in Jewish communal affairs. Just as America has long been seen as "Protestant,
Catholic, and Jewish," as if Jews constituted something like a third of the
religious population and Muslims did not exist, so American Judaism is often perceived as "Orthodox, Conservative, and Reform," as if these are
three more or less equal sectors of the religious community.

It is not easy to generalize, even by sectors, about the role that Judaism plays in the life of American Jews. There are Jews who consider
themselves Orthodox who do not make the hundreds of commandments—ethical and ritual—part of their daily lives, and there are Conservative and Reform Jews who do. But, generally, Orthodox Jews work
harder to observe the letter of scores of commandments found in the first
five books of the Hebrew Bible (= Torah), as interpreted by rabbinic authorities over the past two thousand years, and Conservative, Reconstructionist, and Reform Jews pick and choose from those same commandments. Historically speaking, the non-Orthodox wings of
American Judaism have been more observant of the spirit than the letter
of the commandments. Those who pick and choose from the hundreds
of commandments in the Torah give those they choose to follow a liberal, rather than a literal, interpretation. Traditional Jews, for example, interpret the biblical commandment prohibiting fire on the Sabbath to include the internal combustion engine, and thus they do not ride in
motorized vehicles on that day; Conservative Jews observe this prohibiton for everything except travel to and from the syngogue, while Reconstructionist and Reform Jews, including rabbis, travel on the Sabbath, but (generally) try to limit their travel to those places and activities
they consider (broadly) in the spirit of the Sabbath.

All modern Judaisms—Conservative, Orthodox, Reconstuctionist,
Reform, even ultra-Orthodox—are movements of either the nineteenth or
twentieth centuries, and all emerged as a response to both the Enlightenment and Emancipation. There were deep divisions within Judaism over
the program of the Enlightenment and Emancipation, and they may be
summarized, simply, as a battle between integrationists and separatists, between those who welcomed modernity and tried to adjust Judaism to it, and
those who rejected modernity and tried to not permit its influences to infect
them. Some believed they could reform Judaism and make it consonant
with modernity, though many argued over how much reform should be

permitted. Some claimed, quite erroneously, to have maintained tradition unchanged, but they too adjusted to modernity, although they made every attempt to evaluate it via Torah, to evaluate modern culture by the standards of Jewish law. For a few, this evaluation led them to an absolute rejection of modernity, to as complete a segregation as was possible in our time. Ironically, these resisters have some of the most sophisticated websites of any religious group.

Worship

The varieties of religious expression within the American Judaic community are considerable, even within the same branch or wing. In one Reform Jewish synagogue in Washington, D.C., on almost any Friday evening (Sabbbath eve), the worshippers (men in coats and ties seated together with women in dresses) rise from their pews as the rabbis walk down the aisle of the two-thousand-seat sanctuary toward the elevated pulpit while the choir and cantor sing an English hymn that is found in the 1897 *Hymnal* of the Reform movement as well as the *Book of Common Prayer* of the Episcopal Church. In another Reform congregation, a short walk away, the Sabbath eve worshippers, dressed casually with men and women sitting on folding chairs on a cement floor in a sanctuary only a few years old, join the song leader cum cantor (and the accompanist playing keyboards) as she sings an ancient Hebrew melody with music composed by a contemporary Jewish songwriter of liturgical music.

In an Orthodox synagogue in Los Angeles on a Saturday (Sabbath day) morning, the male worshippers, separated from the women who are upstairs, pray (mostly) at their own pace exclusively in Hebrew with melodies, inflections, and body movements (so they claim) transfered through the centuries unchanged. They bow their heads and bend their knees in an exaggerated fashion, davening—investing each word and melody with all their physical, emotional, and spiritual energy. They seem to know that the perfect prayer is the one that is prayed not only with the soul but by the whole of the human being, body and soul. At another Orthodox congregation, a short distance away, the male worshippers sit on one side of an aisle from the women worshippers, each in full view of the other, the prayer book is in both Hebrew and English, and much of the latter is read, the worship leader periodically announces the page numbers, and before a portion of the Torah scroll (consisting of the Five Books of Moses in Hebrew on parchment) is read, it is passed among the men and then among the women so that every worshipper may be touched by its sanctity.

While the differences are many and significant, a visitor to a typical synagogue on a Sabbath morning would notice that the service is divided into three main parts. The first part, morning prayers, is recited in Orthodox, (most) Conservative, and (some) Reconstructionist and Reform congregations daily, with additions appropriate for the Sabbath. Psalms and the Shema, which is an affirmation of the unity and sovereignty of God (Deuteronomy 6:4—"Hear O Israel, Adonai is our God, Adonai is One"—is one of Judaism's central beliefs), with some blessings, follow. The *Amidah*, the standing devotion that combines individual and communal prayers, is recited silently in Conservative and Orthodox synagogues and chanted together in Reform and (most) Reconstructionist services. All these introductory prayers help prepare the worshippers to pray, to ready their bodies and souls and consciousness for worship. What a Jew does individually will lead her or him to the spiritual strength one derives from praying together in a community.

The Torah reading is the spiritual heart of the liturgy. It begins with the opening of the ark and taking out the Torah scroll. Though sacred, the scroll is usually carried in a procession, with abundant singing, through the sanctuary for all to see and touch. No matter the amount read in a particular synagogue, the Torah is read consecutively each Sabbath throughout the year. The rabbi (or a bar/bat mitzvah candidate) usually gives a synopsis of the weekly reading, which is further divided into seven smaller sections. Members of the congregation or family of a bar/bat mitzvah are honored by receiving an *aliyah* (going up) to recite blessings before and after each section is read, or, in rare occasions, to read a section themselves. When there is a bar/bat mitzvah, the young man or woman chants the final portion, known as the *maftir*. Following this, the Torah is usually lifted (*hagbah*) and redressed (*g'lilah*). Then a congregant, or the bar/bat mitzvah, chants the *haftarah*, an additional reading from the Prophets. The same Torah and *haftarah* portions are read in synagogues all over the world.

The third part of the service is called the *musaf*, or additional service. It contains concluding prayers and hymns that acknowledge the Jews' unique relationship with God and praise God's name, as well as the Kaddish (a mourner's prayer), and a concluding hymn. After the final song it is customary for Jews to greet each other by saying "shabbat shalom," (may you be blessed with) a Sabbath of peace and to move to an adjoining room for abundant food and beverage.

And yet it is very difficult to generalize about Jewish worship. Some congregations pray mostly in English, others mostly (if not even exclusively) in Hebrew; some have cantors and choirs who lead (or even sing on behalf of) the congregation, others have song leaders who maximize participation; some are formal, with directions for standing and sitting, while others have worshippers who know the liturgy so well the service unfolds without instructions. Some read or chant on Saturday morning, in Hebrew, the entire scriptural portion assigned for that week (roughly 1/54 of the Pentateuch), while others read a small portion of the several chapters designated for that week; some synagogues have Sabbath worship at which most (if not all) the worshippers walked to the synagogue (to observe the biblical Sabbath prohibitions against "work"), while others have Sabbath worship in which nearly everyone has left a car in the synagogue parking lot.

Despite this variety—and generally the larger the community, the more diversity—there are some commonalities. More Jews attend synagogues, whether Conservative, Orthodox, Reconstructionist, or Reform, on Rosh Hashanah (the Jewish New Year) and Yom Kippur (the Day of Atonement) than on any other occasion. The equivalent of a "Christmas and Easter" Christian are the (derisive) terms *High Holiday* or *Twice-a-Year Jew*, reserved for those Jews who attend the synagogue *only* on Rosh Hashanah and Yom Kippur. Many Jews feel an obligation to pray weekly (some even daily), but whether the worshippers come weekly or only to a few Sabbath worship services each year, every synagogue places weekly Sabbath worship (Friday evening and Saturday morning) alongside the High Holidays in importance. In most American synagogues the rabbi preaches his or her "major" (formal) sermons on the High Holidays and at least one sermon (less formal) on the Sabbath.

The centrality of the Torah is nearly universal in American synagogues. Bar mitzvah (boys) and bat mitzvah (girls) are the occasions when Jews first read from the Torah. Whether all or only part of the weekly assigned portion is read or chanted during the worship services, the rituals surrounding the removing of the Torah from the ark, the passing of the scroll from person to person (often from grandparent to parent to child), the parading of the Torah around the congregation, the touching of the Torah by worshippers as it passes, the removal of the cover and (later) returning the scroll to its cover, the calling of worshippers to the pulpit to participate in the Torah reading or the blessings surrounding the reading, the actual reading or chanting, the lifting of the scroll in the air following the reading, the return of the Torah to the ark, are familiar to a worshipper no matter which synagogue he or she attends. And in virtually every synagogue in America the assigned Torah portion is read (at least in part) during the Sabbath morning service.

The variety of prayer books found in American synagogues is large. In Washington, D.C., each of the three Reform synagogues uses a different prayer book for Sabbath worship, while in Columbus, Ohio, each of the three Orthodox synagogues uses a different prayer book (they use the Hebrew name for prayer book, siddur) for Sabbath worship. The Conservative and Reconstructionist movements are more uniform in their liturgical texts, but not every congregation will have the latest (revised) edition of their favorite prayer book, and in these synagogues too there will be different books in use. Although the structure of the prayer service is generally the same (the prayers, whether in Hebrew, in a literal English translation, or in a free English rendition generally follow in the same order, whether in full or in an abridged version, whether sung by a cantor, a choir, the congregation, or just read by the worship leader or congregation) from synagogue to synagogue and book to book, the differences are often so great that a Jew who worships regularly in one branch will sometimes be quite confused with a strange book in another branch or sector of Judaism.

Holidays and Life-cycle Ceremonies

In addition to some commonality amidst much diversity in worship, Jews celebrate life-cycle events (circumcision, giving a child a Hebrew name, bar and bat mitzvah, marriage, funeral) and holidays/festivals (Sukkot,

Simchat Torah, Hanukkah, Purim, Passover, Shavuot, Tisha B'Av) in many different ways. Prior to Passover, many Jews will clean their house thoroughly of *chametz* (any one of the five major grains—wheat, rye, barley, oats, and spelt—that has come in resting contact with water for at least eighteen minutes and thus begun the leavening process). They do this so as not to have any temptation to violate the Passover prohibition against eating or drinking anything made from any of these grains or anything in which there may be a prohibited ingredient for the entire week (or eight days) of Passover. Indeed, even the length of festivals/holidays differs from Jew to Jew and congregation to congregation; Rosh Hashanah is celebrated for two days by some Jews (one day by others), Passover is celebrated for either eight days or seven days, etc.

Some Jews will have their son circumcised in the hospital by a pediatrician and give him a Hebrew name at home on the eighth day; others will have a ritual circumciser (*mohel*) perform the operation at the home on the eighth day together with the naming ceremony (*brit* or *brit milah*); others will have the circumcision in the hospital and the naming ceremony (as in the case of girls) at some later occasion in the synagogue.

Variety

In short, not only do Conservative, Orthodox, Reconstructionist, and Reform Jews use different prayer books, arrange their seating diffferently in the sanctuary, and pray at different times (some Jews pray thrice daily, others infrequently; others have Sabbath eve prayers at sunset, most after dinner), but they also observe the special occasions of the year and the special occasions of life in a multiplicity of ways. Rabbi Milton Steinberg, some time ago (1947), described American Jews as strict traditionalists and modernist-traditionalists (or "modernists"). But this division is far too simple; within the Orthodox community alone large numbers of Jews may be described as modern, liberal, neo-, centrist, right-wing, sectarian. and much more. And what you see is not necessarily what you get. Many strict traditionalists, who observe every ritual and ceremonial requirement punctiliously, do not wear a head covering (*kippah* or yarmulke) at work or in the public sphere; others, far less observant, cover their heads at all times (a sign of religious respect). What ultimately unites them, and indeed all religious Jews, is an affirmation of being Judaic, of affirming Judaism as their religion. But how they express that affirmation ranges far and wide.

Jewish Versus Judaic

There are, and this is often striking to Christians, Jews who do not affirm Judaism. It is rare, if not improbable, to find someone who says "I am a Presbyterian but I do not have anything to do with the Presbyterian Church or with Presbyterianism," for affirming Presbyterianism is affirming a religion. But Jews are a people, a nationality, an ethnic group, and a religion, and some Jews affirm their Jewishness but not Judaism. They do not consider themselves Judaic. Born of Jewish parents and thus (even if only the mother is Jewish) considered Jewish according to those who observe Jewish law, they have abandoned anything connected to the synagogue or to religious ceremonies, customs, observances, and rituals. They might ask someone to try to secure a rabbi to conduct their funeral and to bury them in a Jewish cemetery, but they have nothing to do with the Judaic, or religious, community. Less than half the Jews in America affiliate with a synagogue, and although plenty of others attend a synagogue from time to time without affiliation (it is not required for attendance at any time), nobody knows how many Jews affirm their Jewishness but reject Judaism. But there are plenty of Jews everywhere in the country who say that they are Jewish and that they do nothing they consider "religious," including attending synagogue.

This book is about Judaism; the beliefs, doctrines, history, institutions, and leaders of the religious community. But nobody asked the millions of Jews who came to this country whether they affirmed Judaism, and no official document records whether a Jew is just Jewish or Jewish *and* Judaic. Hence, the story of Jewish history (the Jews) and the story of Judaism (the Jewish religion) have been inseparable in Jewish history. So the story of Judaism in America necessarily includes the Jews.

This book will continue with a chapter on beliefs, festivals, and lifecycle events, for nearly all Jews who consider themselves "religious," or who affiliate with a synagogue, define their Judaism by creed and doctrine and/or by their observance of holidays and sacred occasions in the life of a Jew. Broadly speaking, American Jews divide into "traditional" or "nontraditional" groupings, so we will discuss these topics by lumping everything into one of these two divisions. Of course, many Jews will be traditional in one area (e.g., fasting for twenty-four hours on Yom Kippur, eating matzah at the Passover seder) but nontraditional (e.g., driving to the synagogue on Yom Kippur, not worrying about whether the flour from which the matzah has been prepared has been specially supervised from the time the wheat is cut) in the same area, so these divisions are for purposes of discussion rather than making a claim that they describe any specific Jewish man or woman.

From this description of what Jews believe and what they do, we will move to a survey of the history of Judaism in America, beginning with the arrival of the first Jews about 350 years ago. Their European context will occupy us briefly, but we will primarily trace the broad evolution of Judaism through the several centuries, highlighting the emergence and development of the four branches or sectors of American Judaism: Conservative, Orthodox, Reconstructionist, and Reform Judaism. At the very end of this discussion, we will look at the emergence of women rabbis, a phenomenon of the last quarter-century, but only in the nontraditional wings of the community, and at the high-energy level and good health of the American Jewish religious community.

Each of the branches, sectors, or wings of American Judaism has an umbrella organization that governs the movement. Each national office coordinates the activities of the hundreds of synagogues (only about one hundred for the Jewish Reconstructionist Federation) that are members of the association, and thousands of synagogue members wait enthusiastically for the biennial conventions of their national movement. The national office might provide programs to convene and train new synagogue presidents, publications for use in youth and adult education, placement bureaus for selecting a new rabbi, regional leaders skilled in conflict management and synagogue fund-raising, or a comprehensive guide to "Kosher for Passover" foods. We will look separately at each of these central addresses of the four wings of American Judaism.

Jews gather in synagogues of all kinds to read or sing together the rabbinically ordained recitation of the Amidah and the biblically ordained recitation of the Shema, as well as other blessings, poems, prayers, psalms, and readings that fill the prayer books of each branch of American Judaism.

The two holiest vessels in a synagogue (in order) are the people and Torah scrolls, but even the Torah service—the most immediate and palpable interaction between Jews and their Scripture—has wide variations from wing to wing as well as within a single wing. Conservative Jews, for example, wonder who is entitled to be called to the Torah. Can women receive such an honor? What errors disqualify a Torah and what does the congregation do if such an error is found? What are the occasions when a congregation departs from the usual practice in the Torah reading and the Torah service? One chapter will consider the varieties of worship in the American synagogue, what has happened to the sermon in the past few decades, and how members of synagogues reach out to and respond to non-Jews.

We will follow this discussion of the American synagogue with some of the concerns that currently engage the religious community, especially spirituality, converts, "GLBT" (gay, lesbian, bisexual, and transsexual Jews), Jewish education, synagogue architecture, and the relationship to Israel. Of course, these are not independent of the synagogue, but they are featured in a separate discussion because they dominate the bulletins, leadership conversations, newsletters, and sermons across the denominations. The most common topic of dialogue and debate, the increase of "tradition" in every branch of American Judaism—or what some call the "move to the right"—is reserved for the final chapter.

Dozens of thinkers have contributed to the development of Conservative, Orthodox, Reconstructionist, and Reform Judaism in America, primarily by significantly influencing the thought of rabbis and/or laypersons, but we cannot discuss them all. The three women and five men that we have chosen to discuss appear on the "Top Ten" list of nearly every rabbi and congregant the author consulted about the most important intellectuals in American Judaism. One or two others (e.g., Rabbis Leo Jung and Joseph Soloveitchik) will be briefly discussed in the historical chapter on Judaism in America.

As mentioned above, the final chapter explores the turn (or return) to tradition that has been unfolding in all wings of American Judaism for the past few decades. While the author is a historian and not a prophet (the postbiblical Judaic tradition reserves prophecy for children and/or fools), it seems a good hunch that this phenomenon will continue, for the near future, to engage the attention of members of all branches of American Judaism.

CHAPTER TWO

Beliefs, Festivals, and Life-cycle Events

Beliefs

Few American Jewish thinkers have written anything resembling what Christians call systematic theology, or even—what was so popular in nineteenth-century Europe—a theology that collected and arranged, under various headings, scriptural and rabbinic passages with an interpretation or two added to contemporize the "theology." Even among the group with (seemingly) the most unified belief system, there are, as Emanuel Rackman has noted, "the existence of different orthodox approaches." He rightly concluded that "orthodoxy," the true or established doctrine, is "no more monolithic than the non-orthodox movements."[1]

To whom are we to listen when trying to delineate the beliefs of American Jews? The professional "thinkers"? The rabbis of the various branches? The members of synagogues? Each of these does, in fact, contribute to the beliefs of American Judaism; the rabbis may issue a platform with the "official" position of the movement, and surveys may reveal that few members of that wing actually affirm such a belief. This summary, however, will rely less on what a survey of Conservative, Orthodox, Reconstructionist, and Reform Jews might reveal than on official statements by rabbinical groups and the published thinking of rabbis and scholars. From time to time, we will supplement these printed statements of beliefs with sermons we have heard or read and discussions we have held with rabbis.

We could generalize and say that American Judaism is much less concerned with beliefs and theology than American Christianity. Every rabbi knows numerous Jews that tell her or him that although they do not believe in God, and although they do not believe in prayer, they like coming to worship services.[2] Such sentiments, so Protestant and Catholic colleagues report, are much less commonly voiced among American Christians, most of whom have been raised in an environment in which belief is more central to their religion.

Finally, I reduce Judaic beliefs to "traditional" and "nontraditional." I do so because most of Jewish thought is not rigidly bound by denomination. Nontraditional encompasses a very large part of modern Jewry (including many Orthodox), while traditional includes a sizable number of Conservative, Reconstructionist, and Reform Jews. Whether in publications or in public addresses, most rabbis and Judaic thinkers are a combination of traditional and nontraditional.

God

For the traditionalists God exists and is the one, unique (i.e., nothing can be compared to God), omniscient, eternal, wholly good Creator of the universe and of humans. Or, as one Philadelphia rabbi explained to his congregation in 2000, God is "omnipotence, sovereign wisdom, supreme justice, and incomparable goodness." God is, according to Samuel Belkin, "Possessor of the world, Overseer of the world, and Caretaker of the world." He is also, for traditionalists, the Creator of the world:

> The Holy One blessed be He created days, and took to Himself the Sabbath; He created the months, and took to Himself the festivals; He created the years, and chose for Himself the Sabbatical year; He created the Sabbatical years, and chose for Himself the Jubilee year; He created the nations, and chose for Himself Israel; He created Israel, and chose for Himself the Levites; He created the Levites, and chose for Himself the priests; He created the lands, and took to Himself the Land of Israel as a heave-offering from all the other lands, as it is written, "The earth is the Lord's and the fulness thereof."[3]

God's creation of men and women includes the formation of one's body and spirit (i.e., aspiration, belief, feeling, ideals, imagination, thought). So both the spiritual and physical life come from God, both represent the divine, both are holy. The Torah expresses this by noting that women and men are created in "God's image," i.e., that the inner capacities of humans—intelligence, mind, morality, soul, spirit, spirituality—are in God's image, not (literally) arms and legs. The Jews' intellect and emotions affirm God—the Jew knows with the mind and feels with the heart God's relation to him or her as well as the sense that the Jew has something to do with God. For the traditionalist, the Jew is bound to God and God affects the Jew.

Of course, the traditionalist knows that there has not been a uniform God concept among all Jews of all ages, and that "God" may mean one thing in moments of thought and another in moments of prayer and action. But the affirmation from Deuteronomy 6—"Hear, O Israel, Adonai is our God, Adonai is unity"—is meant to unify all the various levels (historical, mystical, personal, philosophical) of traditional religious belief. God is the Sovereign, the Ruler of the universe, who is very much concerned with the moral government of the world and the individuals in that world.

For the nontraditionalists, there is much less certainty that God is omniscient, omnipotent, and wholly good. God is, as the Conservative Jewish "platform" of 1988 expressed it, "a source of great perplexities and confusions," as well as "doubts and uncertainties."[4] The result is that nontraditionalists, in their liturgies and creedal statements, affirm a belief in God but leave the particulars to the worshipper and individual. Indeed, even among the most traditional, certainties about God are often infrequent. Norman Lamm, Orthodox rabbi and president of Yeshiva University, observed that "simple, wholesome, unquestioning faith has largely vanished."[5]

Some affirm a God much like the deity in the Bible: omnipotent, omniscient, and omnibenevolent. Others, such as the late Levi A. Olan of Dallas, part of a "generation which witnessed Auschwitz," rejected "the omnipotent view of the deity [as] a vestigial hangover from the childhood of the race" and the view of God as "both good and powerful," affirming instead that "God seems to be a limited deity who is also a suffering being along with man."[6] There are those who affirm "a presence and a power that transcends" them, but is not totally independent of them, and that emerges when they find meaning, goodness, and justice in the world. For others, as in the 1937 Reform Jewish "platform," God "is the indwelling

Presence of the world" who provides men and women with their "ideal of conduct."[7] There is no small number of Jews, affiliated with religious branches of Judaism, who believe that the supernatural, personal God of the Hebrew Bible—the one who created the world, entered into a uniquely intimate relationship with one man (Abraham) and eventually his descendants, and redeemed the descendants from slavery—was a myth that enabled the Israelites to understand their world. It is not objectively true.[8]

Still others, like Eugene Borowitz, while unable to affirm God as incomparable, omnipotent, sovereign, and supreme, have no doubt God's "Hand" may be "regularly discerned touching me and shaping my life in many ways I cannot call my own, conscious or unconscious." For him, "God redeems," and "some great historic moments" (the civil rights struggle, the Six Day War, the collapse of the Iron Curtain) were "shaped as much by God as by human agency."[9]

Revelation

The traditionalists believe that there is only one explanation for the composition of the Torah, and all "other approaches are error, distortion, heresy or even pretense." What matters is that God gave it. "Revelation . . . is meaningless," wrote one traditional Jewish theologian, "unless the revelation explicitly includes the implication of divinely given Torah."[10] God revealed the Torah—every word of all five books: Genesis, Exodus, Leviticus, Numbers, Deuteronomy—to Moses at Mount Sinai in a single revelation. Moses and the Israelites actually stood at Mount Sinai and heard the commanding voice of God; thus the Torah is also called the Five Books of Moses, as he served as the vehicle of God's revelation. Samuel S. Cohon described the revelation traditionally when he noted that "God descended in His glory amid thunder and lightning on the smoke-covered mountain, and proclaimed to Israel in a voice that all heard clearly, the flaming words of the Torah."[11] Abraham Joshua Heschel called biblical revelation "an event, not a process."[12] And Eliezer Berkovits explained the revelation at Sinai in this way: that the living God is God invisible and yet encountered. And this encounter itself is revelation—God revealed His presence to men and women. So Moses was saying to the Israelites: "At Sinai, you knew God, of His presence, of His word and command, by actual experience, in which all your senses were involved." Thus revelation for traditionalists was an event, an experience, and this experience "remains capable of being experienced" by future generations.[13]

As a result, the Torah is perfect, and all its laws (mitzvot), which traditionally number 613, are unchangeable and "forever binding" on Jews. W. Gunther Plaut expressed this succinctly: God is "their author and He has set these laws for His people to do, but not question or alter."[14] While God is the Author, and the Revealer, it was Moses who "wrote it while in direct communication with God."[15]

Without this revelation at Sinai, a non-negotiable or fundamental belief of traditionalists, "creation is revealed to be a purposeless venture" and "Jewish existence is a conclusion without a premise, a fallacy."[16] As for the second (Prophets) and third (Writings) parts of the Hebrew Bible, traditionalists generally speak of the prophets as hearing God's word and of the subsequent authors as under the "influence" of the holy spirit.

Nontraditionalists distinguish themselves most fundamentally by their radical critiques of the traditional doctrine of revelation and its reinterpretation as a human discovery. Nontradtionalists believe that modern historical research has made it certain that the so-called Five Books of Moses were not Sinaitically revealed, and they regard the Torah as the work of numerous authors over many centuries, and while it is still sacred, it is so because of the reverence demonstrated by Jews rather than by its divine authorship. It is not, as the tradionalists believe, the "record of God reaching out to man," but the results of men (and perhaps women) trying to understand God, of the Jewish people's "ever-growing consciousness of God and the moral law."[17] The Torah is the product of Israel's spiritual creativity in the course of many centuries. If "verbal formulations" result, declares the 1988 Conservative *Statement of Principles*, it is "by human beings," not God, from "an ineffable human encounter with God." It is thus imperfect, and its statutes and regulations are of varying degrees of importance and, because they are human in origin and "culturally conditioned," changeable.[18]

And since they are changeable, nontraditionalists speak of revelation as a "continuous process"[19] or the product of historical processes, with (usually) greater insight and understanding into the relationship between God and the Jewish people. Indeed, "Sinai" may not even be a specific time or place but, in the words of Plaut, "a succession of moments or . . . a succession of places," a "burst of spiritual reaching." Does this minimize its significance for Plaut? Not at all. Revelation "constitutes both the birth and the explanation of the riddle of the Jew."[20] Other Jews who deny the Sinaitic revelation, or limit the use of the word *revelation* to the Decalogue, speak of God's revelation in acts of creation, in laws of nature, in the events of history, in the minds of men and women, and in the spiritual commands God gives to women and men of special endowment.

Torah

The manner in which the traditionalists and nontraditionalists speak of Torah follows from their understanding of revelation. The former, for whom the Torah represents the revealed will of God, use the word not just for the Pentateuch or even the Hebrew Bible as a whole but in its widest sense, claiming that classical or rabbinic Jewish literature (Mishnah and Talmud), compiled more than a thousand years after the revelation at Sinai, is also (Oral) Torah. By this they mean that God gave Moses a second revelation—called Oral because, unlike the Pentateuch, written down by Moses, it was passed down orally for more than a millennium until it was put in writing early in the common era. Together, the Written and Oral Torah, "the essence of traditional Judaism," are "sufficient for all time and should control and guide the entire life and destiny" of the Jewish people.[21]

Nontraditionalists, for whom the Torah resulted from the efforts of Jews to understand God rather than from an effort to record God's word, use the word *Torah* not as the whole of Jewish teaching, revealed by God in the Bible and rabbinic literature, but as just the first five books of the Hebrew Bible. For them, Torah awakens the Jews' "sense of the holy, fosters ethical consciousness, and vitalizes the practice of religion." It is certainly "not a final deposit of truth," but it does represent "a continuous process of intellectual, moral and spiritual growth in religion."[22]

Nontraditionalists are convinced by historical investigations of the nineteenth and twentieth centuries that Judaism is an evolving faith and that the Torah had a long history. So these Jews speak of progressive revelation. Reform Jews have suggested that God conveys enough truth to satisfy the needs of each generation, and that Jewish men and women have continually grown in their understanding of God. So there was no single "flash of revelation," but "for millennia, the creation of Torah has not ceased." The Jews' "knowledge of right grew, and grew slowly, under the guidance of, and impulsion from, God."[23] Thus "rabbis and teachers, philosophers and mystics, gifted Jews in every age amplified the Torah tradition."[24] It often surprises traditionalists to discover that non-traditionalists too venerate the Torah scroll, handle it with care, hug and kiss it out of affection.

Jewish Law

For the traditionalists Jewish law is embedded in the 613 biblical commandments (mitzvot) and their explication and expansion by rabbinic authorities from the Mishnah and Talmud early in the common era to our own time.[25] Halachah is the system of Jewish behavior codified as religious law whose origins are in Torah, and "the fulfillment of *mitzvot* reaffirms a man's belief in the governship of God, in the sanctity of creation, and indirectly brings him to a state of holiness."[26] Halachah is, for them, indispensable, because it is the fundamental basis of God's will, of how God wants the Jew to live, of how to be a good Jew. All of the commandments are "divine law" (Lamm) or divine revelation, and the Jewish tradition insists on not only observing the mitzvot but understanding them as *God's* commandments. All must be obeyed, although every age requires modifications and even new interpretations of words such as *work* ("You shall do no work on the seventh day") and countless other words imbedded in the laws.

For traditionalists a Jew may have legitimate questions about cognitive faith, about how the intellect may "prove" faith statements, but not halachic practice. As Norman Lamm put it, "One can suspend intellectual judgment; one cannot suspend action." Jews may not violate a halachic norm on the basis of a cognitive doubt. The laws of the Torah, as interpreted by recognized legal authorities, are "absolute and unconditional."[27] In what lies the authority of these legal interpreters? For the traditionalists the divine authority behind Jewish law was bestowed on Moses, transmitted by him to Joshua, by Joshua to the elders, and so on down the line, up to and including the latest duly ordained Orthodox rabbi who is authorized to decide questions of ritual and civil law. And no part of life is left out of the range of these laws.

Nontraditionalists recognize that "practice is our chief means to holiness,"[28] but deny the divine origin of the commandments and thus their binding authority. No matter the degree to which they affirm Jewish law as evolving and thus subject to considerable change—and many agree with the platform of Conservative Judaism that Jewish law is "indispensable for each age" and for "authentic Jewish living"[29]—the authority for religious practice is either in each congregation (Conservative Judaism: where it resides in its rabbi) or in each individual Jew (Reform Judaism: where each individual is encouraged to make "informed choices"),[30] not in the Written and Oral Torah.

All nontraditionalists, in some manner, distinguish between the essential or abiding laws and the secondary or transitory ones. They reject the traditional interpretation of the biblical prohibition against "work" on the Sabbath as including the automobile. Some (Conservative Jews) declare it a mitzvah to use a car for the sake of attending public worship (if home and synagogue are too far apart for walking), while others (Reform Jews) acknowledge the present as more determinative than the past and ignore traditional interpretations of what constitutes "work" in trying to be religious Jews. And all declare the system of Levitical laws of purity—the foundation of the rabbinic community of antiquity and the traditional community today—to be "applicable only to by-gone ages."[31]

Covenant/Chosenness

For traditionalists the "electing call of God,"[32] or God "choosing the Jews," is based upon the covenant the Hebrew people of the Bible made with God, a covenant in which Israel took upon itself to fulfill the commandments, those hundreds of duties not required of the rest of humanity. Chosenness then, above all, means the commitment or dedication of the Jewish people to the service of God. Those Jews who strive to achieve a deeper sense of belonging to God by observing the beliefs, ceremonies, customs, moral precepts, and rituals of the Torah often refer to themselves as the "chosen people." They do not mean "privilege, but service and responsibility."[33]

Indeed, election means distinctiveness and separation, and this is the result of the greater degree of responsibility the Torah places on Jews than on others. This is, for Samuel Belkin, "the *raison d'être* of the Jewish people."[34] God "personally elects [Abraham] through a promise and establishes a perpetual covenant with him and his progeny."[35] And later, the events at Sinai "constituted a fundamental pact between God and the people."[36] For traditionalists, therefore, it is "binding upon all Jews for all time, at all times in all places."[37] Michael Wyschograd calls it the "carnal election of Israel";[38] Arnold Jacob Wolf succinctly put the position of traditionalists: "I believe that Israel is still chosen, still obligated."[39]

To nontraditionalists the concept of God "choosing" Abraham and Moses is not to be taken literally. They cannot affirm that "Israel was God's chosen"[40] or that "in His grace He singled out Israel as His special people,"[41] because they cannot affirm the notion of revelation. Israel was not God's chosen, but Israel (the Jewish people) chose Yahweh as its God. The Jewish people has chosen to try to understand God and God's ways.

These Jews are uncomfortable with phrases such as "You have chosen us," which are commonplace in the liturgy, and numerous nontraditional prayerbooks amend (e.g., "covenantship") or delete such phrases.[42] Nontraditionalists also emphasize the ideas and ideals associated with the traditional concept of covenant: "The people of Israel shall keep the Sabbath, observing the Sabbath in every generation as a covenant for all time," or "Help us to grow in loyalty to our convenant with You and to the way of life it demands: the way of gentleness and justice, the path of truth and of peace."[43] They are also concerned that non-Jews may mistakenly conclude that the concept of chosenness implies that the Jews' laws and customs are inherently better than those of others. Since nontraditonalists feel that the Enlightenment and the following two centuries undermined the "faith in the divine authorship of the Mosaic Torah,"[44] the concept of chosenness has no meaning beyond a human choice of God.

Mordecai M. Kaplan once wrote that chosenness indeed has meaning for modern Jews although they cannot reconcile the idea of a traditional covenant with post-Enlightenment thought. There are, according to Kaplan, Jews who do boast of being the "Chosen People," by "scanning every bit of news from the sport sheets to the financial columns for success stories of Jews that might serve to bolster up [their] pride."[45]

Prayer

The author asked Jews all over the country, as they would nosh (snack) following worship, why they prayed. Although a few responded that praying was a way to send an email to God and hope for a response, most offered other reasons. Among the most frequent were that prayer provides the worshipper with an opportunity to express appreciation for all that is magnificent in the world, to give thanks for life and all its bounties, to affirm Judaic values, both individual and collective, and to provide solace in a time of grief and sorrow. Rarely did I meet a Jew who engaged in spontaneous or private prayer; nearly everyone I met at synagogues felt uncomfortable praying without a fixed liturgy or with spontaneous prayer.

The fixed liturgy (the Hebrew word for prayer book is *siddur* and the Hebrew word for liturgy is *tefillah*) that traditionalists use became the official substitute for the central service of the Temple in Jerusalem after the Romans destroyed the Temple and thus eliminated the sacrificial cult. The daily regimen of three services (morning [*shachreet*], afternoon [*mincha*], and evening [*ma'areev*]) parallels the two (morning and afternoon) daily offerings in the Jerusalem Temple, as does the extra service on Sabbath morning (*musaf*), but the precise origin of the evening service is unknown. Spontaneous prayer (*avodah she'b'lev*, "service of the heart") is, of course, always permissible and welcome, but for traditional Jews the fixed liturgy (unchanged for centuries) and set services are obligatory. If one is not near a synagogue at the appropriate time for worship, one just faces East and recites his or her prayers.

The proper ambience for the act of public prayer is maximum concentration on the words (Hebrew) and the object (God) of the liturgy. Assisting the worshipper in concentrating is the separation of the sexes and the absence of distractions. While it is permitted to pray in any language, traditional Jews prefer to use as much Hebrew as possible in their prayer services. Since traditional Jewish women are not bound to the obligation of fixed prayer services, they are free either to remain at home when the men go to the synagogue to carry out their obligation of public prayers or to join them in prayer.

Traditional Jewish prayer books have two primary sections of the liturgy, the Shema ("Hear O Israel"—Deuteronomy 6:4) and its blessings (before and after), highlighting the themes of creation, revelation, and redemption, and the Eighteen Benedictions (it is known in Hebrew as the *Amidah*, "standing," *Tefillah*, "*the* prayer," or the *shemoneh esray*, "eighteen"), although the Amidah, highlighting the themes of praise, petition, and thanksgiving, is the core of every worship service, whether in its long (daily) or abbreviated (Sabbath) form. Reading from the Torah, the third part of the liturgy, is an important part of the Sabbath morning and festival services (it is also read by traditional Jews on Monday and Thursday), and traditional Jews have numerous customs associated with the reading of Scripture (e.g., to touch it at the place where the individual will begin reading with one's prayer shawl and then kiss the prayer shawl).

Among traditionalists, it takes ten adult (thirteen or older) males to initiate public prayer (of course, any number may engage in private prayer), for only adult males have this religious obligation. They wear a skullcap (Hebrew: *kippah*, Yiddish: yarmulke), a mark of piety, at all times in the synagogue. And, since for them prayer is obligatory and they thus attend Sabbath worship (if not even more) without fail, they frequently have "reserved" places in the sanctuary, seats that they occupy week after week in a ritual often as regulated as the rituals of the liturgy.

Nontraditionalists write and edit prayer books that retain only part (large or small) of the traditional fixed liturgy that among traditionalists is unchangeable. For them a siddur may modify, delete, and add to the "classic Jewish prayer book traditions" in order to "meet the needs . . . of American congregations," and "to endow the traditional Jewish service with all the beauty and dignity befitting it."[46] While some worship three times a day, once a week on the Sabbath (Friday evening or Saturday morning) is far above average for nontraditional Jews.

Men and women sit together at all nontraditional services, and customs about wearing headcovering vary widely. There is far more English in these services than among traditional Jews, though many congregations of nontraditionalists will sing and read a liturgy almost entirely in Hebrew. And since there is no sense of religious obligation among these Jews, there is no more reason to expect men than women to attend public worship.

Nearly every nontraditional prayer book has liturgies that revolve around the same two primary sections as the traditional siddur, but there will be free translations, additional Hebrew and English prayers and poetry, and (generally) the absence of some parts of the fixed liturgy. When the Torah is read, some nontraditional congregations decide how much of the weekly portion to read (traditionalists read 1/54 of the Torah every Sabbath with a fixed lectionary in order to complete the reading in one year), even, in some cases where the Leviticus or Numbers assigned portion is considered archaic, substituting more "interesting" portions. This is especially the case among nontraditionalists when it comes to the haftarah, or fixed, prophetic reading following the Torah reading, as many congregations look for a more explicit connection than is sometimes obvious in choosing the reading from the Prophets to accompany the weekly Torah portion.

Some nontraditional congregations have hardly anyone wearing a kippah, while in others nearly every male (and some women as well) will have their heads covered. Nearly every nontraditional congregation uses a gender neutral prayer book, where words such as *Father, King, Lord,* and *Master* are replaced by neutral language. Some offer a choice between exclusive male-gendered and exclusive female-gendered prayers within the liturgy men and women use together, i.e., one page where women read about God in the feminine and mention the matriarchs, and another where men may pray in the masculine and mention only the patriarchs. Some use single-gendered liturgies but think double-gendered. Others (most Reform worship services) include one special addition to the gender-neutral liturgy, naming the matriarchs in the first blessing of the Amidah. In addition, these Jews are far more likely to use melodies (if not sometimes words) with roots in contemporary popular culture. In short, nontraditionalists seek "inspiration, understanding, and *kavanah*" with their liturgies, or what they all call "spirituality."[47]

Messiah

For centuries traditional Jews have tried to discover the exact year (if not day and hour) of the Messiah's arrival, and "calculating the end" or messianic calculations were an integral part of nearly every one of the dozens of messianic movements that have erupted in the history of Judaism. All these movements, and their accompanying messianic performers, have been rejected by the Jewish people, while many of the claimants converted from Judaism. The symbols and ideas (as well as the slogans) of thse movements are biblical in origin, as is the term *Messiah* (the anointed one), and they have mixed, in varying degrees, "political aspirations, religious imperialism, and moral vindications."[48] Most often these claimants promise an imminent redemption of the Jews from their inescapable oppressions, a termination of history, and interpret current events in cosmic terms. A recent claimant, Menachem Mendel Schneersohn, who died in

1993, announced to his followers in the early 1990s that he was the "Messiah-to-be," and interpreted the fall of Communism and the war against Iraq in cosmic terms, as signs of the end of history as it has been known. Ten years later, in spite of Schneersohn's death, some of his followers continue to distribute literature that proclaims him the "Messiah-king."

Baruch M. Bokser was correct when he noted that we cannot impose a single messianic view on the varieties of Judaic messianic movements,[49] but, generally, traditionalists believe that the Messiah will be a descendant of King David (this would be impossible to prove, as there has not been a davidic family—"David and his seed" or "son of David"—in the common era). They are confident that God will eventually end the exile of the Jews from their land (a reference to the ingathering of Jews from the diaspora), restore His people to greatness, inaugurate a new era of history and time (death will be conquered, along with disease and poverty and persecution), and realize all this through a Messiah.

This combination of divine and human activity[50] will also produce miracles,[51] as the world is dramatically transformed and perfected. Just as Schneersohn felt he saw the hand (or finger) of God in current events, so messianic performers have discerned God's work in events of their own era and tried to "hasten the end."[52] Indeed, in traditional synagogues throughout the diaspora, Jews declare that the State of Israel is "the beginning of the sprouting of our redemption" and that it constitutes the beginning of the messianic process.

Nontraditional Jews do not speak or write of a Messiah, but have transformed the idea of an individual redeemer to a vision of a messianic age, one in which, to use the most popular biblical image, the lion and the lamb will lie down together. The liturgies of these Jews are filled with messianic hopes and dreams but eschew the language of a Messiah, substituting exclusively human effort:

> It is up to us to hallow Creation, to respond to Life with the fullness of our lives. It is up to us to meet the World, to embrace the Whole even as we wrestle with its parts. It is up to us to repair the World and to bind our lives to Truth. Therefore . . . we set for ourselves the task of redemption. . . . And then all will live in harmony with each other and the Earth and then everywhere will be called Eden once again.[53]

In every area of Jewish belief the categories of traditional and non-traditional are frequently intertwined; many Jews who think and write about Judaic beliefs straddle the fence that for some separates traditional and nontraditional. Joseph A. Lookstein of Congregation Kehilath Jeshurun in New York City (Orthodox) affirmed the traditional concept of Messiah while simultaneously yearning for a messianic age. In his sermons he would urge his congregants to bring the Messiah by their acts of justice and mercy, by teaching what they preached, by infusing love into their hearts and character, and by practicing tolerance and compassion for all human beings.[54] Many traditional thinkers used traditional *and* non-traditional ideas to explicate their Judaic thought.

Evil

Traditionalists think of God as omnipotent, all-powerful, as have, historically, Moslems, Christians, and Jews. A limited God (sometimes called "self-limiting"), as some modern philosophers and theologians have proposed, has not been the God of the Jewish people. Only an all-powerful or absolute God can guarantee that the world is (ultimately, if not always presently) good, and a traditional Jew trusts in this. If God is all-powerful, of course, God made, as the medieval philosopher Maimonides explained, not only good but also evil, for evil—of every sort—exists side by side with good in the world created by God. Isaiah said it nearly two thousand years before Maimonides: "I am the Lord, and there is none else; I form the light and create darkness; I make peace, and create evil" (45:5–7). The world may be imperfect, but God is the creator of the world's imperfection. So the traditional Jew is forced to ponder why did God create evil, why does God permit it to exist? Or, as Jeremiah put it, as he cried out to God, "Why does the way of the wicked prosper?"

The traditionalists answer these questions in several ways. An Orthodox rabbi in Cleveland recently argued (2002) that what we think is evil is not always evil; a pain in our body might signal to us that we need to see a doctor, and that visit might lead to the discovery that our appendix needs to be removed. So this pain is not "evil." And is death the greatest evil? As early as the Genesis creation story, traditionalists note, someone imagined a world in which man, and woman, live forever. But if that were the case, there would only be first man and first woman, for neither would have discovered the tree of knowledge of good and evil, and hence sex, and hence reproduction, and hence the generations. First man, and first woman, would live forever, but there would be nobody after them to tell their story! So even death may not be evil.

For traditionalists goodness is only possible because we know evil. If we had no temptations, we would not understand the meaning of holiness. And traditionalists have an explanation for moral evils—antisemitism, genocide, prejudice, and racism—as well. Moral evil is wrong: against God's will and against God's commandments. But God created women and men free, free to do good and to do evil, and moral evil is the price God (and man) must pay for this creation. For if God forced women and men to be good, then they would not be free.

Although we may find numerous approaches to evil among Jews with nontraditional views, most of these positions reject the notion that God is all-good, that God is all-knowing, and (especially) that God is all-powerful. It follows, therefore, for these Jews that God is limited in many ways; as Milton Steinberg put it, "God is limited in His power" and "if man is to have real freedom, God's control cannot be complete."[55]

For nontraditional rabbis, thinkers, and laypeople with a view of a limited God, it follows that God is unable to deal with the problem of evil in the world. Man's cruel, destructive, and irrational impulses and the ignominy, indignity, misery, and sordidness of the world are simply part of the universe, part of the world from which "God is exempted."[56] There are things God cannot do, such as intervene in the world, and God's limitations shift the responsibility to women and men to conquer evil. And women and men have the intellectual capacity, moral awareness, and skills to overcome their destructive tendencies.[57] A world of good *and* evil gives freedom a choice.

Festivals

Judaism is much more a religion of doing than of believing. Countless American Jews, traditional as well as nontraditional, observe life-cycle events and festivals but do not affirm many of the beliefs summarized above. It has long been commonplace to point out that American Christianity emphasizes belief rather than practice, while American Judaism makes practice a higher priority than belief. And this generalization contains considerable truth. There are many examples of this contrast, but one will suffice. When most Christians join a church, they will participate in a program for new members that outlines for them the doctrines of the religious tradition of which they are now part. American Judaism has no equivalent, for Jews hardly ever speak of creed or doctrine. In contrast, however (just picking three programs at three synagogues in Houston offered during 2002), there might be a class offered to new members on how to make a Passover seder, how to build a sukkah, or how to prepare for bar and/or bat mitzvah. American Judaism is primarily a religion of doing, celebrating festivals and holidays, and participating in life-cycle events.

Rosh Hashanah

The two Hebrew words mean the New Year, and it occurs on the first day of the Hebrew month of Tishri. This name, Rosh Hashanah, comes from the Mishnah (late second century C.E.) and is based on a tradition that God completed the creation of the world on that day;[58] in the Hebrew Bible it is called a day when the shofar[59] is sounded (Numbers 29:1) and a sacred occasion commemorated with loud blasts (Leviticus 23:24). The holiday continues a season of self-examination, begun during the previous month of Elul with morning penitential prayers, as it is during this time of the calendar year that God remembers the deeds and decrees the destiny, at least for the coming year, of each Jew. It is thus also a day of judgment, not only when God judges the Jew but when each Jew must judge himself or herself. And it is also a day of remembrance, not only of great events in the history of the Jewish people but in the past year of the life of each Jew.

The season is known as the Days of Awe (*yamim nora'im*) or High Holidays, the solemn season that concludes, for some Jews, ten days later, with Yom Kippur, and for others, not until Hoshanah Rabbah, the seventh day of Sukkot. Given its importance—matters of life and death—it is observed by Orthodox and Conservative Jews for two days, even in Israel where no other holiday is doubled. Rosh Hashanah is dominated by three themes: the sovereignty of God, the manner in which God remembers all of the past and relates to humanity, and God's redemptive powers.

An interesting custom on Rosh Hashanah is *tashlich* ("thou shalt cast"), taken from the verse in Micah 7:19, "And You will hurl all their sins into the depths of the sea." On the afternoon of the first day Jews go the banks of a river, or any body of water, recite special prayers, and either empty their pockets or toss some bread crumbs into the water, thus showing their resolve (albeit symbolically) to cast away their transgressions.

On the day before Rosh Hashanah many Jews visit the graves of loved ones, and on the evening of the first day of Rosh Hashanah (Jewish holidays all begin at sundown because in the lunar calendar a "day" lasts from sundown to sundown), Jews eat a special holiday meal. It includes apples dipped in honey, a way to wish each other a sweet New Year. Traditional words do the same: "May you be inscribed and sealed for a good year in the book of life."

Yom Kippur

The ten days from Rosh Hashanah to Yom Kippur are the ten days of penitence, or return (*teshuvah*), days spent in earnest self-examination and devotion so that the Jew will make a sincere desire to turn a new leaf in the book of life. Repentance, or returning to God, is not easy, but it is made easier by taking stock of one's spiritual liabilities, sincerely regretting the mistakes committed, asking for atonement, and vowing to change one's ways. The Sabbath that falls within these days is called the Sabbath of returning (*shabbat shuvah*), and its theme is penitence.

The climax of these days of introspection (the tenth of Tishri) is Yom Kippur, the Day of Atonement, the most sacred day of the Jewish holiday year. To fast, and abstain from all bodily nourishment and pleasure, from sundown to sundown, together with sincere repentance ("He who says, 'I will sin and repent, sin and repent'—he has no chance to do repentance."),[60] maximizes the possibility of God's forgiveness. But this must be combined with every effort to rectify the wrong: "For transgressions between man and God, the Day of Atonement atones. For transgressions between man and man, the Day of Atonement atones only if the man will obtain the good will of his fellow."[61]

The liturgy for Yom Kippur, which covers nearly every waking hour from the evening of Yom Kippur (the Kol Nidre service) to the final service (*neilah* or closing), contains abundant confessional prayers (during

which traditional Jews beat their breasts), but these are written in the plural and recited by the whole community collectively, even by those who
might not have committed any specific sin enumerated. All assume re-
sponsbility for falling short during the year that has passed, even if they
are free of one or more of the many transgressions delineated in the short
(*ashamnu*) and the long (*al chet*) confessional prayers.

Sukkot

The pilgrimage festival of Sukkot (booths) falls five days after Yom Kippur, on the fifteenth of Tishri, and reminds the Jew of those years of
desert wandering recorded in the Bible when the people lodged in temporary shelters or booths. Thus the command to dwell in *sukkot*, or
booths (*sukkah* is the singular), for seven days (Leviticus 23:34). These
booths, temporarily erected immediately after Yom Kippur (usually
against the house), are covered (*sechach*) with detached branches of trees
or leaves and filled with fruit; other names for the holiday are the feast of
the harvest and feast of the ingathering, a reminder of the agricultural origins of the festival.[62]

The agricultural character of Sukkot is symbolized by the *etrog*, or citron, the *lulav*, a branch of the palm tree, as well as myrtle (*hadas*) and willow (*aravah*) branches (Leviticus 23:40). The lulav, three myrtles, two wil-
lows and one palm branch, are bound together by leaves of the palm tree,
and they, together with the etrog, are used ceremonially in the sukkah and
in the synagogue during Sukkot. Meals are eaten in the sukkah, and some
Jews even sleep in it during the festival.

Shemini Atzeret and Simchat Torah

In Israel, at the conclusion of Sukkot, these two festivals are celebrated
together as one day, but throughout the diaspora they take place on separate days. A particular feature of Shemini Atzeret is a prayer for rain
(this would be inappropriate during Sukkot because the roof of the booth
must be open sufficiently to see the sky!), while Simchat Torah is distinguished by completing the reading of the Torah (Deuteronomy) and beginning it once again (Genesis). Its name, "rejoicing in the Torah," gives
license for an abundance of dancing, singing, and general merriment with

the scrolls of the Torah on this day, as they are carried around the synagogue seven times with much rejoicing by adults and children.[63]

Hanukkah

The Jews celebrated the victory of Judah Maccabee and his Hasmonean family over the Syrian-Greeks, under Antiochus IV, on 25 Kislev, 165 B.C.E., by entering the Temple in Jerusalem and rededicating it to Jewish worship.[64] According to legend the jar of oil, sufficient for about one day, lasted for eight days, and thus the eight days of dedication, or *hanukkah*.[65] Jews light a Hanukkah candelabrum (*chanukiyah*) that holds eight candles, one for each night, as well as a ninth candle (*shammash* or "helper") with which they light the other candles. On the first night the light at the right end is lit; on the second night an additional light is added to the left, and so forth for each night, as the new candle is always the first to be lit. On the first night three blessings are recited before the candle lighting; on the other nights the opening blessing is eliminated. Many Jews also eat special foods (latkes, or potato pancakes), play special games (dreidel), and exchange gifts on each night of Hanukkah.

Tu B'shevat

Celebrated primarily in Israel on the 15th (*tu*) of the month of Shevat, this is the new year for trees as, according to the Mishnah and Talmud, the winter season comes to an end and the sap of the trees becomes active, stirring the trees into new life.[66] In Israel Jews fulfill the biblical commandment ("When you come into the Land you shall plant all kinds of trees"[67]), and in many Jewish communities in the Diaspora similar tree-planting ceremonies are celebrated or, alternatively, contributions are collected for tree planting in Israel.

Purim

Celebrated on 14 Adar, Purim takes its name from the word *pur*, or lot, recalling, from the book of Esther in the Hebrew Bible, the lots that Haman cast to determine the most favorable month and day for the execution of his plan to exterminate the Jews of Persia. On Purim Jews read the book of Esther, or, as the Mishnah calls it, the megillah, or scroll. In some synagogues Jews hear the chanting of a special tune that suits the narrative, and the listeners, while making Purim "a day of feasting and gladness,"[68] hoot and jeer (and make loud noises with *graggers*) every time they hear the name of the evil Haman. In addition, Jews present gifts of food to friends and the needy (*mishloach manot*) before the reading of the megillah and eat a special three-cornered pastry filled with poppy seeds or prunes (hamantaschen).

Special Sabbaths

Between the end of the month of Shevat and the beginning of the month of Nissan, in which the holiday of Passover occurs, Jews have four special Sabbaths. Each has become known by the name of the special portion read from the Torah and Prophets on that day, *shabbat shekalim* (the Sabbath before the first of Adar), *shabbat zachor* (the Sabbath preceding Purim), *shabbat parah* (the Sabbath that precedes the last special Sabbath), and *shabbat hachodesh* (the Sabbath preceding Nisan). Each is connected with a special event or historic occasion.

Pesach

One of the three pilgrimage festivals, more American Jews celebrate Passover than any other Jewish festival. Called the festival of matzot or festival of unleavened bread (as well as Pesach) in the Bible, it begins on 14 Nisan and continues, for traditional Jews, for eight days or, for non-traditional Jews, for seven days. Most Jews follow the biblical command to eat matzot during the festival, and, concomitantly, many Jews remove all bread products (*chametz*) from their homes as well.

It is a celebration of both the season when the Israelites obtained liberty from Egyptian slavery as well as the early, or spring, harvest, and it records the birth of the free nation of Israel. Most Jews hold a seder or meal with a special liturgy (Haggadah) on the first two nights of the festival, and the primary task of the liturgy (divided into two parts and separated by the festive meal) is to retell and explain the history of the exodus from Egypt. The readings are primarily about freedom and joining with others in the redemption of the world, hoping to bring closer the messianic era. The liturgy is accompanied by numerous special food items (bitter herbs; *charoset* [a mixture of apples, almonds, nuts, and wine], etc) that serve as reminders of the time of Egyptian bondage. Four cups of wine are consumed at the seder; the Cup of Elijah is placed on the table as a symbol of welcome for strangers, and most Jews use this occasion to invite family, friends, and even strangers to share the festival.

Shavuot

On the second day of Passover the Israelites brought an offering of the winter barley to the Temple in Jerusalem, and this offering was known as the *omer*. In rememberance, Jews now count the *omer* for forty-nine days,[69] from the second night of Passover, the last day being Shavuot, or [seven] Weeks.[70] This pilgrimage festival of Weeks has many names in the Bible and Jewish literature and is celebrated on 6 and 7 Sivan, by traditional Jews, and on only 6 Sivan by nontraditional Jews. It marked the season of the wheat harvest, but American Jews celebrate it as the day of the giving of the Torah on Mount Sinai and in synagogues frequently tie it to the confirmation ceremony.

Because of its agricultural setting, the book of Ruth is read on this festival, and many Jews eat dairy products on this day, perhaps in response to the verse in Song of Songs (4:11): "Honey and milk shall be under your tongue." Even in nontraditional synagogues text study on Shavuot night is popular, and the confirmation ceremonies usually combine a number of these Shavuot themes in their liturgy and presentation.

Tisha B'Av

According to the Mishnah, the destruction of the First Temple (586 B.C.E.) and the Second Temple (70 C.E.) took place on the ninth of the month of Av, and later traditions attached the expulsion of the Jews of England (1290) and Spain (1492) to this date as well. Thus, together with Yom HaShoah, it is the darkest day in the Jewish calendar. It is commemorated by fasting and by reading Lamentations, the vivid biblical account of the First Temple destruction.

Yom HaShoah

This is Holocaust Day, the time when Jewish communities commemorate the Nazi destruction of six million Jews during World War II. It is, of course, the most recent of Jewish holidays, and occurs five days after Passover ends, on 27 Nisan. Although the holiday is too young for American Jews to have developed one standard ceremony or prayer acceptable to all, they observe this day mostly by thinking about the events of 1941–1945. Some light one (or, alternately, six) yellow memorial (*yahrzeit*) candle(s) in their homes in the evening, and attend one of the many synagogue, church, and institutional programs held throughout the country on this day. The latter usually feature a survivor, child of survivors, or a Righteous Gentile speaker.

The Sabbath

There is no scholarly consensus about how the Sabbath (or day of not working) began, unless one is a traditionalist and affirms that it began at the end of the sixth day of creation when, according to Genesis, God finished working and began a day of not working (2:2). Unlike all the other biblical festivals, it is not part of the lunar calendar but occurs every seven days.

Not working is not equivalent to rest, because God not only ceased work on the Sabbath, God also "was refreshed" (Exodus 31:7). So spiritual replenishment, which is far from "rest," became a central feature of this day, and includes (this is but a short list) worship, studying a text, attending a lecture, visiting a museum, enjoying the beauty of nature, visiting friends, reading, marital sexual relations. Thus it is not just a day of not doing work but a day of doing many things.

The Bible prohibits kindling a fire (Exodus 35:3), and from that traditional Jews derive a prohibition on driving (creating sparks) and switching on electric lights or any electric object (computer, radio, television). The text also states that none are to leave their place on the Sabbath (Exodus 16:29), and from that traditional Jews derive prohibitions on walking beyond a fixed distance (Sabbath boundary). Nontraditional Jews generally usher in the Sabbath (Friday at sunset) with special ceremonies (kiddush or sanctification) involving candles, wine, challah, or twisted bread, and a special meal, while traditional Jews observe special rituals at the beginning and the end (*havdalah*) of the Sabbath.

In Judaic literature since ancient times the Sabbath has been personified as a bride, with the Jewish people as the groom. And just as the groom rejoices as his bride approaches, and the prophet Isaiah called the Sabbath a joy (58:13), so Jews are to fill the Sabbath with joy (*oneg*). This Hebrew word, *oneg*, is so essential to the concept of the Sabbath that when food follows a Sabbath evening or Sabbath morning worship service, the food is simply called *oneg*. Abraham Joshua Heschel put it well: "To observe the Sabbath is to celebrate the coronation of a day in the spiritual wonderland of time, the air of which we inhale when we 'call it a delight.' "[71]

Life-cycle Events

Birth

A Jewish male baby has a *milah* or circumcision on the eighth day of his life, accompanied by a ceremony (*brit*, "covenant") that declares him part of the Jewish people and announces his Hebrew name.[72] The milah is performed by a *mohel*, or ritual circumciser. While technically any Jew is eligible to do this honor, all branches of American Judaism have programs to train *mohalim* (pl.) and encourage their followers to use a mohel from that branch. It is customary to make a festive meal on the day of the ritual circumcision, because every commandment is enacted with joy.

There is no specific time for naming a girl, so customs vary greatly in American Judaism. Some do this on the day of her birth, some in the synagogue when the mother or father is called to the Torah, and some (perhaps most) give a Hebrew name at the end of her first month. Among Ashkenazic Jews both boys and girls are customarily named after deceased relatives.

Bar and Bat Mitzvah

Jewish parents are obligated to give their children a Jewish education, and for most American Jews this culminates with a bar or bat mitzvah ceremony. Among the Orthodox, a girl has a bat mitzvah at the age of twelve, and in all other branches of American Judaism both boys and girls have their ceremonies at the age of thirteen.

Whether bar or bat mitzvah (except among the Orthodox),[73] the child, now considered an "adult" in Judaic responsibilities, accepts his or her new status publicly in the synagogue. He or she conducts some of the Sabbath morning liturgy, chants or reads a portion from the Torah in Hebrew and the accompanying prophetic reading (haftarah) in Hebrew, and presents a discourse on his or her understanding of Scripture and the meaning of the ceremony. A festive meal or party usually follows the ceremony.

Marriage

A Jewish wedding ceremony has two parts: betrothal or sanctification (*kiddushin*), which includes a ring ceremony, and marriage (*nissuin*), which takes place under a canopy (*huppah*) and includes the recitation of seven ancient blessings (*sheva berachot*). Each part of the ceremony includes a blessing over a cup of wine, a symbol of the couple's joy. The two parts of the ceremony are divided by the public reading of a marriage contract (*ketubah*) which the couple has signed and witnessed prior to the ceremony. It is customary to break a small glass, recalling the destruction of the Temple in Jerusalem by the Roman in 70 C.E., and signaling the end of the ceremony. A festive meal usually follows the ceremony, for it is a religious obligation to make the bride and groom happy.[74]

Among the Conservative and Orthodox, a "marriage" of a Jew and non-Jew is not religiously valid, and no rabbi from those branches will officiate at such a union. Among Reform and Reconstructionist rabbis there are hundreds who officiate at such ceremonies, conducting a "Jewish" wedding ceremony although either the bride or groom is not Jewish.

Death and Mourning

It is customary for the body of a deceased Jew to be ritually washed, for men to be buried in a prayer shawl (Tallith), and for both men and women to be buried as quickly as possible.[75] It is meritorious to accompany the deceased to their grave and to bury the deceased in the earth following a service. No funerals take place on the Sabbath or on Yom Kippur.

A mourner is not expected to prepare meals immediately following a funeral, so it is a religious duty for friends and family to supply the mourner with food. The first meal is the Meal of Condolence, and subsequent meals are frequently provided during the period of mourning. This period commences as soon as the deceased is buried and includes segments of seven days (no work, no laughter, as well as other prohibitions, a candle or lamp kept burning, public prayers in the home of the mourner that include the mourner's prayer, the Kaddish, for the deceased), thirty days (may not attend weddings or other festivities), and eleven months (recite the mourner's prayer, Kaddish, for a parent). In addition, in all branches of American Judaism one recites the Kaddish on the anniversary of a parent's death (yahrzeit), and many Jews kindle a light on the eve of the yahrzeit and keep it burning for twenty-four hours.[76] Finally, it is customary to set up a tombstone at the head of the grave twelve months after the death.[77] Many Jews will leave a small stone on the grave, or on the tombstone, as a marker of their visit.

CHAPTER THREE

A History of Judaism in America

The Seventeenth and Eighteenth Centuries

Hard-pressed to escape the clutches of the Inquisition during the two centuries following expulsion from their Spanish and Portuguese homelands in 1492 and 1497, respectively, many Iberian Jews fled to the Netherlands where the Dutch enthusiastically welcomed these (mostly) businessmen and their families. While thriving in Amsterdam—where they became the hub of a unique urban Jewish universe and attained a status that anticipated Jewish emancipation in France by over a century—they began in the 1500s and 1600s to establish themselves in the Dutch and English colonies in the New World. These included Curaçao, New Amsterdam, Recife, and Surinam (Dutch) as well as Barbados, Jamaica, and Newport (English). In these European outposts their years of mercantile experience and networks of friends and family throughout the Atlantic world enabled them to play a significant role in the merchant capitalism, commercial revolution, and territorial expansion that developed the New World and established the colonial economies. This Jewish-Caribbean nexus enabled West Indian Jewry to enjoy a centrality North American Jewry would not achieve for a long time to come.[1]

Jews arrived in Recife in the seventeenth century when the Dutch conquered (1630) this part of northeastern Brazil from the Portuguese. With the reconquest by the Portuguese in 1654, Jews no longer felt secure, and thus twenty-three Jews stepped off the *St. Charles* (or the *St. Catherine*)[2] onto the soil of New Amsterdam (later, New York) that same year. They were the first Jews to settle in what would become the United States.

European Parallels

The initial experience of the Jews in America reminds one of the difficulties faced by Jews in Christian Europe on numerous occasions. The local governor, Peter Stuyvesant, together with his Calvinist clergy, did their best to restrict Jewish opportunities for assembly, burial, livelihood ("closed door" and "public-store," i.e., private and public), participation in the militia, and public worship. They were unsuccessful, largely because the parent Dutch West India Company placed economic benefits before religious discrimination, and the activities of the fledgling Jewish community (Stuyvesant called them "a deceitful race") revealed a commitment to the new land and a tenacity of effort that would be repeated in the subsequent centuries.[3]

As Jewish life unfolded in America in the next 350 years, it had many parallels to the western European experience, especially England, France, and Germany. Nearly all over, Jews responded to modernity in similar ways, but freedom from communal restraints such as those Governor Stuyvesant tried to apply came quickly and much more easily in America. Separation of church and state, so fundamental to the American experience, came to France only in 1905, and restrictions on economic and social opportunities remained, in varying degrees, everywhere in Europe.

But the most salient difference between the American and the European experience was the quantity of antisemitism; in this country it was always marginal and insignificant. No matter whether one looks de jure or de facto, Jews faced few liabilities because they were Jews or because they professed Judaism. Especially in the American imagination was this true; political leaders and parties rejected antisemitism, social and economic elites rejected antisemitism, and even religious leaders and (for the most part) Americans of other faiths also desisted from antisemitic statements and actions.[4] In Europe the Jew was frequently the "Other"—here whether one was a Jew or practiced Judaism was always a private decision and largely ignored.

Religious Developments in the New World

The Jewish communities of Charleston, Newport, New Amsterdam/ New York, Philadelphia, Richmond, Savannah, and smaller centers as well grew slowly in the first century or so of their settlement in America. The first federal census, in 1790, counted only 1,243 Jews out of a total population of 2,810,248—less than one-twentieth of 1 percent. Although Ashkenakic Jews (Central European) outnumbered Sephardic Jews (whose ancestors left the Iberian peninsula in the late fifteenth, sixteenth, or seventeenth centuries),[5] the Sephardic ritual dominated American synagogues in the seventeenth and eighteenth centuries, with the officiant (hazan) standing on a podium in the middle of the men's floor (the women sat in the balcony).

The Jews of New York established a congregation before the end of the seventeenth century, but the Jews of Charleston, Newport, Philadelphia, Richmond, and Savannah did not establish congregations and build synagogues until the eighteenth century. All followed the Sephardic ritual, even when (increasingly) the majority of their members were Ashkenazic Jews. The Sephardic ritual of these congregations, as well as the organizational structure and architectural style, modeled itself on London's Bevis Marks or Amsterdam's Spanish-Portuguese synagogue. In 1757 the "Elders and all the members" of New York's Shearith Israel resolved that the elders should ask the "*Parnasseem* [officers] and *Mamad* [*sic; Mahamad*, council]" to write to Shaare Shamayim in London and request that they send them "a proper hazan."[6] Mordecai M. Mordecai of Philadelphia's Mikve Israel sought approval (with letters in Hebrew!) from both London and Amsterdam for the Sephardic design of its 1782 buildings[7]—a design quite similar to those of synagogues in Newport and New York—featuring a women's gallery upstairs as well as the above-mentioned reader's table, which would enable the hazan (facing the worshippers) to lead services *with* the congregation (rather than *for* the congregation if he faced the ark as in Ashkenazi ritual) seated on each side of the table.

The Sephardic synagogues of North America were tightly controlled by laymen. The *parnas*, or president, together with his board of directors,[8] determined who received honors (e.g., was called to the Torah), approved marriages and burials, maintained attendance, decorum, and observance by fining violators (e.g., a man elected to the *adjunta* [board of directors] and refusing to serve would be fined, as would a board member who did not attend worship on the Sabbath), set the order and time of worship as well as Torah reading, supervised the baking of matzah for Passover and the proper ritual slaughtering of kosher animals, assigned and sold seats in the synagogue, and ruled the hazan and/or "minister." The "reach" of the leadership extended a considerable distance. In 1782 the adjunta of Philadelphia's Mikveh Israel pressed formal charges against Ezekiel, a Philadelphia dry goods merchant, who was seen shaving (= "working") on the Sabbath in Baltimore, one hundred miles away.[9]

The hazan (sometimes used interchangeably with minister) read and chanted the liturgy, chanted the scriptural readings, officated at all life cycle events, and instructed the children. He took orders from the parnas (and directors), usually well aware that he was merely a layman who knew some Hebrew and had a pleasant voice. In addition to hiring the hazan, the directors hired (when available) the *mohel* (circumciser), the *shochet* (slaughterer), the *melamed* (teacher), and the *mashgiach* (supervisor of dietary observance and Passover matzah preparation), although usually the low level of compensation required one man to do double (or, sometimes, triple) duty. This would be true in the nineteenth century as well. Buffalo's Beth El sought a minister in 1853 who was a hazan, shochet, and sexton.[10] When "Rabbi" Mordecai Tuska (who was not an ordained rabbi at all) came from Hungary to Rochester's Berith Kodesh in 1849, he served as rabbi, hazan, shochet, mohel, and teacher.[11]

Although bitter about the low level of congregational satisfaction with a hazan (rather than an educated rabbi), Isaac Mayer Wise (1819–1900) was more right than silly when he poked fun at the demands placed upon the hazan:

> The *chazan* was the Reverend. He was all that was wanted. The congregations desired nothing further. The *chazan* was reader, cantor, and blessed everybody for *chai pasch*, which amounted to 4½ cents. He was teacher, butcher, circumciser, blower, gravedigger, secretary. He wrote the amulets with the names of all the angels and demons on them for women in confinement, read *shiur* for the departed sinners, and played cards or dominoes with the living; in short, he was a *kol-bo*, an encyclopedia, accepted bread, turnips, cabbage, potatoes as a gift, and peddled in case his salary was not sufficient. He was *sui generis*, half priest, half beggar, half oracle, half fool, as the occasion demanded.

The congregations were satisfied, and there was no room for preacher or rabbi. Among all the *chazanim* whom I learned to know at that time, there was not one who had a common-school education or possessed any Hebrew learning.[12]

The Sephardic congregations of the eighteenth century certainly did not hesitate to try to force observance. Directors legislated, fined, threatened, and even considered excommunication to raise levels of worship participation and ritual observance. In New York in September of 1757, the officers and directors delineated the details of excommunication for anyone who "continues to act contrary to our Holy Law by breacking any of the principles [*sic*] command."[13] Whether such methods increased the level of observance is hard to tell. But since the excommunication included loss of burial privileges in the Jewish cemetery, it may have worked.

The Nineteenth Century

For the most part the trickle of Ashkenazi Jews who came from Central Europe in the eighteenth century found acceptance in the Sephardic congregations; with the exception of Philadelphia at the very end of the century, no group of Ashkenazic Jews left a Sephardic congregation to start their own synagogue during the eighteenth century. Philadelphia became the first American city to have an Ashkenazic congregation when some recent immigrants left Mikve Israel, about 1795, to establish the German Hebrew Society or Rodeph Shalom. But its members had internalized the Sephardic structure; they used the Spanish term *junto* to describe the board of directors.

Only in 1825, when a group of acculturated Ashkenazim, members of New York's Shearith Israel, formed a new congregation (B'nai Jeshurun), did another Ashkenazic synagogue ("German and Polish *minhag* [ritual]") emerge.[14] In the next few decades numerous central European congregations or synagogues took root in eastern and trans-Allegheny communities.

The leaders of these Ashkenazic synagogues also instituted a system of warnings, fines, and threats to maximize attendance, decorum, and observance, suggesting (again) that there was much lacking in every one of these areas among Early Republic and Antebellum American Jews. When the first ordained rabbi to come to live in the United States arrived in Baltimore in 1840, he discovered that his congregants generously ignored the commandments. When he resigned in 1849, he wrote home to his former teacher, Wolf Hamburger, "The character of religious life in this land is on the lowest level; most of the people are eating non-Kosher food, are violating the *Shabbos* in public . . . and there are thousands who have been assimilated among the non-Jewish population, and have married non-Jewish women."[15]

At Philadelphia's Rodeph Shalom, Friday evening and Saturday morning attendance was required, or else one paid a fine, while Buffalo's Beth El had fines for nonattendance and for undecorous behavior when one did attend. Bene Jeshurun fined members up to $25 for using "improper" language against the trustees, denied admission to services to a congregant who opened his or her store on the Sabbath, and prevented an intermarried member from serving on the board of directors. The Baltimore Hebrew Congregation imposed fines during the 1850s and 1860s for talking during services, singing louder than the hazan, "using snuff," "shewing" tobacco (although spittoons were everywhere in eighteenth and nineteenth century synagogues), leaving during the Torah reading, putting away one's prayer shawl before the end of the service, leaving the synagogue without the permission of the president, and "read[ing] or sing[ing] any prayer loud during the services."[16]

Religious Growth

The first significant growth in the American Jewish community took place in the middle decades of the nineteenth century as Ashkenazic Jews left central Europe, especially the German states, and spread throughout the East, Middle West, South and even California, ranging far from their points of entry for economic opportunity. The 1850 federal census enumerated 30 synagogues (there were likely even more), with more than half in New York and Pennsylvania, a geographic concentration that would not change for more than a century. Bertram Wallace Korn estimated that the Jewish population in America tripled in one decade (1850s), from 50,000 to 150,000.[17] By 1880 there were about 250,000 Jews in America and nearly

300 synagogues, figures that would explode in the next few decades (1,000 synagogues in 1900) with the massive east European Jewish immigration.

The central European Jewish immigrants were highly concentrated in the commercial life of town and cities everywhere. The author traveled through a series of small towns in Georgia, North Carolina, Ohio, Pennsylvania, South Carolina, Virginia, and West Virginia, and he constantly saw evidence of and heard tales about the Jewish merchants of the middle decades of the nineteenth century. In Macon, Georgia, a Jewish merchant was quite accurate when he told the author that "Jews had a store in nearly every midwestern and southern town during the time of the Civil War, and often they owned the majority of groceries and dry-goods stores."[18] They peddled throughout the countryside, obtaining their goods from wholesalers in the cities, and many eventually were sufficiently successful to open their own stores in a small town. In many of these towns their Jewish descendants still own the stores 150 years later, as each generation has found a small synagogue somewhere in the county (e.g., the Fitzgerald [Georgia] Hebrew Congregation) and maintained their connection to Judaism. In Savannah and Atlanta one frequently meets Jewish couples composed of a husband from one small town and a wife from another, who have finally left the drygoods store behind in Albany, Almay, Bainbridge, Columbus, Rome, Valdosta, Waycross, and the like. But without these small-town synagogues (some, like the Conservative congregation Beth Israel, with its kosher kitchen in Beaufort, South Carolina, valiantly carrying on today), there would probably not have been so many seventh-generation Jews throughout the state of Georgia, as elsewhere, settled by their Jewish immigrant ancestors.

These Jewish immigrants, and their American-born children, created not only synagogues but communal, cultural, philanthropic, religious, and social institutions in every community in which they settled, even when their numbers were small. Usually patterned on those models they knew from central Europe, the synagogue served as the focal point of the community, the hub from which the spokes of other organizations radiated.

The synagogue usually held title to the town's Jewish cemetery; when kosher meat was available it was distributed through the synagogue; and the mid-nineteenth-century synagogue hosted cultural (literary, dramatic, and musical societies), fraternal (B'nai B'rith), philanthropic (Hebrew Benevolent Societies), religious, and social activities (by the 1850s, confirmations were commonplace in many synagogues, and weddings were almost always solemnized in the synagogue) much like a combination of a twentieth-century synagogue and community center.

Most important, individuals and governments left the Jews alone to develop their religious institutions and express their Judaism however they wished. Nobody much cared how Jews hired their rabbis (there was no ordained rabbi in the United States before 1840 and no seminary to train rabbis until 1875), how they conducted their worship, how they built their synagogues, or how they distributed their philanthropy. In fact, in nearly every community that has been studied, synagogue building campaigns were communal efforts, with Jews constantly appealing to their non-Jewish neighbors (generally in the local newspapers) for financial support. And American Jews had no reason to think this support would not be forthcoming.

We know most everything we wish to know about the cultural, economic, philanthropic, and social life of these Jews, except how to appropriately label their religious life. It is a truism in the history of Judaism to point out that before circa 1800 there was (very generally speaking) just rabbinic Judaism, the religious system formulated by the rabbis of the first few centuries of the common era and developed during the following millennium and a half. Although this system faced attacks earlier, it was not until the late eighteenth and early nineteenth centuries that central and western European Jews began to create alternatives and, following the creation of institutions, formulate ideologies. To do so they had to negotiate a complex set of interlocking ethnic, linguistic, national, regional, and religious identities. Out of these challenges would emerge a plethora of modern Judaisms, most notably Conservative, Orthodox, Reconstructionist, and Reform Judaism, whose beliefs, festivals, and institutions occupy our attention in other chapters.

It is difficult to describe the Judaism of American Jews in the seventeenth, eighteenth, and early nineteenth centuries, but it was loosely an adaptation of the centuries old rabbinic Judaism as it unfolded in a newly settled and rather vast country. Food prepared according to biblical and rabbinic laws was not always easy to find in Charleston, Newport, Philadelphia, Richmond, and Savannah, but imagine the challenge when these Jews traveled to smaller towns and rural areas of the Carolinas, Delaware, Georgia, Kentucky, Maryland, Tennessee, Virginia, and many other places. The absence of any ordained rabbi, the lack of ritual specialists such as a mohel or shochet, the absence of Jewish cemeteries and of ritual objects, not to mention prayer books, made observance, even when desired, difficult. That fifteen hundred to two thousand or so Jews in 1776 managed, while spread around the thirteen states, to maintain a modest level of ritual and ceremonial observance is much more amazing than whatever omissions are to be found in their Judaism.

With the arrival of the thousands of central European Jews in the middle decades of the nineteenth century, old synagogues expanded and new synagogues emerged. By the mid-1850s every major American city had at least two established congregations, and some had more. The overwhelming majority of these congregations were, in some sense, "traditional," like Philadelphia's Mikve Israel where Isaac Leeser (1806–1868) served as a "moderate innovator."[19] Neither an ordained rabbi nor a college graduate, he nontheless delivered regular sermons in English (1838), established a Jewish day school, high school, and a Jewish college (Maimonides), prepared catechisms, translated prayer books and the Bible, founded the Jewish Publication Society, and edited as well as published a weekly Jewish newspaper (the *Occident*).[20] He battled, on behalf of a very liberal "traditional" Judaism, against Reform.[21]

Attempt at Reform

Although the label *Reform* was only slowly emerging, no other label yet existed. In the few congregations which used the term *Reform* in their literature and, seemingly, wished to make thereby a statement of self-definition, traditional practices dominated. But even without the presence of central European Jews in significant numbers, reform had emerged as a central congregational issue. In the early 1820s Charleston contained the young nation's first- or second-largest Jewish community and boasted of being the cultural and commercial center of America. On 21 November 1824 a group of members of Kahal Kodesh Beth Elohim, probably the second-oldest congregation in the United States,[22] met to petition the leaders of the synagogue; they sent their "Memorial" to the president of the congregation on 23 December. It was returned to them on 10 January 1824—rejected by the parnassim—with a letter noting that since it was contrary to the constitution of the congregation, it was not debatable.

So, on 16 January, the petitioners established a Reformed Society of Israelites; they drew up a constitution a month later and set about to carry out the details of the petition. These included a weekly sermon in English, English prayers, a commentary on the weekly scriptural portion, and a more solemn, decorous service.

The society did not survive for even a decade, but when it folded and some of its members returned to K.K. Beth Elohim, they (together with a new minister, Gustavus Poznanski) would steadily introduce reforms, beginning with an organ (1841) in the newly built, colonnaded, Greek Revival temple (still standing and one of Charleston's primary tourist attractions).

To some extent the petition continued a pattern that had already emerged in Europe. When the petititoners made mention of a "reformation which has been recently adopted by our brethren in Holland, Germany, and Prussia," they surely had in mind the founding and liturgical reforms of Amsterdam's Adath Jeshurun (1796), Westphalia's Seesen Temple (1810), Berlin's Ber Temple (1815), and the Hamburg Temple (1818). With Enlightenment and emancipation recently behind them, many Jews had already concluded that traditional Judaism was, as the petitioners expressed it, without "decency . . . beauty . . . dignity . . . intelligibility . . . reason . . . enlightenment . . . [and] understanding," and that Judaism must offer a "more rational means of worshipping the true God."

The petition was also a response to American Protestantism. The context of the Charleston petition is the eager expectation, unbridled enthusiasm, and restless ferment of the period. "We are all a little wild here with numberless projects of social reform," Emerson wrote to Carlyle. The American environment—with its absence of tradition and its sense of individualism, nonconformity, and pregnant possibility—encouraged a spirit of experimentation. Successive waves of revivals and open rebellions against the Protestant ecclesiastical establishment by Millerites, Mormons, members of the Oneida community, Shakers, Spiritualists, Transcendentalists, Unitarians, and the like left many torn by a sense of anxiety and disunity.

Not only the challenges to traditional theological formulations, which shook the churches, but also the attraction of Protestant brevity, dignity, decorum, and simplicity, and, most immediately, the local upheavals in Charleston churches provided the impetus for the petition. The Second Independent Church of Charleston broke off from the First

Independent Church in 1817 over a doctrinal dispute; the church's minister, himself a Unitarian, had cordial relations with Charleston Jewry. Such upheavals undoubtedly gave the petitioners courage to present their own demands, a sense of the justice of their demands, and the firm belief that they were, as their leader Isaac Harby stated, "enlightened descendants" of ancient Israel.[23]

But the religious reforming spirit increased everywhere with the arrival of central European Jews in large numbers. It grew more dramatic, even radical, when these same Jews joined congregations but feared that their American-born children might be lost to Judaism. "Here," Rabbi Isaac Mayer Wise would note, "everyone does as he chooses, preaches as he thinks fit, and expounds the Law as he understands it." And the direction of change was quite clear in the middle decades and, as we will shall see in another chapter, precisely the opposite of the changes widely observed in the last decades of the twentieth century. In almost every congregation thus far studied, reforms had been introduced and, in many, would continue to be introduced. These reforms were largely ceremonial in nature, and they included adding an organ, mixed-sex choirs, family pews (i.e., mixed seating), Sabbath services on Sunday, scriptural readings in English rather than Hebrew, and a "recess" in the middle of the day of Yom Kippur prayers, as well as eliminating the second day of some holidays (Wise abolished the second-day celebration of the three biblical "pilgrim" festivals in his Cincinnati synagogue in 1859 and of the Jewish New Year in 1873),[24] head covering requirements for the synagogue, repetitive prayers, selling of honors and Torah chanting. Some of these additions and or removals were more widespread than others, some were more significant than others, but each of them indicated that the synagogue was moving away from tradition and toward what we loosely call Reform.

Some reforms were merely in the area of decorum and dignity, and these would characterize nearly every synagogue service in the nineteenth and twentieth centuries, no matter the branch of American Judaism. Isaac Leeser, the supporter of "traditional" Judaism in the nineteenth century, complained about "loud and boisterous slamming of the door," the "noisy manner of taking [a] seat," and those who "drop in at the Synagogue before or after the commencement of the service, as it may suit their tastes or convenience." Together with most other rabbis, he was especially conscious of what Christians, who "hasten to their churches when the time for meeting is about to arrive," would "imagine" about Jewish worship.[25]

Other reforms were more radical, such as eliminating head covering, as this custom had become as inviolate as any biblical commandment found in the Torah. The most serious, in moving a synagogue out of the orbit of "traditional" congregations, was altering the liturgy (eliminating some prayers). Once alteration took place in the fixed liturgy, including the elimination of even one prayer, a window had been opened for more significant changes.

Many synagogues began to call themselves Reform in the mid and late nineteenth century but required men to wear head covering, continued to seat the men and women separately, and forbade the use of an organ. But the adoption of a common liturgy, the *Union Prayer Book* (the High Holiday volume appeared in 1894; the Sabbath and festival volume in 1895), made one "a full-fledged Reform congregation"[26] and clearly delineated "*UPB* congregations" from those that identified themselves as traditional. But before the late 1890s it is difficult to label a synagogue because the "reforms" that had been insititued varied so widely.[27] Liturgical reform, however, eventually (in the twentieth century) separated Reform congregations from Orthodox and Conservative synagogues.

The Late Nineteenth and the Twentieth Centuries

Immigration

The dramatic increase in Jews (fourfold) and synagogues (fourfold) from 1880 to 1900 came from east European immigration that began (lightly) in the 1870s and reached gigantic proportions in the next three and a half decades. World War I brought it to a halt, but it resumed again in 1919, only to be closed once and for all in the early 1920s with the passage of the National Origins Act.

The American press labeled 9 September 1881, when the first group of eighteen pogrom refugees arrived in New York, as the precise date when the mass migration of east European Jews began and emphasized the sharp distinction between this east European period and the previous cen-

tral European period of Jewish immigration to America. Although the
two migrations differed in their composition, they were similar in their
motivation and in their content.

The geographic origins of those immigrating to America shifted
markedly in the late nineteenth century. The five million immigrants who
composed the pre–Civil War wave, and the ten million who arrived between 1860 and 1890, came predominately from the British Isles, Central
Europe, Scandinavia, and western Europe. Between 1890 and 1924 15 million emigrated from Austria-Hungary, Greece, Italy, Romania, Russia
(and what was once Poland), and Turkey. More specifically, of the approximately 650,000 Europeans who arrived in the United States in the
year after 1 July 1881, more than 80 percent emigrated from Germany, the
British Isles, and Scandinavia; of the 1.2 million European immigrants of
1906–7, more than 80 percent came from southeastern and eastern Europe. Only scattered east European Jews arrived with the central European Jewish immigrants before 1870, and only 1 percent of the "east European" immigrants consisted of central European Jews. By 1906, when
Jewish immigration to America peaked at more than 140,000, central European Jews numbered less than 1 percent of the newcomers.

The east European Jews came from Galicia, Hungary, Lithuania, Romania, Russia, and adjacent areas. They had a keen sense of pride about
their unique origins, and the city, province, or country where they had
lived usually served as an organizing principle for their cultural, religious,
and social lives. But these distinctions were not quite so great as they appeared to the individual immigrants. The enormous population explosion, the changing national boundaries of eastern Europe, the "intermarriages" across national borders, and the continual external migrations, all
combined to so thoroughly mix these Jews that precise national origins
are often indistinguishable.

But they inundated the quarter-million or so Jews in America in 1880,
as two million arrived by 1914. They did not come primarily because of
pogroms, although these atrocities surely accelerated the movement and
frequently provided the last necessary prod toward emigration. Rather,
the context of mass emigration from east Europe differs little from that of
the earlier central European migration, as both consist of diverse threads:
the revolution in transportation, the constantly increasing population
which could not be absorbed into productive sectors of the society, the

economic aspirations of persons whose occupational advancement was limited, the search for political freedom or the desire to escape from persecution, and America's favorable image all provide the background of east European Jewish immigration to America.

The transition from sail to steam made mass migration to America possible, as the journey was now measured in days rather than weeks. In 1846 Isaac Mayer Wise sailed from Bremen to New York in sixty-three days; fifty years later the trip took nine days, and thirty-two hundred American offices of the Hamburg-Amerika line stood open to help someone already in America book passage for relatives and friends. Indeed, the United States Immigration Commission noted that between 1908 and 1910, 58 percent of the "Hebrew" immigrants had prepaid tickets from relatives in the United States.[28]

Concomitant with the development of new transportation facilities came the economic and social dislocations generated by the industrial revolution that spread southward and eastward in the last decades of the nineteenth century, as in western Europe earlier. The 1869 famine in the Suwalk area provided the initial catalyst for east European Jewish emigration, an exodus dominated by Lithuanian Jews. Nearly forty thousand Russian Jews arrived in America in the 1870s, before the east European Jews began to come in even larger numbers.

The enormous growth of the Jewish population in modern times peaked during the years of the east European mass immigration. Despite the movement of more than two million Jews from eastern Europe to America between 1881 and 1914—and more than 300,000 others to additional lands—the Jewish population actually increased in Austria-Hungary, Romania, and Russia. While the emigration wave crested between 1881 and 1897, the net population increase among Russian Jews totaled 22 percent. Overall, with a birth rate alone of 2 percent annually, the Jewish population of Russia tripled after 1847, swelling to over 5.2 million in 1897.

This growth made absorption into the economy tenuous, and the desire to improve one's economic position was intimately connected with the growing overpopulation. By the late nineteenth century the Pale of Settlement included Lithuania, New Russia, White Russia, and certain cities of the Ukraine—the 15 western gubernias of European Russia and the 10 gubernias of Congress Poland. From 1890 to 1892 tens of thou-

sands of Jews were forced into the overcrowded Pale by the czarist government that expelled them from the great cities of the Russian interior.
Lodz had 2,775 Jews in 1856, 98,677 in 1897 and 166,628 in 1910; Warsaw
jumped from 127,917 Jews in 1882 to 219,141 in 1897. By 1897 4.9 million
or 95 percent of all Jews in the Russian Empire lived in a *gorod* (city) or
mestechko (town) of the Pale; in these densely populated communities the
competition, the overcrowding and squalor, and the absence of ways and
means to earn a livelihood encouraged many to migrate.

Antisemitism too played a role. Jews were excluded from a long list
of trades and professions, and rigid quotas for Jewish students restricted
opportunities for higher education. Nevertheless, the extreme poverty of
the east European Jews, the pressure of mounting population and the
constant narrowing of economic opportunities, probably caused more
Jews to leave than did antisemitism. In Galicia, from 1890 to 1914, over
three hundred thousand Jews came to the United States although there
were no pogroms and modest civil and religious freedom. Pogroms
alone drove few away, but rather a combination of all the factors delineated above.

By the time the east European Jews arrived, the earlier community of
central European Jews, and their children, had made a generally comfortable adaptation to American economic life. In 1889 John S. Billings of
the Bureau of the Census surveyed eighteen thousand employed Jews
(four-fifths of whom were immigrants from German-speaking countries
or their descendants) and discovered a heavy imbalance in favor of trade
and commerce. Indeed, 80 percent of the Jews were agents, bankers,
bookkeepers, brokers, clerks, collectors, petty merchants, retailers,
wholesalers, or the like, and another 5 percent were professionals. Even
more striking: two-thirds of all the Jewish families in the United States
had at least one servant! Jews had clearly achieved a comfortable position
in American society.[29]

But this profile was hardly descriptive of the newcomers who moved
largely into manufacturing concerns as a proletarian labor force. The garment trades in the late nineteenth and early twentieth centuries were
dominated from top to bottom by Jewish immigrants: 60 percent of employed immigrant Jews worked in the garment industry in 1890, and 85
percent of men's clothing and 95 percent of women's apparel were being
produced by Jewish manufacturers in 1900. These immigrants saw the

garment industry as a source of immediate employment, for themselves and often for the entire family.

The total involvement of the family was made possible by the emergence of the "outside shop" or "sweat shop" (sometimes called "putting-out industry" or "home industry"): a small, overcrowded, poorly maintained workplace, often no more than a tenement loft or room. These "shops," which dotted Baltimore, Boston, Chicago, Los Angeles, Minneapolis–St. Paul, Newark, New York, Philadelphia, and St. Louis, were operated by contractors who obtained unfinished garments from manufacturers and found groups of immigrants to complete the work. These contractors made a profit by subdividing the finishing of the clothing and lowering to a minimum the cost per piece, or the wages per task. As a result, the positive benefits of working close to (or at) home with family and friends and maximizing the labor resources of the household members were more than offset by the continuous downward pressure on piece rates, the long seasonal hours of hectic labor followed by stretches of unemployment, and the exploitation of immigrant men and women and their children as entire families fought for a share of the work.[30]

While industrial technology brought Jewish workers together during the day, the urban technology of the second and third decades of the twentieth century made possible a steady movement to dwellings some distance from work. The upwardly mobile products of immigrant homes began to leave the immigrant neighborhoods for the expanding suburbs during and after World War I, and this movement into areas of "second settlement" produced a major transformation of an urban ethnic group. Subways, trolleys, elevated trains, and the automobile made the countryside more easily accessible. New apartment complexes and single row houses—the latter available with a small down payment and a thirty-year, 3 percent mortgage—sprang up overnight. Asphalt paving, gas ranges, improved sanitary plumbing, and brightly lit rooms combined to make the new residences even more appealing. Tens of thousands of Jews left Manhattan for Brooklyn, the Bronx, and parts of Queens, while Jews everywhere were leaving downtowns (usually described by contemporaries as a ghetto) and moving to the emerging suburbs of Birmingham, Chicago, Cincinnati, Cleveland, Detroit, Indianapolis, Los Angeles, Miami, Phildelphia, Pittsburgh, St. Louis, San Francisco, and numerous other places.[31]

For these immigrants from eastern Europe, their religion was far more than a confession or faith as it had become for the majority of central European Jews in America by the late nineteenth century with their choirs, decorous and solemn worship, formal English sermons, mixed seating, and organs. Central European Jews in America spoke of themselves as Israelites or Hebrews (rarely as Jews), and centered their faith (much like Protestants) around their religious institutions. One could speak of these central European Jews, and their congregations, much like a denomination in the Protestant sense of the term, as they were not identifiable culturally or ethnically and their Judaism was expressed primarily by their occasional synagogue attendance.

The religion (some call it folk religion[32]) of the immmigrants of the late nineteenth and early twentieth centuries was traditional, no matter how much the forces of enlightenment and secularization might have battered some of them (e.g., Hungarian Jews), and this meant that it consisted of "traditional" ways of celebrating, dressing, eating, speaking, and, of course, praying. The synagogue was only one of their Judaic institutions—so even if they did not always keep the biblical or rabbinic dietary laws as the most rigorous Jews in Europe might have done, and if their ideology was a bit confused, they combined Jewish and religious practices in ways that identified them as a distinct cultural, ethnic, and religious group.[33] In Birmingham a single block of the east European Jewish "ghetto" (Northside), where "new immigrants had very little contact with non-Jews," had a synagogue, ritual bath, Jewish bakery, Talmud Torah, and Young Men's Hebrew Association.[34]

When the institutions themselves were not abundant in a neighborhood, the immigrants nonetheless mixed the ethnic and the religious in imaginative ways. The author's grandmother would buy nonkosher chicken from a Jewish butcher for a "traditional" Jewish chicken soup she served on Sabbath eve in both her "kosher-style" Los Angeles restaurant and to her children for the special Sabbath eve dinner.[35] In Macon, Georgia Congregation Sha'arey Israel's adult Bible class was "conducted entirely in Yiddish" from the first decade of the twentieth century to at least World War II.[36]

At first these immigrants established synagogues intimately tied to the *lansmanschaften* (fraternal) organizations they created. These organizations, like the Voliner lansmanschaften in Columbus, Ohio, aided those who were sick, provided death benefits, offered modest loans to those in need for such purposes as Passover relief and endowment of brides, established tuberculosis sanitaria, homeless shelters, homes for orphans, and havens for the aged, and provided a social network for those from one geographic area. Thus, in Columbus, early lansmanschaften synagogues included the Hungarian synagogue, or as it was known at the time, the First Hungarian Hebrew Church, whose founders were (mostly) from adjacent Hungarian villages;[37] in other cities there was a Romanian synagogue, a Russian synagogue, a Polish synagogue, and the like. There were eventually synagogues from more specific locales (the Neziner synagogue, from a town in the Ukraine) rather than a region, or synagogues that defined themselves by a particular liturgical variation (*Nusach Ha-ari*, named after a sixteenth-century mystic, Isaac Luria). Everywhere, the immigrants first organized their synagogues mostly by east European geography. After some years, as they moved to areas of second settlement, and their children reached adulthood, they organized their synagogues mostly by neighborhoods within the American city. Generally, the lansmanschaften synagogues remained in the area of first settlment, and as the immigrants moved out of the ghetto or area of first arrival they established what became known simply as Orthodox synagogues whose membership more frequently than not consisted of Jews from the neighborhood, no matter their east European place of origin.[38]

Orthodoxy

These synagogues of the immigrants were Orthodox in liturgy (e.g., they did not abbreviate the service); the occasional sermons were in Yiddish; and the worshippers were unlikely to be punctilious in their observance of ceremonies, customs, holy days, and rituals. Occasionally, several congregations brought a distinguished rabbi to the community from eastern Europe, and while he might formally be the rabbi of one of the congregations, he would also serve as the religious authority of the community and would alternate his preaching, weekday classes, and responding to questions of Jewish law among the several synagogues.

Since education is a religious obligation in Judaism, these Orthodox congregations would frequently unite to establish a Talmud Torah, or after-school and Sunday Jewish education program. The focus of their curricula was Hebrew language and literature (the vehicle of Judaic texts), not Yiddish, the spoken language of the immigrants; girls were rarely included in the classes (*hadarim*); and these schools were usually staffed by ill-trained and poorly compensated immigrant teachers. These religious schools appealed to traditional families who hoped to provide their children with a modicum of a traditional Jewish education while the latter attended public school during the main hours of the day.

We may distinguish, very broadly, two types of Orthodox synagogues and two types of rabbis. One is represented by the east European-born immigrants and their rabbis, painstakingly trying to recreate a synagogue as they remembered or had been told it had been in the Old World; the other by the children of these immigrants, raised in an American Orthodox environment, who had no real or even imaginary east European model to imitate but constructed an Orthodox Judaism heavily influenced by the environment in which they were raised and educated.

The former group, what a historian of Orthodox Judaism in the United States has repeatedly called "resistors,"[39] was small in number even at the height of east European Jewish immigration. Although all the resistors were no more identical than all the accommodators, for sometimes the lines blurred considerably between them, typical of the resistors was the Slutzker Rav (he opened a yeshiva in Slutzk, Lithuania), Jacob David Willowski (1845–1913), who arrived in the United States in 1903 (he left suddenly in 1905 for Palestine) and immediately declared that English sermons had no place in the synagogue (much less the English language in the worship service). East European born and already a distinguished Talmudist while in his teens, he and rabbis like him not only insisted on Yiddish sermons but rejected every attempt to accommodate tradition to the American environment, especially in the area of synagogue decorum, mixed seating, Sabbath observance, and secular studies. He went so far as to condemn the sermon itself, arguing that it contained "no guidance for the Jewish people . . . mak[ing] them like the rest of the nations . . . [and] open[ing] the gates leading to . . . Reform Judaism."[40]

Yet another frequently cited model of resisting, if not rejecting, America was Jacob Joseph of Vilna (1848–1902), who came to the United States as the "chief rabbi" of New York City. He was given the unenviable task of rallying the immigrants and their children to affirm the world of east European Jewry. A fine scholar, good preacher, and active organizer who

received an enthusiastic welcome from the immigrant Jews when he arrived in July of 1888, he faced an almost hopeless task. Despite a small and
appreciative following, he was quickly reduced to being no more than the
chief rabbi of the Association of the American Orthodox Hebrew Congregations (actually, a few synagogues on the Lower East Side of New
York City) and more accurately just the employee of those kosher butchers who accepted his authority. Most did not; his reforms (taxing meat and
poultry to pay for additional supervision; removing incompetent slaughterers; etc.) were met with hostility from butchers, consumers, and ritual
slaughterers. This was less a reflection of the skills of Rabbi Joseph than
divisions within the immigrant community and, more important, the ten-
sions between an Old World rabbi meeting an immigrant community en-
countering America.

The New York correspondent of Isaac Mayer Wise's *American Israelite*, even before Jacob Joseph arrived, described him as a man "whose
vernacular is an unintelligible jargon," while Dr. Henry Pereira Mendes
(1852–1937), rabbi of New York's Shearith Israel (1877–1920) and the
first president of the Union of Orthodox Jewish Congregations in America (1898–1913), who supported Rabbi Joseph, doubted that his Old
World authority would enable him to "have success in America." Indeed,
he represented, to thousands of new immigrants, precisely what they had
traveled a great distance to escape. A bearded, Yiddish- and Hebrew-
speaking chief rabbi had little appeal to Jews breathing in the fresh air of
North American religious voluntarism.[41]

Similarly, men such as Abraham Jacob Gershon Lesser (1834–
1925), the first president of the Union of Orthodox Rabbis and the head
of the Cincinnati Orthodox community from the time this native of
Poland left Chicago in 1898, "never learned to talk English and the only
words in English that he could write comprised his name. As a result,
he did not take part in the civic life of the community." He agreed with
his colleague Rabbi Willowski who, when visiting the United States,
criticized the immigrant rabbis of the Union of Orthodox Jewish Congregations for "having emigrated to this *trefa* [impure] land."[42] These
immigrant rabbis, struggling to maintain the traditions of the Old
World, may have rallied some of the immigrants, but they were ill-
equipped to meet the religious needs of an emerging second generation
of American Jews.

The accommodating or modernized Orthodox rabbis, beginning with the American-born and educated children of the east European Jews who affirmed both the Enlightenment and modernity, were much more open to secular studies alongside Judaic studies, to the use of English in sermons and even the liturgy, and to a style of dress and appearance influenced not by Poland or Lithuania but by America. They were equally open to the "amenities—aesthetics, decorum, manners" and the fundamental and unswerving belief that the typically undecorous service threatened the future of an American Orthodoxy,"[43] to participation with Conservative and Reform rabbis in communal forums, and much more relaxed about levels of observance, even (frequently) agreeing to serve mixed-seating congregations with (always) the long-term goal of convincing the worshippers that separate seating by sex is more appropriate for meaningful worship.

The model, par excellence, of the Americanized Orthodox rabbi, was Leo Jung (1882–1987) of the Manhattan Jewish Center, a flagship Upper West Side Orthodox synagogue. The son of a distinguished Orthodox rabbi, Meir Tsevi Jung (1858–1921), who combined an education at three European yeshivot (talmudic academies) with a love for Goethe, Kant, and Shakespeare, he too was a product of the religious Enlightenment (Hildesheimer Rabbinical Seminary in Berlin) and secular Enlightenment (the universities of Berlin, Vienna, Giessen, Marburg, London, and Cambridge—he spoke of the last as his "most beloved *alma mater*"—from which he received several degrees).

He came to the Jewish Center in New York in 1922 (remaining there for sixty-five years) and immediately tried to shape what he called "modern Orthodoxy" or "Torah-true" Judaism, an orthodoxy for the children (and grandchildren) of the east European Jewish immigrants that would accommodate traditional Judaism and the values and culture of modern, urban America. He would quote widely from Dickens, Ibsen, Henry and William James, Shaw, Tennyson, Whitman, French, Greek, and Latin authors as well as a broad range of rabbinic literature to establish a series of patriotic programs, celebrations of American holidays integrated with Jewish values, odes to Lincoln, Washington, Jefferson and even the Pilgrims. "There is nothing graceful and worth having in modern life," he once said, "which the Orthodox Jew may not enjoy."[44]

Joseph B. Soloveitchik (1903–1993), also known as "J.B." or simply the "Rav" (rabbi of rabbis), was another accommodator of Jung's generation. He came to the United States (Chicago, briefly, and then Boston) in 1932, already distinguished as a Talmudist, but with a Ph.D. dissertation on the epistemology and metaphysics of Hermann Cohen from a German university as well, and would dominate Talmudic studies at Yeshiva University's Rabbi Isaac Elchanan Theological Seminary (RIETS) for four decades after the death of his father in 1941. Equally at home in Western philosophy, science, psychology, and religious phenomenology as in Talmud, he stood for a modern or accommodating American Orthodox Judaism with deep roots in both traditional Judaic and modern secular scholarship.[45]

Just as Orthodox rabbis—even immigrant rabbis—differed greatly in how they responded to modernity, especially in the form of secular studies, the English language, and the American environment, so did the members of Orthodox synagogues. Some Orthodox worshippers preferred a small cell or room, often without decorum or English explanation; others, estranged from the Old World synagogue of their parents, emphasized beauty, congregational singing, order, responsive reading, and a (formal) sermon. The former, "exclusionary" congregations, usually sought resistors to lead them; the latter, "inclusionary" synagogues, turned first to graduates of the accommodating rabbinical school of RIETS and, not infrequently, graduates of the Conservative branch's Jewish Theological Seminary. Indeed, the lines of demarcation between accommodating Orthodoxy and emerging Conservative Judaism were frequently blurry in the eyes of these second- (and even third-) generation American Jews.

Conservatism

An interesting attempt in the first decade of the twentieth century to bridge the two worlds of east European and American Orthodoxy, by a Jewish Theological Seminary student, Elias L. Solomon (1879–1956), was the Jewish Endeavor Society's Young People's Synagogue in the immigrant neighborhood of New York City. Solomon, Russian-born, Jerusalem-raised, but American-educated, sought an Americanized Orthodox worship setting: a traditional Hebrew prayer service but the use of a book with English translations. The YPS did not last beyond 1910, and its founder would serve as a transition to the emerging Conservative movement. He received his ordination at the JTS, and, as many rabbis of his generation, he moved back and forth between two Orthodox and two Conservative congregations.

Graduates of JTS would serve Orthodox congregations; graduates of RIETS would serve congregations with mixed seating and late Friday evening (a hallmark of Conservative Judaism) worship services; and the designation Orthodox or Conservative often became as blurry when applied to rabbis as to congregations. Beth Abraham of Nashua, New Hampshire, a Conservative congregation, had a succession of "ordained rabbis who came from various orthodox rabbinical schools" while "men and women would sit together." Beth El of Rochester formally joined the Conservative movement in 1920, implemented both "strictly traditional" daily services and mixed seating, and was served by both Conservative and Orthodox rabbis.[46] A historian of Miami's first synagogue to "elect the Conservative route," noted that "there were also strong Orthodox influences within Temple Beth David."[47] Indianapolis's Conservative Beth El, organized in 1915, was first served by students from the Conservative seminary, then by ordained Orthodox rabbis who presided over a 1,100 seat sanctuary with family pews (and a separate-sex section). At the dedication of the sanctuary, the president of the Union of Orthodox Jewish Congregation of America (Rabbi Herbert S. Goldstein) was one of the two guest speakers, and the Orthodox rabbi who was installed at that time went on, a few years later, to head Congregation Baron Hirsch of Memphis, the largest Orthodox congregation in America.[48] Atlanta's Ahavath Achim's 1936 constitution declares it to be a synagogue of "Orthodox Jewish ritual," yet in the 1940s mixed seating was instituted. Atlanta's Orthodox Shearith Israel installed a microphone for Rabbi Sidney K. Mossman's Sabbath sermons (1956), adopted the Conservative movement's "Silverman" *Sabbath and Fesitval Prayer Book*,[49] and added late Friday evening bat and bar mitzvah services (1960) to attract more worshippers.[50]

The fluidity of the boundaries, as well as some of the issues at stake in delineating those boundaries, are indicated in the discussion that took place at Atlanta's Shearith Israel in April 1958, as the congregation wrestled with the layout of the sanctuary in the new synagogue. It is explicitly about seat arrangement but also about how to define oneself Judaically in a pluralistic society.

Many ideas, both pro and con, were brought up and discussed. For the negative point-of-view, the question was brought up whether by having mixed seating we would violate our by-laws by being a conservative, rather than an orthodox congregation; it was also suggested that Rabbi [Tobias] Geffen would possibly not have let his name be used for a testimonial dinner if he thought the new building would be for a conservative congregation. From the positive angle, the suggestion was made that if Shearith Israel wished to grow in the future, it would be necessary to change with the times; also that nowhere in our religion is it specifically written that there shall be separate seating of the sexes; also that while our by-laws say we shall be an orthodox congregation, in practice we're not really so as many members ride to services on Sabbath and other days; also that while Shearith Israel had originally been set up so that only men who observed the Sabbath could be members, that if this were strictly enforced, there possibly would be no Shearith Israel today. Many other ideas were brought up and discussed, and very pertinately, Rabbi [Sidney K.] Mosmann pointed out that most of the orthodox synagogues in the Mid-West have mixed seating, and that these synagogues have orthodox rabbis.[51]

The indecisive Elias L. Solomon himself did finally identify permanently with Conservative Judaism, serving New York's Shaare Zedek for more than three decades beginning in 1922.[52] Although this indecision rarely occured in late twentieth-century or early twenty-first century American Judaism—RIETS graduates no longer migrated to Conservative congregations—in the first decades of the twentieth century, as Conservative Judaism emerged and solidified in the United States, the odyssey of Rabbi Solomon was not so striking. Today, when Orthodox rabbis mock the ideology of Conservative Judaism and Conservative rabbis disparage the refusal of Orthodox rabbis to permit the mixed seating once so common in Orthodox synagogues, it is not even guaranteed that Orthodox rabbis will join with Conservative rabbis on *nonreligious* communal issues.

Just as the labels *Conservative* and *Orthodox* are confusing when applied to numerous synagogues in this period (there were Orthodox congregations, such as Atlanta's Ahavath Achim, with mixed seating and there were Orthodox synagogues with late-evening Friday services and even—in the case of Atlanta's Shearith Israel—late Friday evening bar mitzvah ceremonies,[53] in imitation of the Conservative movement), so too is the label *Orthodox* or *Conservative rabbi*. Indeed, it is no more clear what we mean if we say RIETS graduate or JTS graduate, for the lines separating these two branches—unlike the thick boundaries today— were once quite thin if not totally dissolved.

Conservative Judaism is usually portrayed as a reaction to Reform Judaism: the Jewish Theological Seminary emerged at the same time that the Reform rabbis, meeting in Pittsburgh in 1885, issued a platform in which they rejected all the "rabbinical laws" and "Mosaic legislation" other than the "moral laws," for the ceremonies, commandments, customs, and rituals of Judaism "obstruct" rather than "further modern spiritual elevation." Or else it is viewed as the new branch of Judaism that ministered to "the new immigrants, whose Orthodoxy was of so unbending a nature that all the forms of Judaism in America . . . seemed little better than heathenism."[54]

The key fact about Conservative Judaism, no matter how it emerged, is that its leaders always distinguished it from Reform and Orthodox Judaism—what the *Atlanta Georgian* called the "middle ground."[55] In contrast to Reform, the movement insisted that males wear head covering during worship and that the truncated, heavily English Reform *Union Prayer Book* be prohibited. And it distinguished itself from Orthodox Judaism by rejecting a European form of tradition; insisting on modern, scientific biblical criticism, minimizing (sometimes rejecting) the traditional notion of divine revelation of the entire Torah at Mount Sinai, supporting (quite early) those congregations that wished to have mixed seating. challenging the traditional authority of Jewish law and thus developing an openness to moderating and even changing laws (e.g., driving on the Sabbath, ordaining women as rabbis, counting women as part of the quorum required for public worship, and permitting women to participate in the reading of the Torah) that remain sacrosanct for Orthodox Judaism. and by responding to what it perceived as a lack of aesthetics in Orthodox worship among east European Jewish immigrants, namely, private conversations, walking around the sanctuary, "passing around snuff (which always led to paroxysms of sneezing) during the allegedly solemn prayer service."[56]

But what disparate congregations had in common is hard to retrieve. Many had organs, mixed choirs, family pews, only one-day festival observance, men who met twice daily for public worship, abundant English translations of prayers, the reading of the prophetic selection (haftarah) in English; some had none of these. The Conservative pattern, from city to city and, sometimes, within the same city, would vary significantly and be, sometimes, quite similar to Reform worship, other times much like Orthodox worship.

These Conservative congregations grew steadily from the 1920s through the 1950s and 1960s; by the end of the 1960s there were more Conservative synagogues than synagogues affiliated with the Reform movement. With 229 congregations in 1927, the United Synagogue of America (the national organization of Conservative congregations) had increased by more than 200 synagogues from its origins in 1913. In the decade after the Second World War the movement from cities to suburbs exploded. Already by 1950 the national suburban growth rate was ten times that of central cities, and in 1954 the editors of *Fortune* estimated that 9 million people had moved to the suburbs in the previous decade.[57] The United Synagogue was overwhelmed with applications from (mostly) new congregations. Indeed, in 1956 and 1957 alone, 130 new congregations joined the organization. By the end of 1965, when the exodus from cities had stabilized, 800 synagogues (compared to 500 ten years earlier and less than 400 fifteen years earlier) belonged to the Conservative movement.

Reform

Reform Judaism too felt the impact of children and grandchildren of immigrants who had journeyed from city to suburb and from immigrant Orthodoxy to American Reform Judaism, as hundreds of Reform congregations, like their Conservative counterparts, experienced a significant influx of Jews of east European ancestry. In 1947–48 there were 364 Reform congregations with 100,000 member units, less than a decade later there were 520 congregations with 255,000 memberships, and by 1963 the Union of American Hebrew Congregations (the national organization of Reform congregations) reported 646 congregations. In one twelve-month period alone (1954–55) 50 congregations joined the union.

For most of those affiliating with Reform for the first time, the ideology of the movement was less significant than the convenient location of a synagogue, the attractiveness of the local rabbi, the reduced time commitment for religious education and bar/bat mitzvah preparation, and the form and style of worship services.

Until these children and grandchildren of the east European mass immigration began to join Reform congregations, and slowly but steadily transformed their ritual and customs, Reform synagogues everywhere were part of the "classical" Reform movement—with its minimum of ceremonial practice. Scores of Reform rabbis may be designated as "classical Reformers," so a brief listing is hardly exhaustive. But representative of different parts of the country were Joseph Krauskopf at Philadelphia's Keneseth Israel (1887–1924),[58] Max Landsberg of Rochester's B'rith Kodesh,[59] Leon Harrison of St. Louis's Temple Israel (1891–1928),[60] San Francisco Emanu-El's Jacob Voorsanger (1889–1908),[61] and Richmond, Virginia Beth Ahabah's Edward Nathan Calisch (1891–1945).[62] All were anti-Zionists, fierce opponents of the dietary laws, Sukkot, the bar mitzvah ceremony, blowing the shofar on Rosh Hashanah, chanting the Torah, eating unleavened products for seven days during Passover, using a *huppah* (canopy) at weddings, and most everything else considered sacred by traditional Jews.

Rabbi Landsberg called the Jewish prayer for the dead, the Kaddish, a "base superstition," and instructed that the anniversary of his death (yahrzeit) be ignored. The trial version of his 1884 prayerbook, *Ritual for Jewish Worship* (the first fully idiomatic, English-language radical Reform service—a twelve-page Sabbath eve liturgy), which would be used for more than fifty years, contained no Hebrew characters.[63] Rabbi Calisch spoke for his radical, or classical, Reform colleagues when he said that he sought to strip Judaism of the "foliage of ritualism and ceremonialism."[64] He was a leader among the Catholics as well as the Jews. On the twenty-fifth anniversary of his arrival in Richmond, a Catholic leader wrote to him, in part, "In my opinon, no man has done so much for the spread of Catholic ideals and the Catholic spirit among us . . . as you have done."[65] Like so many Reform rabbis of his generation, he spoke of Jews and Christians as members of the same family and spoke of the time when "distinctions between church and synagogue, between Christian and Jew, shall be merged into the great

temple of the brotherhood of Man."[66] And, like dozens of his colleagues, he wished to celebrate the Jewish Sabbath on Sunday, the day
of the "American Sabbath."

When the east European descendants joined Reform congregations,
they demanded head covering in previously hatless congregations, bar
mitzvah ceremonies instead of, or in addition to, confirmation, congregational singing instead of choir-led (mostly Protestant) hymns, fasting
for twenty-four hours on Yom Kippur rather than just until the "lunch
break,"[67] programs connected to the newly created Jewish state, Israel, in
congregations that had been, mostly, non-Zionist or anti-Zionist, and increasing amounts of Hebrew despite a widely used prayer book that had
subordinated this traditional language of prayer in favor of English.

Historians of Judaism debate exactly when significant amounts of tradition entered the Reform movement. Jeffrey S. Gurock believes that in
the interwar period, circa 1920–1940, the "ritual traditionalism" that
characterized Reform in the last decades of the twentieth century was already present in considerable amounts. He finds Reform rabbis, here and
there, who comment on the "revival of interest in ceremonials" and the
"return to the old practices [like] investing themselves with the skull cap
and talith" at worship services in Reform congregations.[68] There is as yet
no agreement as to how much "tradition" signals a dramatic return to rituals and customs once discarded by Reform Jews, and thus when to place
the beginning of the turn toward significant amounts of increased ritual,
but all agree it came from these Jews of east European ancestry. By the
1970s, at the very latest, most observers began to detect a steady movement in Reform Judaism toward tradition, so much so that by the start of
the new millennium the casual observer would not be able to notice much
difference between a Sabbath eve worship service in a Reform and a Conservative congregation, most anywhere in America, despite different
prayer books.

Nearly every Reform rabbi wore head covering during worship, incorporated generous amounts of Hebrew into the service, encouraged the
congregation to sing Hebrew melodies, paraded the Torah around the
congregation after it was removed from the ark and before it was read, and
felt comfortable inserting traditional ceremonies and rituals, long ignored
by Reform congregations, into occasional holiday and festival celebrations. Increasingly, elderly Reform congregants would complain to their

rabbis that the worship had become "too Orthodox," a sure sign of dramatic changes in the direction of increased tradition.

Orthodoxy's Rebirth

At the same time that Reform and Conservative congregations increased exponentially, Orthodox Judaism looked like a goner. In the middle decades of the twentieth century commentators noted its virtual demise, and wondered if—aside from some small sectarian communities—it would survive. Careful observers noticed that in addition to small numbers of Jews who declared or identified themselves as Orthodox, significant numbers of those that did so identify were not punctilious observers of Jewish ceremonies, customs, and rituals.

Even the son of the Rav, Haym Soloveitchik, who grew up in an Orthodox environment in Boston, recalled that he "grew up in a Jewishly non-observant community, and prayed in a synagogue where most of the older congregants neither observed the Sabbath nor even ate kosher." His neighbors were eastern European Jews, but "most of their religious observance . . . has been washed away in the sea-change, and the little left had further eroded in the 'new country.'" Indeed, "the only time the synagogue was ever full was during the High Holydays," and "most didn't know what they were saying."[69]

This began to change in the late 1960s and early 1970s, although the number of Jews declaring themselves Orthodox did not increase. But those that did so identify began to observe the rituals of Judaism more strictly, so that by the start of the new millennium a smaller but much more dedicated group of Orthodox Jews vigorously articulated a Judaism that put complete Sabbath and holiday observance, kashrut (dietary regulations), traditional worship (e.g., complete separation of men and women), and full-day Jewish schooling in the forefront of their religious lives.

While it is clear that levels of observance have increased among the slightly smaller number of Orthodox Jews in America in 2000 than in 1990, it is wrong to picture Orthodoxy as any more homogeneous than the extremely variegated Reform movement. The diversity in belief is tremendous, and the varieties of practices hardly less. Modern Orthodox rely on different sources deemed authoritative than do, say, sectarian or right-wing Orthodox, so that whereas some Orthodox will buy strictly kosher foods anywhere they are sold, others will shop only at stores that carry nothing that is not kosher. Some pursue secular education and participate in modern culture while concomitantly participating in Orthodox life; others will attend only sectarian Orthodox-sponsored shcools and avoid areas of secular culture. Some Orthodox rabbis will join communal organizations in which Conservative, Reconstructionist, and Reform rabbis participate; others deny their designation as "rabbis" because they do not observe all of Jewish law and hence shun association (and, implicitly, approval) with them. Orthodoxy, in sum, is much less monolithic than Conservative Judaism.

Reconstructionism

In the two or three decades after World War II, as Reform and Conservative congregations increased dramatically, and Orthodox Judaism seemed to most observers moribund, a fourth branch of American Judaism began to attract the attention of first rabbis and then laypeople. Reconstructionist Judaism may have begun in 1922 when Mordecai Kaplan (1881–1983) started to "reconstruct" Judaism while serving as rabbi of the newly formed Society for the Advancement of Judaism in New York City. Or it may have begun in 1934 when Kaplan's enormously influential *Judaism as a Civilization: Toward a Reconstruction of American Jewish Life* appeared. Kaplan dated its beginning to 1935 when he launched the influential *Reconstructionist* magazine.

Determined to construct an American Judaic civilization or culture or community without supernatural revelation or supernatural "choosing" of the Jews, and yet with considerable respect for traditional ceremonies, customs, and rituals, Kaplan affirmed Jewish observances not because they were divinely revealed commandments in the Torah but because they were the "sancta" of the Jewish group, the sacred or holy aspects of Judaism that had been cherished through the centuries.

For the most part, throughout the 1920s, 1930s, and 1940s, the Reconstructionist movement viewed its objective as infusing the three wings of American Judaism with its messsage; to provide, in Kaplan's words, "a rationale and a program . . . of Jewish unity which might enable Jews to transcend the differences that divide them."[70] There were only a few independent Reconstructionist synagogues (they preferred the term *fellowships*), as members of Reconstructionist organizations (fellowships, study groups, "centers") were encouraged to belong to an existing Conservative, Orthodox, or Reform congregation. But by the end of the 1950s Reconstructionist Judaism had become a fourth branch, or wing, of American Judaism, for a discernible "movement" had begun to take shape. With the founding of the Federation of Reconstructionist Congregations and Havurot in 1954 and the ascendancy of Mordecai Kaplan's son-in-law, Rabbi Ira Eisenstein, to the presidency of the Jewish Reconstructionist Foundation in 1959, we may speak of the Reconstructionist movement. In the following decade (1968) the movement's leaders founded a seminary to train Reconstuctionist rabbis (Reconstructionist Rabbinical College), the Reconstructionist Federation aggressively recruited new synagogue memberships and sustained old ones, and the movement was on the brink of a rabbinical organization (Reconstructionist Rabbinical Association or RRA, established in 1974) of its seminary graduates. By the end of the 1970s there were more than forty synagogues in the federation and close to ten thousand members of those congregations.

Havurot

Concomitant with the growth of Reconstructionist congregations, and clearly related, was the emergence in the 1970s of *havurot*, or fellowships, in Reform and Conservative congregations. Small, independent groups of ten-to-fifteen-member units (usually families) that ate, celebrated, studied, and worshipped together (at least once a month) mostly independent of the institution to which the members belonged (using homes or rooms other than the sanctuary of the synagogue), they were especially popular in large congregations where some members, feeling alienated, sought decentralization, intimacy, revitalization, and a stronger sense of community.[71] In the congregation in which they first emerged—Valley Beth Shalom in the San Fernando Valley outside of Los Angeles as a response to a 1970 Rosh Hashanah sermon by Rabbi Harold Schulweis—there were thirty havurot by 1973, and in Los Angeles, in 1975, exclusive of Valley Beth Shalom, two

researchers counted more than one hundred havurot in Conservative congregations alone.[72]

Women Rabbis

Another dramatic change has taken place, one that is greatly transforming
even those congregations that appear more formal in worship atmosphere—the emergence of four hundred women rabbis.[73] Although there
are yet no women who have been ordained as Orthodox rabbis—the latter
understand Jewish law as prohibiting this—they have dramatically
changed the face of Conservative, Reconstructionist, and Reform Judaism.

In the synagogue there is a level of emotion and intimacy that is dramatically different than three decades ago, when there was not a single
woman rabbi in America (the first, Sally Preisand, was ordained in 1972).[74]
Women rabbis introduced much more hugging and kissing when congregants ascend the pulpit, and this has characterized congregational worship
everywhere now for two decades or so. These same rabbis have revolutionized the sermon too, introducing more confessional and personal topics that have, to a large extent, replaced the emphasis on national and international themes of a previous generation of sermons. Women rabbis
have dramatically changed the way in which "the rabbi" talks to congregants, in every area of synagogue life, exchanging a much more reserved
and abstract level of conversation with a greater interest in sustaining conversations about congregants' feelings, joys, and worries. They have also
created and implemented a wide variety of blessings and liturgies for significant moments in a women's lifetime. Unlike their male counterparts,
they are far more likely to call women to the Torah with the Hebrew *feminine* forms of nouns, adjectives, and verbs ("grammatical etiquette")
rather than the centuries-old "traditional" form for calling a male to the
Torah. And women have encouraged substantial dialogue on balancing
one's professional and personal life, on intimacy, and on empowerment.[75]

Most interesting, women rabbis have changed the theological dialogue in congregations. Uncomfortable with the patriarchal tradition,
they have pushed the Conservative, Reconstructionist, and Reform
movements to consider truly inclusive prayer. Toward this goal, nontraditonalists have altered liturgical texts by using feminine pronouns and
verb forms as well as adding the matriarchs to prayers traditionally in-

voking Abraham, Isaac, and Jacob.[76] Men usually spoke of God as ultimately concealed, hidden, indescribable, infinite, unfathomable, and unknowable. Women rabbis, in sermons and classes, draw far more easily on the rich Jewish mystical and literary vocabulary of God's feelings: God is aging, embracing, hurt, lonely, longing, lost, studying, tired, and weeping. Although metaphors and allegories, to be sure, are never meant to be taken literally, a generation of women have greatly expanded the Judaic possibilities for answering questions such as who is God, what is God, where shall Jews look for God, and what are the implications of a male or masculine image of God.[77]

Ironically, women rabbis in the nontraditional branches of American Judaism have been asking these stimulating questions at precisely the same time that the role of the rabbi is being slowly transformed. When the author attended rabbinical school in the 1960s, the integration of Jewish studies into university and college departments had not taken place, so rabbinical students included those interested in serving congregations as well as those intent on academic careers. This has long since changed, and rabbinic students, even the most academic, plan on congregational careers, while young men and women interested in teaching Judaica in the academy enroll in one of the numerous graduate programs in Jewish history, literature, philosophy, or Judaic studies. The result has been that the rabbis of the past two decades or so are much less academically oriented than previously.

Indeed, the congregational rabbi of the opening years of the new millenium is far less either an intellectual or a community leader than in previous generations and far more a facilitator of countless activities—most of them part of the Judaic sacred calendar—within the congregation. It was, of course, the women who traditionally worked in the facilitating professions, such as counselor, social worker, and teacher, and they have entered the Conservative, Reconstructionist, and Reform congregational rabbinate at precisely the time that the role of the rabbi has been moving steadily away from leader and in the direction of helper.

Orthodoxy has been little influenced by the hundreds of women rabbis who have entered Conservative, Reconstructionist, and Reform synagogues as leaders, or by the equal number of women synagogue presidents who have made such a phenomenon now commonplace.[78] Orthodox congregations remain committed to excluding women from leading services or reading from the Torah when men are present. And the more sectarian or resistant the synagogue members feel toward feminism, the more male-centered will be its worship and activities. This is highlighted in the increasing (not declining) number of rigid separations (sing. *mechitzah*) between men and women in Orthodox sanctuaries. Today there are very few Orthodox synagogues without separate seating, and one Orthodox congregation in Columbus, Ohio, with mixed seating, found it nearly impossible in 2000 to hire an Orthodox rabbi who was willing to serve the congregation.

Jeffrey S. Gurock has pointed out that one need only study *mechitzot* (pl.) to understand the varieties of Orthodox Judaism in America. There are congregations where the separation is merely an aisle, and men (or women) can look right or left and see the other sex. There are other synagogue sanctuaries where the mechitzah is an actual partition; some partitions prevent worshippers from seeing the other sex while seated; others (generally called "right-wing" by the more modern or centrist Orthodox) separate the sexes even while standing. At one of the most aesthetically pleasing sanctuaries in the United States, B'nai B'rith Jacob, an Orthodox synagogue in Savannah, Georgia (four murals, two on each side of the ark containing the signs of the zodiac, adorn the pulpit; Jewish law strictly prohibits the picturing of God, but art has long been welcome in synagogue sanctuaries), the center section of the twelve-hundred-seat sanctuary seats men only, and the women sit in two raised sections on the right and left. Although elevated, the author recently watched (8 June 2002) many wives sit in a spot on the side that enabled them to make direct eye contact with their husbands, not to mention the majority of males seated in the center. Finally, there are synagogues where the women are seated in the balcony, with great sight lines to the pulpit but not to the men who are worshipping below.

Vitality

What strikes the contemporary observer of the synagogue is its vitality. Whether modern or ultra-Orthodox, Conservative, or Reconstructionist, the synagogue is alive, and many are doing quite well. Religious observance has been continually raised to new levels (among the Orthodox even to new heights or rigor). There are synagogues where worshippers pack prayer services, even early in the morning. One Detroit Orthodox synagogue was so crowded during prayers that it spawned a separate congregation in 1997 while enlarging its own building and remaining crowded. A Detroit yeshiva enlarged its main study/prayer space and in 2001 is still packed with worshippers from the neighborhood for Saturday morning services despite an 8:15 starting time. It is almost impossible to find a seat on a Friday evening if one comes late to the service at Conservative B'nai Jeshurun in Manhattan, and hundreds of worshippers regularly pack the sanctuary at the late Sabbath service at San Francisco's (Reform) Congregation Emanu-El. Everywhere the liturgy has moved in directions maximizing congregational participation in unprecedented ways. Even among the Reform worshippers, where there is yet no sense of an obligation to pray regularly and Friday evening takes precedence over Sabbath morning, head covering has become the rule rather than the exception, Hebrew now predominates over English, and the Torah is more and more read and discussed. The embourgeoisement of American Jewry may be a certain fact, but their worship patterns resemble more and more a religious group seeking spirituality. And perhaps this is not at all a contradiction.

CHAPTER FOUR

Institutions, Organizations and American Jewish Religious Activity

Like so many Protestant demoninations, Conservative, Orthodox, Reconstructionist, and Reform synagogues are each linked to a denominational "umbrella" organization that coordinates the movements. In some branches this organization establishes policy; in others it merely coordinates the multiple programs of the members institutions, but in each case the national organization has a strong presence within the American Judaic community. From time to time its leaders (e.g., Rabbi Alexander Schindler) have been among the most well-known American Jews.

The Conservative and Orthodox synagogue organizations established policy for the hundreds of congregations affiliated with those movements. By joining the United Synagogue, all Conservative congregations agree to observe the dietary rules (kashrut) within the confines of the synagogue. A Jewish worshipper at a Conservative congregation anywhere in the United States can be quite confident that shrimp or egg rolls with pork will not be served at a Sabbath lunch following worship services. And no Conservative congregation will host an intermarriage, e.g., a wedding of a Jew and a Christian. Similarly, the Union of Orthodox Jewish Congregations of America (OU) demands that every member synagogue observe the separation of men and women in the sanctuary during worship services or (in a rare case) that the congregation affirm that it is "moving in the direction of such separation."

For Reform congregations no authority of any kind resides in the umbrella organization. The Union of American Hebrew Congregations coordinates festival observances, fund-raising efforts, mitzvah projects, youth and adult educational programs, and much more, but it is prohibited from demanding anything of the congregations. The very principle of Reform Judaism is congregational autonomy, and if a congregation wants to serve ham and cheese sandwiches at a luncheon, or if a congregation wants to host a marriage ceremony of a Jew and a Presbyterian, the national organization has no authority to tell an individual congregation how to interpret Judaic ceremony, custom, or ritual.

The Union of American Hebrew Congregations

Moritz Loth (1832–1913), a prosperous Cincinnati Jewish merchant and president of Bene Yeshurun, convinced the other Cincinnati congregations in 1872 to issue a call to northwestern, southern, and western synagogues "with a view to form a union of congregations" to assemble in Cincinnati. Loth excluded the eastern congregations because they included "radical" reformers, and his goals were modest: to establish and financially support a seminary to train American Reform rabbis (every rabbi in the United States in 1872 had been ordained in Europe), to publish educational texts for children (these were virtually nonexistent), and to agree to hire only moderate Reform rabbis.

Loth's committee sent the formal invitation in March of 1873 and in July, in Cincinnati, thirty-four western and southern congregations formally agreed to the first association of American synagogues committed to religious goals: the Union of American Hebrew Congregations (UAHC). Although the meeting was mostly organizational, the delegates made a critical ideological decision to guarantee congregational autonomy by agreeing not to "interfere in any manner whatsoever with the affairs and management of any congregation." This has continued to be the fundamental principle of the union (and of Reform Judaism), to guarantee maximum individual freedom to each congregation. This would be tested from time to time in the next 125 years—much like the American Bill of Rights—but always reaffirmed. In 1943, when Houston's Beth Israel congregation, by a vote of 632 to 168, approved a resolution that denied voting rights and elected office to all members who would not subscribe to the congregation's "Basic Principles," one of which opposed "a return to Palestine,"[1] there was nothing the other congregations in the Union could do, no matter how distasteful they found this decision, but reaffirm the right of Beth Israel to remain a member of the union. In 1994, when the union's board of 180 members—representing 865 congregations—met to discuss Cincinnati Beth Abraham's membership application, they were faced with a request from a congregation that refused to explicitly mention God in its liturgy. If an existing congregation announced they were dropping certain traditional prayers because they were too "God-intoxicated," few ripples would flow through the union. But this congregation forced the union to declare, reluctantly to be sure, that its autonomy indeed had some limits and some beliefs and practices went beyond the pale.

Why did Beth Abraham seek admission to the UAHC? It sought access to the umbrella group's various educational, leadership, social, social action, and summer camp programs, and the opportunity to engage in dialogue with other congregations in regional and national gatherings. Among the departments of special interest to most of the congregations in this large national organization are Adult Jewish Growth (= adult education), Israel Programs, Jewish Education, Jewish Family Concerns, Outreach, Religious Action (= social action), Small Congregations, Synagogue Management, and the Youth Division (= youth groups and summer camps).

Most of these departments emerged slowly during the 125 years of the union's existence. The UAHC grew steadily in the late nineteenth century, from its original 34 to 72 in 1875 to 95 in 1894, and continued its growth well into the twentieth century. By 1920 the UAHC counted more than 200 congregations, nearly 300 by 1930, and passed the 400 mark by the beginning of the 1950s. Its main activity in the early years centered around Sunday schools or religious education, especially efforts to help small congregations and those in smaller Jewish communities and more Jewishly isolated areas where resources, such as qualified teachers, were lacking. The Committee on Circuit Preaching, established in 1895, arranged for rabbis to make visits to small towns—for worship and religious education—approximately every other month.

The union's Board of Delegates on Civil and Religious Rights (established in 1859 by twenty-four congregations) sought to "keep a watchful eye on all occurences at home and abroad,"[2] while the Committee of

Social Justice, recreated in 1929 to aid "those who are struggling for more equitable and just conditions of life in fields and industry, commerce and social relations," constantly took vigorous (and often bold) positions on numerous national and international issues. The Commission on Jewish Education published books for nearly every grade level of Reform religious schools. Philadelphia's Mikve Israel and Charleston's Beth Elohim are credited with the first Jewish Sunday schools (1838), and by the 1880s nearly every UAHC congregation had a religious school. The union tried its best to encourage a "uniform course of instruction," to provide materials for teachers as well as texts for students, to constantly survey the curricular and personnel needs of the member congregations, and to organize conventions for teachers and educators. The National Federation of Temple Sisterhoods (founded in 1913 and later called Women for Reform Judaism) and the National Federation of Temple Brotherhoods (founded in 1923) established cultural, philanthropic, religious, and social programs in nearly every UAHC congregation.

The "religious revival" of the 1950s caused dynamic growth in Reform congregations, as the number of UAHC synagogues increased by more than 50 percent in that single decade! According to the Department of New Synagogues, between 1946 and 1958 sixteen new Reform temples emerged in northern New Jersey, four in Rockland County (N.Y.), six in Westchester (N.Y.), and thirty-one on Long Island. Growth took place much more slowly in subsequent decades (about 15 percent in the 1960s and 7 percent in the 1970s), though by the end of the century the UAHC could claim more congregations than the parallel umbrella organization of Conservative synagogues.

The UAHC headquarters moved to Fifth Avenue in New York in 1951 from its long residence in Cincinnati, and in the 1990s it moved to a large and generously staffed center on Third Avenue in New York. Thirteen regional centers (Chicago, Cleveland, St. Louis, San Francisco, etc.) were led by Reform rabbis and professional administrative staffs, and numerous Reform rabbis headed national departments in the New York office. The UAHC ran at least ten Reform summer camps at the end of the century, sponsored a potent Religious Action Center in the nation's capital, and supported a rapidly growing network (more than twenty) of Reform Jewish day schools (The Progressive Assocation of Reform Day Schools) from Florida to California.

This network was supported by nearly two million members of UAHC congregations who contributed a portion of their synagogue membership dues to the union. From the end of World War II to the mid-1960s, the Combined Campaign raised large sums of money and, as at all other times, divided the proceeds equally between the Hebrew Union College (Reform rabbinical seminary) and the UAHC. Every year, as congregations and members increased, the campaign raised more money, and its funds came from annual congregational dues (50 percent), individual supplementary gifts (40 percent), and various communal grants (10 percent). For some years members of Reform congregations paid a flat amount, about $6 per member in the 1950s, but there was increasing pressure to "tax" congregations more equitably. By 1958 the [Louis] Broida Dues Plan went into effect, which mandated that each congregation would send 10 percent of the dues collected to the union. The plan (with a name change to Reform Jewish Appeal) worked successfully for years, although from time to time the percentage increased (e.g., to 12 percent in the early 1980s). The highest rate charged in 2001 was 8 percent, but in 2002 some congregations paid as much as 12 percent of their budget to the union.

Congregational minutes in many parts of the country indicate that "the cost of UAHC membership is a major operating expense," and most congregations handle this by implementing a member-family surcharge. One congregation in Texas, for example, calculated a flat dollar amount of $8,475 (based on a per member unit cost of $17.33) and passed this on to its members in a separate billing of $17.33 per month in 2001. This congregation had $487,000 in self-assessed dues income and contributed nearly $40,000 annually in UAHC dues.

We noted earlier that the UAHC was created, in part, to establish a seminary, and two years after its inception it established the Hebrew Union College in Cincinnati to train rabbis for UAHC congregations. From the start (the first rabbis were ordained in 1883) its graduates served Reform Jewish congregations. The college grew dramatically in the twentieth century, relying on the "tax" or a percentage of a UAHC congregation's budget, as well as private endowments, for its support. In 1949 the HUC merged with Rabbi Stephen S. Wise's Jewish Institute of Religion (New York), and soon the HUC-JIR had campuses in Cincinnati, New York, Los Angeles (1954), and Jerusalem (1963). In 1970 a mandatory first year in Jerusalem (following a B.A. degree) was instituted, with the final four years now possible at any of the three American campuses. The college supplied American Judaism not only with rabbis but with Jewish professionals of many kinds, including administrators, cantors, educators, and social workers.[3]

During the tenure of Rabbi Maurice Eisendrath (1943–73) as president of the UAHC, its most prominent activity was its commitment to social action. He was the driving force behind the creation in 1949 of the Joint Commission on Social Action of the UAHC and the Central Conference of American [Reform] Rabbis. Eisendrath relentlessly pushed congregations to engage in more and more social action ventures, especially civil rights and desegregation in the South in the 1950s and withdrawal from Vietnam in the 1960s, as he called upon Reform Jews "to apply the precepts and practices of prophetic Jewish faith in combating all forms of injustice and bigotry." Previously, it was individual rabbis who stood out in social action pursuits; by the time Eisendrath's presidency ended it was congregations, rather than their rabbis, who were in the forefront of religious action programs in the community and the nation.[4]

Eisendrath encouraged the UAHC to rally behind the freedom rides to Mississippi by northern and western Jewish volunteers, a significant percentage of whom were Reform Jews. He also urged participation in the 1964 Mississippi voter registration campaign, even though the Reform Jews in the South, many of whom vigorously attacked Eisendrath, trembled at the thought of white reprisal against them as they watched some of their hooded southern neighbors burn freedom buses and beat the freedom riders and southern police react mostly by arresting scores of them.

It was during Eisendrath's presidency that the UAHC approved a Social Action Center in Washington, D.C. (1959, and again in 1961), and in 1961 the Emily and Kivie Kaplan Center for Religious Action (now the Religious Action Center) opened in the capital with only the opposition of four or five (of more than 600) UAHC congregations. From the start, the center vigorously lobbied on Capitol Hill on behalf of civil rights for Negroes and gave strong support to both the Congress of Racial Equality and the National Association for the Advancement of Colored People. Eisendrath hated racism and the "vast miasma of venomous racial hatred and segregation which rises like a stink in God's nostrils."[5] Unfortunately, like most Northern whites, neither the center or the UAHC did little to fight racial segregation outside the South, and the racial separation in the North, West, and East mirrored the South but without the legal structure.

The Religious Action Center kept social justice in the forefront of Reform congregations throughout the last decades of the century, and the congregation members passed resolutions at their biennial conventions on behalf of troubled Jewish communities around the world (Ethiopia, Iran, Iraq, Soviet Union, Syria) and against apartheid, investing in South Africa, and the Vietnam War, and especially those Jews and non-Jews in the United States (AIDS victims, elderly, gays, lesbians, and the poor) in need of support.

The union also turned inward in the 1980s and 1990s with an intensive twelve-week course to certify physicians as Reform *mohalim* (ritual circumcisers),[6] as well as vigorous outreach to the non-Jewish partners of Jewish congregants and to non-Jews enrolled in Reform-sponsored conversion courses and intensive programs of adult Jewish education. As gentiles married to Jews joined synagogues in record numbers, and individuals with birth names such as Chung, Kelly, and Rodriguez carpooled their children to religious school, Rabbi Eisendrath told the UAHC Board of Trustees in 1978 that Reform Judaism should define a Jew as someone with *either* a Jewish mother or a Jewish father ("patriarchal descent") and that it should "reach the unchurched."[7] Since that time congregations have constantly debated the limits of non-Jewish membership (may non-Jews be full members? may they be committee members? may they be officers?) and amended by-laws to reflect clearer boundaries between Jews and non-Jews, while the union has reached out to them with abundant programs and materials.

In 1989 the union initiated a four-day national adult education study program (Kallah), and soon expanded it into numerous national study and spirituality retreats in different parts of the country. In addition it initiated a weekly Torah commentary distributed throughout the movement (primarily electronically), *Go and Study* texts for congregational leaders and committees (study texts have been published for finance, education, and ritual committees), and considerably upgraded its press.[8]

Other affiliates of the UAHC have continued their long-standing work in areas such as synagogue education (the National Association of Temple Educators, 1954), synagogue music (the American Conference of

Cantors), brotherhoods (National Federation of Temple Brotherhoods) and sisterhoods (Women of Reform Judaism),[9] synagogue administration (National Association of Temple Administrators), and youth work (National Federation of Temple Youth, 1939).

With the support of ARZA (American Reform Zionist Association), the union has demonstrated a considerable activism in building a Progressive, or Reform, movement in Israel, with two dozen congregations and three settlements active at the start of the new millennium. With hindsight, the turning point was possibly 24 October 1986, when, in response to an attack by a local Orthodox rabbi in Jerusalem and his twenty-five followers (they tried to steal the Torah scroll, physically assaulted the Progressive rabbis, and shouted obscenities at the women worshippers), the rabbi apologized (rather than face criminal charges) and the Reform movement began a new willingness to pursue its rights and to argue its case in the public arena.

The union was joined in its support for Progressive Judaism by the Central Conference of American Rabbis, the professional organization of Reform rabbis, which adopted its first platform dedicated exclusively to the relationship between Reform Judaism and Zionism in 1997. The platform encouraged aliyah (emigration to Israel) while concomitantly "affirming the authenticity and necessity of a creative and vibrant disapora Jewry."[10]

Eisendrath's successor, Rabbi Eric Yoffie, who took office in 1996, has emphasized a return to "tradition" and more intensive study for Reform laypeople. In amplifying his understanding of tradition, he has urged synagogue boards to call upon congregants to read and discuss four significant Jewish books each year, for synagogue committees to study a Jewish text during every committee meeting, for synagogues to train Torah readers and to incorporate Torah study into Reform Jewish Sabbath observance, and for Reform Jewish worshippers to consider adopting ceremonies, customs, and rituals discarded by Reform Judaism for a century or more. There is already considerable evidence of his successes.

The United Synagogue of Conservative Judaism

Rabbi Solomon Schechter (1847–1915), the president of the Conservative rabbinical seminary, the Jewish Theological Seminary of America (JTS), together with a number of seminary graduates, founded this umbrella organization of Conservative synagogues (formerly the United Synagogue of America) in February 1913. 22 congregations (half from the cities of New York and Philadelphia) were charter members of the organization, committed to clearly distinguishing their congregations from the Orthodox and Reform movements. By emphasizing "Jewish tradition in its historical continuity, advancing the cause of traditional Judaism, and strengthening the conservative tendency in American Israel," these congregations signaled their commitment to tradition (unlike Reform) and to history (unlike Orthodoxy, which maintains its interpretations have not evolved historically but were there at Sinai).[11]

Its constitution, crafted a few years later, amplified this rejection of Reform while, at the same time, spreading the broadest possible net with which to lure any and all congregations in the United States not affiliated with the UAHC. Indeed, as we have seen, the Conservative movement was already clearly delineated from the Reform movement—all Conservative congregations required men to wear head covering, held late Friday evening services, sat men and women together[12] and rejected the Reform *Union Prayer Book*—but the distinctions between Conservative and Orthodox were not yet clear. All of the congregations that joined the United Synagogue were nominally Orthodox before becoming members; Atlanta's Ahavat Achim, whose 1936 constitution declared it to be a synagogue of "orthodox Jewish ritual," joined the United Synagogue in 1952.[13] Conservative rabbis served Orthodox congregations; Columbus's Tifereth Israel, before joining the United Synagogue, called itself a "modern Orthodox" congregation and hired Jewish Theological Seminary graduates. Some Orthodox congregations (Columbus's Agudas Achim) had mixed seating, some did not. The term *Conservative Judaism* was not yet consistently used by the movement (the United Synagogue often called itself a Union for Promoting Traditional Judaism), but it was clear to every member of these founding congregations—as well as those who joined subsequently—that this movement stood for abundant Hebrew in worship, a decorous service, English sermons, a positive attitude toward "tradition" and traditional ceremonies, customs and rituals, a rabbinate trained in scientific research, and Sabbath and dietary observance. Only the most rigorously observant, and they were few in the 1910s and

1920s, would refuse to visit one of these emerging Conservative synagogues and ponder how they felt about the compromises with tradition (in contrast to the Reform rejection of tradition) that these synagogues were making.[14]

As the national organization defined itself, thanks largely to the careful craftsmanship of Schechter, it emphasized its American dimensions (thus the Jewish Theological Seminary of *America* and the United Synagogue of *America*). The rabbis ordained at the seminary of the Conservative movement were American rabbis, demonstrating to the children of east European immigrants that one could have the best of America's secular education and a first-class rabbinic education, could be a fine English-language preacher, deeply committed to decorum and order in worship, sensitive to the latest developments in American intellectual and cultural life, and, concomitantly, respectful of the authority of Jewish law and tradition.

It was the issue of authority that prevented Conservative Judaism from being the only alternative to Reform Judaism, for, increasingly, Orthodox congregations rejected the compromises with tradition of Conservative Judaism. Conservative synagogues have a respect for authority (unlike Reform they did wish to "conserve" tradition) but not an absolute commitment to it (unlike Orthodoxy), as they have always been willing to modify, change, and even discard some of the traditional laws. Indeed, the Conservative movement has little commitment to Jewish law beyond the areas of the Sabbath and kashrut. Conservative rabbis emphasize less the rootedness of Jewish law in divine revelation than its growth and development historically, and this means its changeability. And nearly every change Conservative congregations, laity, and rabbis have made in the century or so of their existence has found them at odds with Orthodox Judaism.

By the time the United Synagogue was established, Reform Judaism had clearly defined itself as an American movement with little interest in tradition. Its prayer book, the *Union Prayer Book*—used in nearly every Reform congregation—emphasized English prayers and the American identity of Reform congregations; it represented a radicalized version of German Reform clothed in an English translation, a liturgy that would have little appeal to east European immigrants and little more appeal to their children. But the United Synagogue congregations felt everything to the right of Reform was there for the taking, and they emphasized conservatism, history, and tradition—all in an American milieu—in a broad, undefined manner that might appeal to every non-Reform Jew.

An example of how Conservative congregations interacted with the American environment, compromised with tradition, and (reluctantly) set themselves off as just another branch of American Judaism rather than, to use Schechter's term, "catholic Israel," was their response to the increasing "number of people who found themselves living in widely scattered suburbs" after World War II. As the opportunities provided by the automobile led to the development of these suburbs, Conservative Jews everywhere moved away from their landmark downtown synagogues. They found it virtually impossible, but certainly impractical, to walk several miles to Sabbath eve or morning worship in order to both worship and observe the Sabbath prohibition against driving. The result was that "attendance at the synagogue on the Sabbath [became] physically impossible for an increasing number of our people."

A solution was proposed by the Conservative rabbinic authorities who made decisions on matters of Jewish law and who responded to the de facto situation of post–World War II Conservative synagogues and their members. They declared, in 1950, that riding to the synagogue on the Sabbath to worship, and only to worship, did not violate the prohibiton on Sabbath travel. By this compromise with tradition, the rabbis (and the synagogues that accepted it) preserved the prohibition on travel (for most of the Sabbath) and the obligation to pray with the community.

In so doing, the Committee on Jewish Law and Standards, and the United Synagogue of America, rejected the Orthodox view that every detail of the law must be observed, absolutely, and the Orthodox view that when a rabbinically forbidden act such as travel on the Sabbath (the Bible, of course, says nothing about Sabbath travel in a vehicle) clashes with the obligation of public prayer, both must be maintained. Thus, unlike the Reform movement, for which Jewish law had no authority, the Conservative movement took Jewish law very seriously and, from time to time, made compromises that alienated, little by little, Orthodox Jews.[15]

Another example of a compromise with Jewish tradition is the role of women in the synagogue. In 1985 the Conservative movement began ordaining women rabbis at the Jewish Theological Seminary, and scores of women now serve as rabbis in United Synagogue congregations. In addition, as in Reform congregations, women are called to the Torah, read from the Torah, and participate in every aspect of the liturgy in the Conservative movement. Here as well, this has set this wing of Judaism apart from the Orthodox who continue to interpret Jewish law as prohibiting the ordination of Jewish women as rabbis, calling them to the Torah, reading from the Torah, or leading the worship service (unless they do so in an all-women worship service).

Conservative Jews are serious about Jewish law; indeed, they speak frequently about law as the "life of Judaism." But they also feel free to change Jewish law—albeit, slowly and carefully—largely because they do not use as their starting point divine revelation of the Torah at Mount Sinai. It is authoritative, but it is not divine, and it is open to alteration by serious rabbinic authorities who carefully inquire about what Conservative Jews are doing and how Conservative Jews might best accommodate an ancient legal system with living in the modern world.

Like other religious umbrella organizations, there were numerous affiliated societies that constituted the United Synagogue. The North American Association of Synagogue Executives (1947) had more than 250 members at the end of the 1990s. The Young People's League (1921) supervised 127 youth groups with 15,000 members by 1927, and was replaced by the United Synagogue Youth in 1951. On its fiftieth anniversary in 2001 it claimed 25,000 members.[16] The National Women's League (1918), founded by Mathilde Schechter (1859–1924), which coordinated Conservative sisterhoods, had less than 30 affiliates in 1918, 70 societies with 6,700 women in 33 cities in 1920, 230 with 20,000 members in 1925, and 800 with 200,000 members in 1968 (it is now the Women's League for Conservative Judaism).[17] The National Federation of Jewish Men's Clubs (1929) served as the central office for 100 brotherhoods with 10,000 members in 1934, and had 350 affiliates with 38,000 men in 1986 (it is now the Federation of Jewish Men's Clubs).

The National Academy for Adult Jewish Study and the Solomon Schechter Day School Association (1964) provided curricular and other materials for synagogue and day school programs. Camp Ramah (1948) opened its newest camp in the South in the 1990s and extended its reach to Israel where its Ramah Israel programs had an annual budget of nearly $4 million in 2000. The World Council of Synagogues (1957) coordinated the internationalization of Conservative Judaism, while social action programs in individual synagogues were united by the Joint Social Action Commission in 1953 (it is now the Commission on Social Action and Public Policy).

A brief summary of Conservative Jewish brotherhood programs in Philadelphia during the twentieth century would highlight annual Good Neighbor Nights (dinner followed by speakers of different faiths), Saturday afternoon meals (called *seudah shleesheet* or third meal) at the synagogue with singing, dancing, and/or study; and Holocaust remembrance programs of various kinds. At the same Conservative synagogue a brief review of sisterhood activities would include adult education of many kinds, communal service programs, especially for the elderly, keeping the synagogue kitchen stocked with (kosher) food and supplies, maintaining a congregational gift ship with Jewish ritual objects, raising funds for the Jewish Theological Seminary library and residence halls, teaching and transcribing Braille, and (after about 1970) increasing programs for women who no longer stayed at home raising families but worked, full-time, outside the home.[18]

In the decades following the First World War, even before a social action commission emerged, the Conservative movement was active in the world outside the synagogue, especially in passing resolutions on social action that were adopted by the constituent bodies of the Conservative movement. These included resolutions on abortion, an antilynching bill, circumcision, civil liberties, civil rights, conversion, disarmament, domestic violence, economic injustice, euthanasia, federal aid to education, genocide, industrial relations, medical ethics, organ donations (the movement strongly supported such donations by informing its members that there is no greater honor for the dead than bringing healing to the living), Palestine and Israel, peace, religion in the public schools, the Vietnam War, and working conditions.

The Committee on Propaganda, in the early years of the United Synagogue, was vigorously recruiting Orthodox congregations for the movement, and had phenomenal success in the first 15 years of the United Synagogue's existence. Membership grew from 22 in 1913 to 50 in 1916 and 229 in 1927. Although less than 200 synagogues belonged to the United Synagogue at the end of World War II, it quickly outdistanced the Reform and Orthodox movements in the postwar years, as it grew to 365 synagogues in 1949, 778 in 1964, and 832 with approximately 1,500,000 members in 1971. In these postwar years, it was "America Jewry's movement."

The United Synagogue provided the primary support for the Jewish Theological Seminary, the institution that supplied rabbis for Conservative Judaism. Established in 1886 in New York as an "Orthodox Seminary" and initiating course instruction in 1887 as a response to the Hebrew Union College and Reform Jewish ideology, its name came from the distinguished Breslau Jewish Theological Seminary.[19] Early in the twentieth century a group of affluent Reform Jews in New York hired Dr. Solomon Schechter of Cambridge University to transform the seminary into an institution that would provide traditional, Americanized (English-speaking) rabbis to serve the rapidly growing immigrant Jewish community. Schechter, who regularly used the phrase *Conservative Judaism* as an alternative to Reform Judaism and Orthodox Judaism, delineated the contours of what he and others, self-consciously, would call a Conservative Jewish seminary.

A bachelor's degree was required for admission, and the JTS emphasized instruction in classical Hebrew or rabbinic texts (HUC emphasized Scripture). It also required its students, unlike HUC (which emphasized individual choice), to observe Jewish dietary laws, Jewish holidays, and the Sabbath. It raised funds through the United Synagogue as well as through private endowments, and at the turn of the twenty-first century it had become an institution of prominence, with programs that provided the Conservative movement and American Judaism with rabbis and other professionals, including academics, cantors, and educators.[20]

In the most recent years intermarriage has greatly agitated the United Synagogue and its constituent member congregations. When a Jewish member of a Conservative synagogue, even one who is raising children in the synagogue religious and educational community, has a non-Jewish spouse (this is a "mixed marriage"), the rights and privileges of the non-Jewish spouse are a source of anxiety everywhere. Is he or she entitled to membership? If so, the spouse could (of course) become a member of (for example) the ritual committee or even, in theory, president of the congregation (there is at least one example of a non-Jewish president of a Reform congregation in New York). Should the Torah be passed to non-Jews on the pulpit? Should they be called to the Torah to recite a blessing (which says, among other things, that God has "chosen *us*")? Should they be buried in the Jewish cemetery of the synagogue? In short, what should be the role of the non-Jew in the life-cycle ritual of a Conservative congregation?

Finally, the United Synagogue of America (now the United Synagogue of Conservative Judaism), has been continually concerned with synagogue attendance, not just at worship services but at all the activities of its constituent members. In a report undertaken just after World War II, the United Synagogue discovered that late Friday evening services, the "rallying point of religious activity," offered the "sorry spectacle of pews regularly empty."[21] Fifty or so years later, a study sponsored by the Ratner Center for the Study of Conservative Judaism at the Jewish Theological Seminary noted that Conservative synagogues were not successful in attracting young adults into their synagogues, and again the United Synagogue responded with renewed and vigorous efforts to ameliorate this situation.[22]

The Union of Orthodox Jewish Congregations of America

Henry Pereira Mendes (1852–1937), hazan and "minister" (= not ordained as a rabbi) of Shearith Israel in New York City (1877–1920), who combined European piety (he grew up in an Orthodox home in London) and secular American culture (he had a medical degree), was the principal founder of the Union of Orthodox Congregations in America (1898), an umbrella group of Orthodox synagogues. Reform Judaism served as the impetus; Mendes noted that he organized the UOJCA as a protest against "declarations of reform rabbis not in accord with the teachings of our Torah . . . and the accepted rulings of recognized sages of Israel."

The constitution of the union makes explicit this response to Reform Judaism, criticizing the reformers' neglect of "ceremonial duty" and their rejection of a "personal Messiah" and of Zionism, while affirming "Divine revelation of the Torah," the "codes of our Rabbis" (i.e., Jewish law), the need to "remain separate . . . in rites, ceremonies, ideals and doctrine" from non-Jews, and the desire to "advance the interests of . . . Rabbinical and Historical Judaism." It did this modestly at first, as the union of mostly small and poor synagogues was run out of Mendes's office and conventions met at his synagogue, and concerned itself initially with "loyalty to Jewish law and custom": kashrut and Sabbath observance (e.g., pushing college boards and boards of examiners to permit students to reschedule college-admission tests that fell on the Sabbath), battling Christian missionaries working the immigrant neighborhoods, and making ritual objects available to Orthodox Jews.[23]

Greenport Long Island's Tifereth Israel is typical of the members of the union in its formative years. It was poor (dues were $6 per year in 1902), and even with the selling (or renting) of seats for worship services, fines of all kinds ($5 if caught attending a celebation of a nonmember) and the selling of various synagogue honors, it could barely afford the one employee who earned $500 annually by leading services biweekly, reading the Torah, and teaching some children in the afternoon and evening after public school was finished for the day. The itinerant *shochet* came every Friday between 7:00 and 9:00 A.M. to slaughter chickens (for a fee) in a ritually correct manner, and others served the needs of the congregants on an occasional basis. The congregation took its Judaism quite seriously; it expelled members who refused to use the shochet, who disturbed divine worship, or who refused to send their children "to learn." And unless such an UOJCA synagogue sought an English-speaking, American-trained traditional rabbi (and only the Jewish Theological Seminary could supply such a man early in the twentieth century), it made do as did the Orthodox Jews of Greenport.

The Union of Orthodox Jewish Congregations of America grew rapidly, from the 50 congregations represented at the inaugural meeting of 1898 to 96 (or 104) congregations two years later, and reported 2,303 congregations in 1933, 3,100 in 1956, 2,500 in 1960, 3,900 in 1962, 3,100 in 1964, 2,000 in 1965 and in 1969. More likely, the union could claim 180 member congregations in 1925, 200 in 1927, 300 in 1942, 500 in 1950, 700 in 1955, 720 in 1957, 1,000 in 1983, and about 925 in 2000.[24]

Much more than Reform or Conservative congregations, the Orthodox union members were located in the largest cities of the United States, especially New York City. In 1947 93 of the 310 UOJCA synagogues were to be found in Long Island, Manhattan, the Bronx, and Brooklyn, while in the same year more than half of all the congregations in the union were in two states (New York and New Jersey) and one city (Philadelphia). Orthodoxy was yet to spread very far from the point of origin of most east European Jewish immigrants and would continue, throughout the century, to be even more urban than its Reform and Conservative counterparts. Today Orthodoxy has transformed itself from what most called "a dying movement" (1950s) to a vibrant (though numerically small) branch of American Judaism.

Its publications, describing these Jews as "Modern Orthodox," take a dual tack: on the one hand, noting "the disastrous state of American Jewry in the 1990s" (i.e., the vitality of Reform and Conservative Judaism) or "tolerance and pluralism when relating to the ideologies of non-Orthodox movements have no place in Torah philosophy," because "there is only one Judaism," Orthodoxy. On the other, reveling in its own vitality. Typical is the enthusiasm of Rabbi Berel Wein, "In a recovery that can only be seen as bordering on the supernatural, the Orthodox movement has become the fastest-growing and most dynamic part of American Jewry over the last decades of this century," or, in the words of Judith Bleich, "the resultant transformation of American Orthodoxy . . . on these shores is well-nigh miraculous."[25]

And though it is not the "fastest-growing . . . part of American Jewry," having actually declined slightly between 1990 and 2000, its vitality is not in question. Orthodox Jews fill the Upper West Side and Upper East Side of New York City, as well as affluent neighborhoods of numerous other North American cities; there are numerous suburbs, everywhere, with thousands of young Orthodox couples, there are numerous Orthodox schools filled to overflowing, and there are yeshiva towns on the model of Europe in previous centuries.[26]

Unlike the Reform and Conservative congregations, which have automatic contributions from member congregations graduated by size and budget, the UOJCA has no clearly defined financial package that takes a percent of the synagogue budget, or a member's dues, for the national organization. Indeed, many of the union synagogues do not even have a formal dues plan, and it is rare to find a member of a UOJCA synagogue who is aware of the financial arrangements between an individual synagogue and the national organization. Thus the national campaigns of the union (the 1938 drive sought $1,000,000—$1 from a million members) are the major source of income for the UOJCA and its activites on behalf of Orthodox congregations and its outreach programs (supporting rural synagogues and Orthodox Jewish education, acquiring a Torah for a new congregation).

Over the years no activity took precedence over supervising kashrut and making kosher products available to observant Jews everywhere. The *Kosher Directory* is regularly updated, provides long lists of kosher products (foods, sweeteners, vitamin supplements, water, and the like) and services, and serves as a guide to the relatively unobtrusive "U" symbol on countless products. In 1925 the UOJCA and the Union of Orthodox Rabbis (UOR) signed an agreement to jointly issue *heksherim* (kashrut approvals) under the auspices of the Va'ad Ha-Hora'ah (appointed by the UOR) and an advisory committee (appointed by the UOJCA). Since this service is done on a fee basis, the two organizations tried to eliminate accusations of payoffs, profiteering, and unethical *mashgichim* (kashrut supervisors) by a joint finance committee that would control the kashrut proceeds and distribute them to the needy. Orthodox publications regularly list new food products elgible to display the "U," while the Kashrut Division of the UOJCA lobbied Jewish leaders to observe Orthodox dietary regulations (although they vary widely among the observant) at communal functions. By 1954 139 rabbis supervised 405 products in 181 plants in 129 firms; in 1955 alone, 113 products, manufactured by 34 companies, were added to the list; in 1963 more than 2,000 kosher products were produced by over 400 companies; and the list continued to expand through the following decades until in 1983 it included 10,000 products and in 2000 it reached 200,000 products from 2,000 manufacturers in almost 4,000 plants in 62 countries.[27]

The UOJCA, and especially its Institute for Public Affairs, like its Reform and Conservative counterparts, was also immersed in programs of social justice, including (moving chronologically through the twentieth century) lobbying for the five-day work week (and thus free time to observe the Jewish Sabbath day), social security legislation, the right of civil service applicants to move Saturday tests to another day, religion in the public schools, federal civil rights legislation, fair housing, freedom of religious expression and exit for communities abroad, Israeli settlements in the West Bank (the UOJCA never used the term *Occupied Territories*), and legislation or programs related to alcoholism, domestic violence, and substance abuse.

Orthodox women also had sisterhoods or ladies auxiliaries, coordinated by the Women's Branch (established in 1922) of the union. It claimed 2,000 sisterhoods in 1952 but only 600 in 1982, and everywhere these women raised funds for Orthodox causes and sponsored events to rally Orthodox women. They were joined, as UOJCA affiliates, by the National Conference of Synagogue Youth (established in 1942 as the National Union of Orthodox Jewish Youth and renamed in 1959), with regions all over North America. These regions, as in the United Synagogue Youth (Conservative) and National Federation of Temple Youth (Reform), divided the country into manageable program units and interspersed local and regional youth programs (conventions, leadership consultation, seminars, weekend retreats) around annual (or more frequent) national (and even international) gatherings. And, recently, the NCSY added a Junior division (sixth through eighth grades), a comprehensive Israeli division, and claimed its membership surpassed 15,000.[28]

Union of Orthodox Jewish Congregations of America synagogues find their rabbis primarily from graduates of the Rabbi Isaac Elchanan Theological Seminary (RIETS) in New York. Although called a seminary, where non-Talmud programs of Jewish learning and practical rabbinics exist together with Talmud (as at the seminaries of the other sectors of American Judaism), it is actually a yeshiva, where Talmud is the overwhelming subject of study, and study (not ordination) is primary. The origins of the RIETS are in 1896–97 on the Lower East Side of New York, and in 1903 the Union of Orthodox Rabbis recognized the RIETS as the only legitimate yeshiva (among several) in the United States, although it served initially as simply a school, with ordination invested separately (unlike the other seminaries). In 1915, with the merger of Etz Chaim and the RIETS, it became solely an advanced yeshiva for training (and ordaining) English-speaking, Orthodox rabbis, and the main conduit for filling UOJCA pulpits. Unlike the Conservative, Reconstructionist, and Reform seminaries, the RIETS does not ordain annually but triennially; by 1968 it had ordained its 1,000th rabbi.[29]

Other affiliates of the UOJCA include the Pardes Project, which coordinates hundreds of discussion groups on current issues in Orthodox union congregations around the country; Kharkov, bringing Orthodoxy to the Ukraine; the National Council for the Disabled/Yachad, which arranged programs for developmentally disabled and deaf children as well as (in Israel) children with cancer; and numerous programs built around Torah or study, such as Torah Tidbits.

While kashrut dominated UOJCA activities and publications for decades, today the issue of feminist Orthodoxy fills the pages of Orthodox publications and countless forums, for this is the first generation of Orthodox Jewish women to reckon with the idea of gender equality. There are new sounds of women and Talmud in academies of all kinds, as Orthodox girls argue for an education commensurate with boys. Women are participating in festivals (such as Simchat Torah, the holiday of Torah rejoicing) in which they were previously onlookers, and young women are chanting the weekly Torah portion at a women's *tefillah* (public prayer group) and *minyanim* (prayer quorums) everywhere, as Orthodox women press for spiritual equality in synagogues, family life, houses of learning, and Jewish communal organizations—always within the framework of Jewish law.[30] They seek to preach from the pulpit, introduce the Torah and prophetic scriptural reading, serve as officers, carry the Torah through the women's section, recite the Kaddish (mourner's prayer),[31] include the *imahot* (matriarchs) in the *Mi sheberach* prayer for the sick, and offer a Torah commentary. One Orthodox congregation outside Manhattan, the Hebrew Institute of Riverdale, has a spiritual assistant (*madreechah ruchaneet*) to the rabbi, and this assistant is a woman. This generation of Orthodox Jewish women argues that there is no mechitzah (separation of men and women in the synagogue) between women and the Torah, that Orthodox women have little spiritual impact on Jewish law, rituals, and customs, and that women have been socialized in Orthodox communities into internalizing and celebrating their innate differences in ways that benefit the men who hold the economic, cultural, and social power in the Orthodox community.[32]

Mainline Orthodox publications, and nearly every Orthodox rabbi, generally object to this feminism, whether in the form of bat mitzvah ceremonies, women's tefillah, or women as Torah readers, largely because it radically challenges well-established gender roles in Judaism. They point to the abundance of spiritual equality and worth in the traditionally mandated women's role and rituals and the nourishment and nurturing available to women by the gender-based differences that prescribe domestic roles for women (children, family purity rituals, food, and *shalom bayit* [domestic tranquility]). It is certainly the issue to watch as the twenty-first century unfolds.[33]

The Jewish Reconstructionist Federation

In an attempt not to create a fourth sector of American Judaism, the earliest Reconstructionist congregations, as we noted earlier, insisted that their members also join existing wings (Reform or Conservative). Reconstructionism's leader, Rabbi Mordecai M. Kaplan, asserted that the movement was a "school of thought," not a new denomination, "a movement *in* Judaism" and not "a movement *of* Judaism," and his followers echoed this. Jacob Agus, rabbi of Chicago's North Shore Agudas Achim, insisted that Reconstructionism was "not a sect but a movement to concentrate and give organizational form to the elements of strength within all sections of American Judaism." Adopting the denominational pattern would only alienate a large and active element in American Jewry. He spoke for those Reconstructionist leaders who put Jewish unity as the highest priority and felt that they could influence existing congregations to intensify Jewish education, create democratic organizational structures, cultivate Jewish arts of every kind, rebuild the homeland in Palestine, experiment with Jewish liturgical changes, and bring some of the aspects of the Jewish community center movement into the synagogue. They were reluctant to become "a fourth religious denomination" and jeopardize Jewish unity because the Reform and Conservative congregational bodies "are indispensable." Rather, Reconstructionism viewed itself as "transcending . . . denominational differences."[34]

By the late 1960s, however, Reconstructionism had become a "full-fledged movement," a fourth denomination of American Judaism, with its own seminary, its own rabbinical organization, and its own congregational union, the Federation of Reconstructionist Congregations and Havurot (FRCH). The latter grew out of the Reconstructionist Federation of Congregations (and would change its name again in 1998 to the Jewish Reconstructionist Federation). With the change of name to FRCH in 1961, this umbrella organization of a small number of synagogues and fellowships (havurot) signaled that it was moving toward independent denominational status and would soon demand that congregational affiliates belong only to the federation.[35] By the early 1980s it numbered 45 member units, by the 1990s 70 affiliates, and by the start of the twenty-first century the membership reached 100. Almost 60 percent of these congregations and fellowships were in eight states: Pennsylvania (12), New York (9), California (9), New Jersey (7), Massachusetts (6), Maryland (6), Illinois (5), and Florida (4).

The programs of the FRCH have a single goal: to promote the Kaplanian idea that Judaism is the evolving religious civilization of the Jewish people. Therefore they emphasize congregational activities that center on diaspora culture (especially music and dance), Hebrew language, Israel, Jewish thought, life-cycle events, and philosophy.

In 1968 the FRCH established a seminary in a Philadelphia suburb—the Reconstructionist Rabbinical College—that ordained seventy-five rabbis in its first fifteen years of existence. It initially combined with Temple University to create a joint graduate program in Judaic studies and rabbinical learning that culminated in advanced degrees from each institution. It was the first seminary to admit women rabbinic students (HUC-JIR and JTS followed in the 1970s and 1980s, respectively) and the only seminary to construct a curriculum based on Jewish "civilization." Like the other seminaries, it received its funding primarily from the congregations (and individual members) in the movement.[36]

In 1999 the Jewish Reconstructionist Federation published a 1,275-page prayer book for the High Holidays, *Kol Haneshamah: Prayers for the Days of Awe*. Deeply influential within a short time after its publication, it combines a strong commitment to tradition with a broad search for contemporary meaning, especially through poetry. It continues the theology of the 1989 Reconstructionist Sabbath prayer book, *Kol Haneshamah: Shabbat Eve* (245 pages), rejecting the coming of a Messiah, concepts of chosenness, the Genesis 1 creation of the world story, individual afterlife, a transcendent deity, and verbal revelation of the Torah.

Reconstructionism is characterized, perhaps most of all, by its insistence that the biblical conception of God is humanly constructed, legendary, and mythic. The Bible does not leave a record of what God said or what God is but, rather, what the Jews of that time and place said God said. For modern Jews, or Reconstructionists, God is men and women's highest aspirations, ideals, and dreams, or, most frequently, ultimate reality. It is this ideology (and primarily, theology) that most differentiates the institutions of Reconstructionism from those of the other branches.

CHAPTER FIVE

The Synagogue

There is a reading found in some Sabbath evening prayer books that begins, "The synagogue is the sanctuary of Israel, born of Israel's longing
for God. Throughout our wanderings it has endured as a stronghold of
hope and inspiration, teaching us the holiness of life and inspiring in us a
love of all humanity." *Israel*, of course, is a term used from biblical days
to the present for the Jewish people, and this text nicely sums up much of
the historic vitality of the synagogue.

At least since the diaspora experience in the Greek and Roman
worlds, where it was ubiquitous and vital, the synagogue has been the
sanctuary of the Jewish people, literally and figuratively: the place where
Jews have offered prayers of petition and gratitude, listened to the reading of their Scriptures, celebrated festivals, studied texts, and found
refuge in times of physical and spiritual difficulty. Rabbis, whether employed by the community or by a specific congregation, preached
and/or taught in the synagogue, primarily through sermons but also by
lessons on the Torah. And it has long been the site of "boundaries," the
place where one ultimately determined whether or not one is Jewish.[1] In
this chapter we will explore the varieties of synagogue worship, the recent evolution of the sermon, and the latest dilemma over boundaries in
the synagogue.

The synagogue has a longer history than the discussion in this chapter will suggest. Yesterday's synagogue was much more a center of wor-

ship and social life for entire families than that of today; small children, parents, and grandparents often occupied adjoining pews until the combination of assimilation, occupational mobility, secularization, and suburbanization caused severe dislocation in the multigenerational family's relationship to the synagogue. And the role of the rabbi and the rabbi's sermon have changed over a period of 150 years as well. The rabbi has become a professional, a specialist, and the highlight of worship services has fluctuated—at different times, in different wings of American Judaism, and in diffferent locales—from the liturgy to the sermon, with the latter sometimes just a pause in the liturgical flow, other times the center of the worship experience. But this chapter is less a study of the historical evolution of the synagogue and more a look at the synagogue during a period of only a few decades.

As the new century unfolds, Sabbath eve and morning worship in American synagogues is extremely diverse. Perhaps the Conservative Jewish Sabbath morning service is the exception, as no matter whether one attends a Conservative synagogue in Seattle or Miami, Boston or San Diego, the Sabbath morning service is virtually identical.[2] But in nearly every other case the varieties are more striking than the similarities.

The Varieties of Worship

The least common is the rather old-fashioned service, usually found in larger sanctuaries with elevated pulpits, hidden choirs, and much solemnity. These are formal, no matter the branch of Judaism, with rare spontaneity or informality at any time during the services. The worshippers at these congregations are more likely to be middle-aged and elderly, and frequently have been attending this type of service for many years. The rabbi constantly gives directions for rising, sitting, reading responsively, the page to be read, and the like, although these are explicit in the text. The rabbi delivers a formal sermon; the setting (pews, decor, physical layout) is permanent; and the officiants, in Erving Goffman's words from another context, "cannot begin their act until they have brought themselves to the appropriate place and must terminate their performance when they leave it."[3] They are "services that were made into performances," in the words of Rabbi Harvey J. Fields of Los Angeles, with "worship leaders who reduce congregants into passive and bored specta-tors,"[4] or, as one study of such Reform worship services calls the congre-gants, "individual auditors" or "spectators of a liturgy performed by oth-ers."[5] Worshippers at such services dress more formally than at other synagogues (rare is the man without coat and tie),[6] and when something new is carefully introduced into the service bulletin and pulpit announce-ments prepare the way so as to cause the least possible stir.

In an age of "spirituality" seekers, where participatory worship is continually privileged, such services usually get low marks (*cold* is the frequent adjective by those who are not regulars). But many are deeply moved by quiet solemnity and a classical concert atmosphere, and may even find God in the constant, in a service that has been the same for years, and express sadness at a new liturgy that uses gender-neutral lan-guage or new English translations for familiar readings. The cadences of such a liturgy can be a warm balm for many, but the numbers are de-creasing steadily. In fact, my interviews with worshippers following serv-ices indicate that few find spiritual sustenance from the liturgy, or even edification from the sermon, but come mostly out of comfort in attending something that rarely changes. They enjoy the community of fellow wor-shippers who also appear regularly and who share weeky socializing at the lengthy refreshment hour after the Sabbath evening and morning services. They complain if the service exceeds the standard length (espe-cially if a guest speaker talks longer than the weekly norm), as they look forward to its completion in the shortest amount of time possible to max-imize fraternizing.

The most common type of Sabbath worship in America is what I will call middle of the road. These services are frequently in medium-sized sanctuaries, with a mixture of (mostly) well-dressed and (some) infor-mally dressed worshippers, and a mixture of young, middle-age and old worshippers. The rabbi delivers a talk, less formal than the sermon at the old-fashioned congregation, but generally from a detailed outline rather than a text. The music, whether led by a cantor or choir, is usually a mix of (mostly) participatory hymns and (some) solo selections. Stage direc-tions are frequently executed through subtle body movements, interfer-ing only modestly with the flow of the liturgy. Spontaneous insertions, while not abundant, are not out of place either, and that includes asking if anyone has any announcements of upcoming events.

These worshippers are more likely to comment on the sermon after the service (more on this later) and to wonder if the type of service they have attended maximizes "spirituality." They are the most comfortable with attending services of other branches; they even (with the exclusion of most Orthodox) find the variety of services interesting. They wonder why there are not more younger worshippers at their own services, but seem to be content with the liturgy and with their fellow worshippers.

The third type of worship experience is a service marked by informality, abundant Hebrew (whether Conservative, Orthodox, Reconstructionist, or Reform), maximum congregational participation, Torah reading (and often discussion), and occasional commentary about, or explanation of, the liturgy by the rabbi. The rabbi hardly needs to give any stage directions, as the worshippers are either expected to read the instructions in their prayer book or simply follow what others (more familiar with the service) are doing. The cantor is much more of a congregant, initiating hymns and responses but rarely singing them alone. The rabbi, or service leader, often greets the worshipppers at the door of the sanctuary before services or, as is common at an Orthodox congregation in Riverdale (the Bronx), New York, works the crowd during "appropriate" parts of the liturgy (when some are wandering around or talking to each other or even dozing a bit).[7] The worshippers tend to dress casually,[8] more younger worshippers are present than in the other worship environments, and the rabbi is more likely to come off the pulpit (usually not elevated in any significant manner) and move among the congregants who themselves are more likely to be in chairs that are movable, in contrast to fixed pews or seats in the other congregations.[9] This is possible, in large part, because these services are held in synagogues built in the past three decades with sanctuaries intentionally designed without fixed pews.[10]

In hundreds of American synagogues there is not one of these worship services but multiple Sabbath morning services in the same synagogue, sometimes at the same time. Multiple Sabbath services have been common in Orthodox synagogues for some time, where the synagogue has long been both a social club and sacred space, but it is a more recent phenomenon in non-Orthodox congregations. An alternative to the late Friday service and the bar or bat mitzvah service on Saturday morning, where some congregants feel like a stranger with so many guests present, is the "alternative" or "minyan" service on Saturday morning. Usually led by laypersons, it maximizes informality and spirituality, creates participants rather than spectators, even when missing the "setting" or "furniture, decor, physical layout and other background items."[11] When there is more than one rabbi at the synagogue, one of them sometimes drops in, but usually as a worshipper, not a leader. And, in many congregations around the country, there are sufficiently knowledgeable laypeople for someone to prepare the Torah reading for that Sabbath. It is this service, overwhelmingly, to which those who come for Torah study (often called Early Torah) and remain for worship will go when they stay in the synagogue beyond the hour or period of learning. And this is clearly the fastest growing Reform and Conservative worship experience as the new millennium gets underway. One Conservative congregation in Southern California has five different Sabbath morning services, all well attended, and this is more the norm than the exception.

In the main sanctuary (this is known as the "regular" service) the rabbi and cantor lead the worship, a sermon is always presented, and bat or bar mitzvah ceremonies occur here. This service lasts about three hours, from 9:00 A.M. to noon. There is a layperson-led early Sabbath service with no sermon, no liturgical repetitions, and no life-cycle events, and it takes place for an hour and a half before the "regular" service. There is a learners service that meets monthly and is primarily a "teaching" service that includes Torah reading, a brief Torah discussion, and an explanation of some part of the liturgy. It is always led by a rabbi who takes and responds to questions throughout the service. There is a service that also meets monthly and has a long Torah reading and discussion, an abbreviated liturgy, and abundant singing. It is lay led. The final service, also lay led, meets monthly and "competes" with the regular service by beginning and ending at the same time. It seems to attract singles and couples in their twenties and thirties who prefer to worship together rather than where there are life-cycle ceremonies.

At Kehillath Israel, a Conservative synagogue in a Boston suburb, there is, simultaneously, a Sabbath morning "traditional" service, an "egalitarian" service, a service for ages two to five (Nitzanim, "buds"), for ages five to seven (Mini Minyan) and ages seven to thirteen (Junior Congregation). On Saturday morning, at the Hebrew Institute of Riverdale, the same Orthodox synagogue mentioned previously, from

8:30 A.M. to noon a worshipper may choose to attend the regular service, the teen minyan, the Sephardic minyan, the beginners service, and (monthly) the women's service. These services are more and more the common pattern in large Conservative congregations, and scores of Orthodox and Reform congregations also hold multiple worship services on Saturday mornings.

This has a parallel in a relatively new worship pattern that has emerged in Reform and Conservative congregations on Friday evening, as if in response to Kaufmann Kohler's 1906 observation that "late Friday evening services are an innovation of a dubious character."[12] In city after city, congregants are adult men and women with careers, frequently in the professions. Even if they live in the city (rare), few are the couples who find it possible to arrive home from work in time to have a modicum of Sabbath dinner and arrive at worship services on time, or even close to the start. And if they live in the suburbs (the norm), this is even more unlikely, as neither husband nor wife is home in time to prepare dinner and for the family to finish eating in time to attend worship.

For the most part this simply eliminates the large majority of congregants from worship attendance, except on special occasions when, with considerable planning, one of the adults is able to leave work early and have dinner ready in time for hurried eating and driving to the synagogue. Since Saturday morning is perceived as a "bar or bat mitzvah service," this helps explain the absence of most Reform members from Sabbath worship. There is, in fact, in at least one area of the country, a strong correlation between those families without children at home and families where one of the parents is home on Friday, or at least on Friday afternoon, and worship attendance on Sabbath eve.[13]

An increasing response to this situation is the "early" Sabbath eve service—paralleling, though not imitating, the Orthodox Friday eve service that is held at sundown, even if sundown is at 4:30 P.M.—an attempt to attract at least one of the two adult members on their way home from work to Sabbath dinner. Starting somewhere between 5:30 and 6:30, depending on the location of the synagogue, the major areas of employment, and the season of the year, this service is much more likely than any other (except the Saturday morning minyan) to elicit a positive response about spirituality from those who attend. Frequently it is mostly sung by the worshippers, with little direction from cantor, layleader, or rabbi, and the "sermon" is, at most, a brief five- or ten-minute message.[14] Sometimes this service replaces the late service;[15] in some synagogues it is in addition to the later service. Everywhere the worshippers are enthusiastic: a brief but meaningful worship exerience, a modest "sermon," and a relaxed Sabbath dinner with spouse, self, or (when appropriate) children lies ahead.

The informality of many of these minyans, alternative, or early services has influenced the pattern of worship in the main sanctuary as well. At one large congregation in Durham, North Carolina, on a typical Sabbath eve, a packed sanctuary of men and women included a rabbi and cantor in suit and tie and approximately 125 of the 135 adult males present wearing open shirts without tie or coat. The worshippers at the smaller Sabbath worship services usually dress casually, and they are part of a revolution in dress patterns at synagogues all over the country. Concomitant with this is an increase in the number of sanctuaries with movable chairs, enabling the rabbi (or worship leaders) to arrange the seating in a pattern conducive to the atmosphere desired for that evening or morning. Of course, this is impossible in sanctuaries with pews, and the majority of congregations at the beginning of the twenty-first century still have such pews.

These more or less informal services attract worshippers who seem much more likely to engage the subject of the rabbi's talk or the themes of the Torah portion following the service, especially among the Reform and Reconstuctionist Jews, who have little commitment to weekly worship irrespective of the type of service. They are also much more prone to be critical of services not like their own, especially those that do not maximize congregational participation or that use a different liturgy.

The latter is a constant topic of discussion, for there are abundant prayer books available within each branch of American Judaism. Some Conservative congregations use a gender-neutral liturgy. some retain the older (1980s) book. Some Orthodox congregations use a prayer book with Hebrew on one page and English on the facing page (even when they read little or no English!), others use a single prayer book that is exclusively in Hebrew, while some encourage worshippers to bring any "Orthodox" prayer book they wish.[16] And among Reconstructionist and Reform Jews the number of liturgical choices are much greater, as each congregation searches for the prayer book that will maximize congregational attendance and spirituality.

Many Conservative, Reconstructionist, and Reform synagogues have Sabbath eve services that one might call an event. The large majority of congregants do not worship regularly, and it takes something special (a jazz service, an ecumenical service, a Holocaust memorial service) for them to consider attending a Friday evening service. There is virtually no sense of an obligation to worship regularly (e.g., monthly, not to mention weekly) among non-Orthodox Jews in America, and whether someone attends or not seems to have little to do with either the type of service or the rabbi's sermon or the Torah portion. Worshippers, when asked after the service about this, express little enthusiasm for the liturgy, or confidence in the ability of prayer to find a listening ear, but emphasize the sense of community, the words of the rabbi, and the music as the attractions.

Attendance, at 8:00 or even 8:30 P.M., requires considerable preparation for an early (and usually rushed) Sabbath dinner as well as travel to the synagogue. But this is hardly the problem; the same adults who do not attend the synagogue manage to complete their Sabbath dinner, if they have one, and arrive at a cinema in time for an 8:45 film. There is simply little motivation for prayer, and without a sense of obligation to pray regularly (as the Orthodox have), most synagogues are poorly attended on Friday evening.

Of course, "poorly attended" is, to some extent, in the eye of the beholder.[17] I assume that a synagogue with 750 member units has at least (and there is abundant information to suggest this is a very low figure) 1.5 adults for each member unit, or about 1,100 adult members. If so, there is rarely a Sabbath, without a featured "event," when there are as many as 10 percent of the adult members present, whether on the East Coast, the West Coast, or in the Midwest, South, or New England.[18] And this figure, consistent with national surveys, is strikingly low when compared to church attendance.[19]

The exceptions are twofold: Sabbath morning worship at small and medium-sized Orthodox congregations, where men have an obligation to pray regularly (this is true of all Orthodox males) and congregants feel a sense of community, and, to a lesser extent, similar Conservative congregations, where the multiplicity of worship services attract substantial numbers of men and women. At such congregations one counts a regular attendance of about 25 percent of the members.[20]

At most medium-sized and large Reform and Conservative synagogues in America, one or more b'nai mitzvah ceremonies take place at the Sabbath morning services. At Reform congregations there is a sense on the part of most of the Sabbath evening worshippers that the following morning is for "bar mitzvah families," so those that do attend worship at such Reform congregations tend to pray on Sabbath eve rather than Sabbath morning. This is not as much a dilemma at Conservative and Reconstructionist and not at all relevant at Orthodox congregations, where the liturgy and Torah service remains much the same whether a bar or bat mitzvah ceremony will occur, and congregants do not think of the Sabbath morning worship as "private."[21]

Curiously, at many Reform congregations, more members attend the Torah study hour, usually led by the rabbi, before the b'nai mitzvah ceremony, than remain for the service. In many places rabbis report that twenty-five to thirty people attend Torah study from 8:30–10:00, and then most of them get in their cars and drive home as the Saturday morning service begins. Lawrence A. Hoffman has observed that "the likelihood that they will appear at a Shabbat service where they do not know the bar/bat mitzvah is only slightly higher than the probability that they will be found at a randomly selected funeral where they know neither the mourner nor the deceased."[22] Reform congregants feel as if the premises have been rented to a specific b'nai mitzvah family for their private celebration rather than joining with the congregational family as is appropriate for a bat or bar mitzvah. Many feel like "outsiders" at these services, although they all know that they are just as public as those on Sabbath eve.[23]

The Sermon

No matter the branch of Judaism, there has been a dramatic change in the role of the sermon at Sabbath worship. In the 1920s, 1930s, 1940s, 1950s—and even into the 1960s—charismatic preachers drew large crowds. In 1962 lectures to rabbinic students at the Hebrew Union College–Jewish Institute of Religion in Cincinnati, Abraham J. Feldman of Hartford, Connecticut, could argue that "the preaching ability of the rabbi is considered first and primary among the qualifications of the modern rabbi."[24]

Even in the 1970s Jerome K. Davidson of Beth-El in Great Neck, New York, could note, in discussing his preparation for Sabbath eve services, that he was "driven to speak well, to enunciate everything, so meticulously, to develop a commanding style."[25]

In synagogue bulletins from Conservative, Reform, and large Orthodox congregations all over America in the fifties and sixties, rabbis regularly announced sermon titles in advance. This is rare today; most rabbis have, as Samuel Karff observed, "devalued preaching"[26] and consistently indicate that they need not write out their sermon; they speak either from a detailed outline or from a few notes.[27]

Among American rabbis homiletics is a dying art. Few would agree with Gilbert Rosenthal's claim in the late 1980s that "preaching is our bread and butter and . . . most of us are judged by our oratorical skills."[28] A Conservative rabbi who taught senior homiletics at the Jewish Theological Seminary in the late 1980s, Rosenthal noted that when he was a student the seminary required four years of homiletics and one year of speech. This had been reduced to two semesters of homiletics and no speech.[29] Rabbinic students at American seminaries (in contrast to many Protestant seminaries where great preachers are videotaped and studied by students) are rarely exposed to great preachers, past or present, and thus serious public speaking is no longer a high priority in the synagogue. Some rabbis justify this by pointing out that congregants, after a week of work, have very short attention spans and seem quite satisfied (here they are correct) with the brief, informal talks of most Sabbath evenings and mornings. Most significant, contemporary rabbis cannot prepare rigorously and mobilize energies, for a good sermon takes eight to ten hours of research and writing and few rabbis can find this time in the midst of a busy schedule of administering, conducting life-cycle events, counseling, and teaching.

The exception to this is the jam-packed High Holidays of Rosh Hashanah and Yom Kippur, where a great many rabbis announce their sermon titles in advance, spending considerable time in preparation, and where congregants, at various venues, often critically discuss the sermons. The most popular forum for such discussions seems to be the "break the fast" following the day-long Yom Kippur fast and worship, either at the synagogue or at various homes. Where once (so older congregants report) they might have discussed what the rabbi's wife wore during the holidays, they are much more likely to talk about the liturgy (what was meaningful, what was boring) and the sermons (whether or not they agreed with the rabbi on some issue about which he or she spoke). There is hardly any constructive feedback for the rabbi, except for the occasional letter, yet most rabbis continue to insist that their sermons "went over well." They draw this conclusion largely from the perfunctory comments made by worshippers as rabbi and congregants greet each other following one or more of the services.

While seating is a constant headache at most synagogues for High Holiday worship services, and sanctuaries are closer to empty than filled on Sabbaths, the American synagogue is a busy place on a daily basis. At a Conservative congregation in a Washington, D.C. suburb, a Monday night forum centered on "Legislative Issues in Bioethics," a Tuesday Sisterhood lunch highlighted "Osteoporosis and Bone Mineral Density," a Wednesday evening meeting planned the annual family camping weekend, a Thursday evening featured an adult b'nai mitzvah class, a monthly book group, and a United Synagogue Youth meeting, but numerous committees (Adult Jewish Education, Brotherhood, Family Education, Fine Arts, Long-range Planning, Membership, Religious Practices, Sisterhood, and Youth), as well as elected officers, held meetings during this same week. In addition, a nursery school (two, three, and four year olds) used the Sunday school classrooms during the weekdays. While study is generally in third place, the contemporary synagogue serves as a house of assembly, a house of prayer, and a house of study.

The well-being of the synagogue seems quite unrelated to rabbinic preaching. Congregations always seem busy, if not frenetic; they flow along independent of the learning and homiletical skills of the rabbi (though not without her or his "managing skills").[30] In the late 1920s, 1930s, 1940s, and 1950s Jews in New York would say they were going to "Jung's synagogue," or "Lookstein's shul," or "Wise's temple"; Jews in Cleveland came from all over the city to "Silver's temple," "Brickner's temple," or "Goldman's center" to hear these three local but nationally celebrated preachers. It was, as Samuel Karff correctly observed, the "power of a charismatic preacher" that drew the people.[31] Today, though plenty of rabbis are equally gifted, it is mostly a dedicated core of members and relatives/friends of the b'nai mitzvah who attend worship. Few are drawn because of the rabbi's preaching; the attachment is institutional. And this attachment is considerable, even if not primarily built around prayer.

Non-Jews and "Outreach"

Fueling this attachment, in Reform and Reconstructionist synagogues, is the increasing number of non-Jewish spouses whose Jewish husbands or wives are members of the congregation. One cannot talk about groups without considering the concept of boundaries,[32] so what to do with the non-Jewish member of the family when life-cycle events are celebrated is an increasingly complicated problem for Conservative, Reconstructionist, and Reform congregations in the early twenty-first century. Should a non-Jewish wife of a Jewish male member of the congregation be required to convert if the couple's son wishes to have a bar mitzvah? Should the non-Jewish parent, especially one who has been supporting his partner's Jewishness and raising Jewish children, participate in the Torah ceremony at the bar or bat mitzvah of his children? Conservative Judaism more or less solves such dilemmas by requiring non-Jewish wives to convert if they or their children wish to participate in the religious life of the congregation, for Conservative Judaism (as Orthodox Judaism) continues to mark Jewishness through the religion of the mother. But Reform and Reconstructionist congregations are much less concerned with making sure that both parents are formally Jewish, preferring to treat the children of a mixed marriage as Jewish if the family designates the children as Jewish. There is, thus, a presumption of Jewish descent, so long as at least one parent is Jewish and the family acts as if (i.e., affiliates with a synagogue) they are part of the Jewish faith and not "actively involved in another religion."[33]

These congregations have, essentially, a "don't ask, don't tell" policy. Few of their membership applications inquire about this, and as long as the child does not suddenly declare, in afternoon or Sunday Hebrew school or during bar or bat mitzvah study, in a congregation where a sizable proportion of interfaith marriages are dual religion, "That's not what they teach us in church school," he or she is presumed to be Jewish. This is so even though synagogue administrators note that many dual religion couples raise their children as "Jewish" in the congregation but celebrate

Christmas and Easter. In Reform and Reconstructionist congregations the non-Jewish mother (or even non-Jewish father) could attend the church of her or his choice (this remains quite rare) and the child be eligible for religious school enrollment and bat or bar mitzvah. This has led one Conservative rabbi to refer to Reform (positively) as providing the "Big Tent" of the American Jewish community, embracing interfaith couples, matrilineal descent, and patrilineal descent.[34] Indeed, a recent study of Conservative Judaism revealed that 429,000 former Conservative Jews were now affiliated with a Reform synagogue, and 31,000 with Reconstructionist synagogues.[35]

Although there is very little evidence of outreach toward interfaith families in the Conservative movement,[36] the new millennium has witnessed a much more aggressive policy, in Reform and Reconstructionist congregations, to encourage the non-Jewish members to become active in the synagogue and to consider conversion.[37] Although neither of the these branches have binding policies, non-Jews generally remain free to stand on the pulpit when the child is given a Hebrew name, to stand next to the baby boy for a *b'rit milah* (circumcision) in the home, serve on committees, and receive burial in the congregational cemetery, and little distinction is made between the Jewish and non-Jewish parent. In fact, aside from the Torah service, where passing the Torah from generation to generation and participating in the Torah blessings (during which one acknowledges in public her or his Jewishness) and reading is generally restricted to Jews, and serving as an elected officer or chair of a committee such as Ritual or Religious School is likewise restricted, little else distinguishes the intermarried couple and their child, including death, in Reconstructionist and Reform congregations.[38] The rabbis and lay leaders worry about intermarriage and declining rates of Jewish identity among a tiny minority population. They know, implicitly, that "the boundary is both the life and the death of a group,"[39] so they have decided that membership in the synagogue sufficiently identified the family as Jewish, notwithstanding one non-Jewish parent. Only when that parent is openly active in another religious tradition is there a problem, and this is rarely investigated.

In fact, there are numerous congregations that go out of their way to encourage the participation of families with a non-Jewish parent and make only a minimal effort to convince this parent to become formally Jewish.[40]

In many communities such synagogues are widely known as places of special welcome to these families, and their literature, programs, and worship services openly encourage intermarried families to participate as Jews. And there may not be any special motivation for the non-Jews in the family to formally study toward and complete the ceremony of conversion, given their place within the ritual life of these congregations.

This phenomenon is primarily a result of an aggressive policy established by Reform Judaism (mentioned previously) beginning in the late 1970s when Rabbi Alexander Schindler, head of the Union of American Hebrew Congregations, created front-page news with his presidential sermon to the laypeople of the movement at the UAHC Biennial in Toronto. He spoke about "outreach," and proposed that the Reform movement consider as Jewish the child of any intermarriage, whether the mother was Jewish and the father non-Jewish or the reverse.[41] Since the Reform movement had consistently acknowledged (along with all other Jewish groups) the child of a Jewish father but non-Jewish mother as non-Jewish, and since this had been the working assumption in Reform congregations in the United States for more than a century (notwithstanding the 1961 *Rabbi's Manual*),[42] Schindler's suggestion was explosive.

Reform rabbis began to deliberate seriously on this delicate matter at their 1980 convention, and by 1983 they were prepared to issue a resolution that declared that the child of one Jewish parent is "under the presumption of Jewish descent, no matter whether the Jewish parent is the father or the mother."[43] "Presumption" meant simply that Jewish identity was not automatic; "appropriate and timely public and formal acts of identification with the Jewish faith and people" would determine whether or not the child of *any* intermarriage would be considered Jewish. And each rabbi would be the judge of whether the "acts" were appropriate.

As more and more rabbis feel comfortable declaring a child Jewish if he or she is enrolled in the religious education program, as long as one parent is Jewish, the number of intermarried parents in Reform congregations (and the same holds true in Reconstructionist synagogues) has been steadily increasing. A survey conducted among a number of congregations in the Mid-Atlantic Region of the Reform movement in 1998 revealed that more than a third of those Reform Jews who were married in the years 1995–1998 and belonged to a congregation had intermarried, and very few of those marriages had resulted in a conversion to Judaism by the non-Jewish partner.[44]

A larger 1998 survey of Conservative and Reform synagogues in the Mid-Atlantic region of the United States uncovered some interesting data about intermarriage. First, only about 40 percent of the members of the congregations surveyed lived in units with one or both parents and children in the same home, which parallels U.S. government statistics stating that, between 1970 and 1996, the percentage of children living with one parent increased from 12 to 28 percent.[45] This reminds us that it is long past the time when Jewish congregations should refer to "families" when enumerating their membership or announcing events in their bulletins. There are increasing numbers of elderly single members (more women, of course, than men), couples cohabiting without formal marriage, and single-parent units.[46]

Second, couples marry at increasingly older ages, magnifying the chances that a Jewish male or female will marry a non-Jew.[47] The delaying of marriage is extremely striking in the survey; a third of all male members and almost 40 percent of women members of Conservative and Reform synagogues were not married before 44 years of age.

Third, the high rate of intermarriage is demonstrable in the Reform congregations in the region. More than a third of those Reform Jews who were married in the years 1995–1998, and belong to a synagogue, have intermarried, and very few of those marriages have resulted in a conversion to Judaism by the non-Jewish partner.[48] The survey also revealed that intermarriage rates increased from 1985–1995, compared to earlier years, and that the rates from 1995–1998 continued the increase as well.[49]

Fourth, in both Conservative and Reform congregations there is a generous attitude toward intermarriage. Generally, the younger the respondent the more open is he or she to intermarriage; but in every age cohort only a minority of congregants oppose their children entering an intermarriage.

When the author interviewed Conservative and Reform congregants and rabbis about intermarriage, he found a dramatic difference between the clergy and the laity. All Conservative rabbis, and the majority of Reform rabbis, were opposed to intermarriage, refused to officiate at such marriages, and were very anxious about the future of Judaism, largely because of the increased intermarriage rates. This was true even though they had little information on whether or not the intermarriages that take place in their region lead to Jewish identification by the Jewish spouse and/or Jewish identification among the children. The Reform rabbis who did officiate at such weddings (they constituted about a third of the rabbis in the region) were much more likely to cite evidence of couples where the Jewish partner later identified with Judaism, where the non-Jewish partner supported raising the children in the Judaic tradition, and (less so) where the non-Jewish partner formally adopted Judaism.

In contrast, the increased intermarriage rates did not make the majority of the laypeople that I randomly interviewed nearly as anxious as the rabbis. They spoke about the happiness of couples, irrespective of religious affiliation, and (naively, perhaps) hoped that the Jewish spouse would continue to affiliate with Judaism and persuade the non-Jewish spouse to raise the children in the Judaic tradition. Nearly all of them believe that synagogues should encourage the participation of families with a non-Jewish parent and that the bulletins or newsletters, worship services, and programs should reach out to the intermarried couples.

Staffing

Congregational programs are generally orchestrated by one or more of four professionals: a rabbi, a cantor, an executive, and an educational director. The attachment of synagogue members to their institution depends not only on the role of the rabbi but the increasing visibility of other professionals.[50] Where once cantors were restricted to providing music during worship services, today cantors work as a team with rabbis in preparing young men and women for bar and bat mitzvah, in teaching children and adults, officiating at congregational life-cycle events, visiting ill members, and even preaching.[51] Religious school principals increasingly have advanced degrees in higher education and Judaica, and the executive director of larger synagogues is, to some degree, the C.E.O. of a large (albeit nonprofit) business, coordinating the activities of every sector of the synagogue. Administrators, cantors, and educators, like rabbis, have their own professional organizations that are divided, for the most part, along denominational lines.[52]

The role of the cantor has increased dramatically in recent decades as bat and bar mitzvah have far exceeded confirmation in priority within the Reform and Conservative synagogue. In the 1940s and 1950s, and to some extent into the 1960s, confirmation was a very Jewishly affirming moment in the life-cycle of a young Conservative or Reform Jew. The rise of bar and bat mitzvah, firmly in place by the 1970s, coincided with the downgrading of confirmation and its moving back, in some cases, to grade nine, or, in other cases, its disappearance.[53] Thus the three or four extra years of intellectual and spiritual growth, combined with the ability to ask cogent questions and demand meaningful responses through study with the rabbi (and, in some places, pass exams on fundamental principles of Judaism), have frequently vanished. It may have been the rehearsals, and the extremely long service in which every confirmand has a part, that doomed the ceremony, and it has still not been replaced despite the proliferation of high school programs in Reform and Conservative synagogues.

One of the areas in which cantors have assumed quasi-rabbinic functions is the increasingly popular adult b'nai mitzvah class, especially in Conservative synagogues. These classes are filled largely by women, and the reasons are many. They are most likely to have missed bat mitzvah, as it is only since the 1970s that Conservative synagogues have routinely trained girls as well as boys to be called to the Torah at the age of thirteen. Women also make up the largest percentage of converts to Judaism, and these "Jews by choice" of course missed the opportunity for a bat mitzvah. Finally, adult women seem more eager than men to join a group of peers that meet regularly (e.g., biweekly) for one or two years to study Hebrew and Judaism.

Cantors, with the assistance of rabbis, frequently teach the adult b'nai mitzvah class. The students range in age from their forties through eighties, and their study of Jewish history, literature, and thought culminates in a ceremony (usually on a Saturday morning) in which they each chant in Hebrew verses from the Torah portion or the prophetic reading of that week and some (if not all) present a brief talk on why they chose to make the commitment to prepare for the bat or bar mitzvah ceremony.

This cantor-rabbi partnership is more common today than in the past because cantors, trained and "invested" at the Conservative and Reform seminaries, have supplemented their intensive Hebrew music training with abundant Judaic studies, either (or both) as an undergraduate and as a cantorial student. This generation of cantors is comfortable teaching the history of Judaism, and rabbis increasingly have relinquished this function with b'nai mitzvah classes. But together, increasingly, they lead congregants in efforts to climb the (metaphorical) ladder God lets down from the aperture of heaven—to seek spirituality.

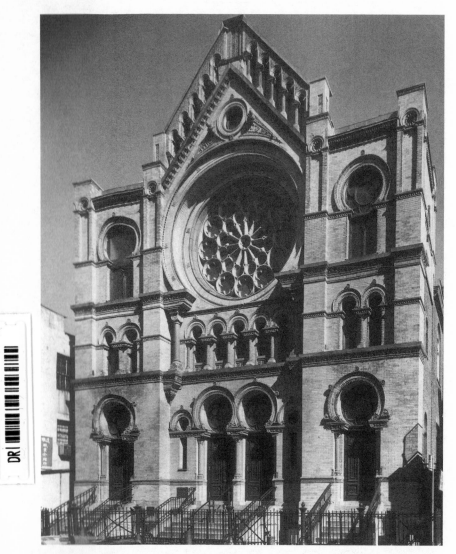

Jewish immigrants from eastern Europe poured into the Lower East Side of New York City during the 35 years prior to World War I. Its heart was the tenth ward, where in 106 acres there were more than 1,200 tenements in 1893 with a population of 74,000, or 702 persons per acre. These Jews established scores of synagogues on the Lower East Side, including the Eldridge Street synagogue (1887), the first building designed and built to be a synagogue by East European Jews, which combined Gothic, Moorish, and Romanesque features. COPYRIGHT © KATE MILFORD

At most traditional synagogues women and men sat separately during worship. The women either sat downstairs with the men, separated by an aisle or a barrier, or upstairs (as at this synagogue) in a womens' gallery. With few Jews left on the Lower East Side the Eldridge Street synagogue's sanctuary closed in the mid-1950s, although worship services have continued unbroken in other rooms. COPYRIGHT © KATE MILFORD

The small Georgian Touro synagogue in Newport, Rhode Island (Congregation Yeshuat Yisrael) was dedicated in 1763 and utilized the Sephardic system of worship. President George Washington visited the synagogue in 1790 and subsequently responded to the greetings of the leaders with stirring words that included the assurance that the government "would give to bigotry no sanction, to persecution no assistance." It is a national historic site. VICTORIA AROCHO/AP PHOTO

Most synagogue sanctuaries in America have fixed seats or pews, as here at Beth El in Tacoma, Washington. JOHN FROSCHAUER/AP PHOTO

Savannah's Mikveh Israel was founded by Jews who arrived in 1733. Its current Gothic building was dedicated in 1878; Gothic (or neo-Gothic) was a popular Victorian style of synagogue and church architecture. COURTESY OF CONGREGATION MIKVEH ISRAEL

Millions of Jewish immigrants left eastern Europe in the late nineteenth and early twentieth centuries for various reasons (economic, political, religious, and social), and they went to many countries in the world. Most, however, came to America and they, as well as their descendants, would embrace this land of freedom. BETTMANN/CORBIS

When the Torah is read in the synagogue, the reader never touches the parchment. To make sure his or her fingers do not touch the scroll, a pointer or *yad* (hand) is used.

A *sofer* (scribe) is a professional expert in writing Torah scrolls with a feather quill and indelible ink in straight lines on ritually proper parchment. The scribe uses a manual that contains the traditional Hebrew text and all the rules for proper calligraphy.

Most synagogue Sabbath services are followed by an *oneg* or refreshment hour during which worshippers not only eat and drink but frequently discuss the liturgy, music, and sermon.
COURTESY SUZANNE GRONEMEYER

The *shofar* (ram's horn) is the central symbol of Rosh Hashanah, the Jewish New Year. It is blown at weekday services prior to Rosh Hashanah and during the New Year liturgy, either by the rabbi or cantor or a layperson. In many synagogues multiple shofars will be sounded simultaneously. BILL ARON/PHOTO EDIT

Following Leviticus 23:34 and 39-43, Jews erect a sukkah or temporary shelter immediately after Yom Kippur, cover it with branches, decorate it with fruit, and use it for meals and even lodging for seven days. DAVID H. WELLS/CORBIS

Israel has often had a powerful impact on American Jewish life, and many Jews celebrate Israel's Independence Day with parades, Hebrew songs, and special foods.

Jews light one candle on the first night and an additional candle for each of the eight nights of Chanukah, and the candles are placed in a *chanukiyah* or menorah. A ninth candle, the *shammas*, is used to light the others. It is praiseworthy for every member of the family to have his or her own menorah for the ceremony of lighting.

JANET HOSTETTER/AP PHOTO

The Passover seder or festive dinner table ceremony is the quintessential Jewish home observance and is usually shared with family and friends. Participants follow the ceremony order (seder) from a Haggadah, a book of prayers, songs, and narratives. INDEX STOCK

A ceremonial seder plate with Passover foods is placed in front of the ceremony's leader. These foods include a roasted shankbone, a green herb, a roasted egg, *charoset* (a spread made from fruits, nuts, and wine), a bitter herb, and matzah (unleavened bread). FOODPIX

Although any knowledgeable Jew may lead worship services in nontraditional synagogues (and any knowledgeable Jewish male in traditional congregations), rabbis frequently read the liturgy together with a cantor. In many synagogues one or more congregational leaders sit on the pulpit during the services. BILL ARON/PHOTO EDIT

The Torah scroll is taken from the ark and carried in procession around the synagogue before and after the reading. During the joyous processions with the Torah scrolls on Simchat Torah, songs are sung and worshippers often dance with the Torah scrolls held up high. COPYRIGHT © BERYL GOLDBERG

A mitzvah is a commandment, and a bar (boy) or bat (girl) mitzvah ceremony signifies that the youth is eligible to fulfill the commandments of Judaism. In a nontraditional community he or she will be trained by a rabbi and/or cantor to conduct some of the service, read and/or chant from the Torah and the Prophets, and give a brief Torah discourse. Among traditional Jews the bat mitzvah ceremony is much different from the bar mitzvah ceremony. BENJIE SANDERS/ARIZONA DAILY/AP PHOTO

In most bar and bat mitzvah ceremonies the young man or woman is joined on the pulpit by parents, grandparents, and siblings. The bar mitzvah has learned how to read unvocalized Hebrew (consonants) from the Torah. BILL ARON/PHOTO EDIT

A Jewish wedding takes place under a *huppah* (canopy), which is often a prayer shawl held up by four poles. It is a symbol of the home the couple will soon make together. Lyn Hughes/Corbis

The often beautifully illustrated *ketubah* or marriage contract is traditionally written in Aramaic, but nontraditional ketubahs abound in Hebrew and English. Pictured is an egalitarian ketubah, increasingly popular in nontraditional Jewish weddings. Published by the American Conference of Cantors, copyright © 1994 Pamela Feldman-Hill

Increasingly, women rabbis (as pictured here) and women laypersons are reading from the Torah during worship services as men have long done. When women do this in traditional congregations they do so in a women's service. BILL ARON/PHOTO EDIT

Rebecca Gratz (1781–1869) COURTESY THE JACOB RADER MARCUS CENTER
OF THE AMERICAN JEWISH ARCHIVES

Isaac Mayer Wise (1819-1900)
COURTESY THE JACOB RADER MARCUS CENTER OF
THE AMERICAN JEWISH ARCHIVES

Solomon Schechter (1847-1915)
COURTESY THE JACOB RADER MARCUS CENTER
OF THE AMERICAN JEWISH ARCHIVES

Mordecai M. Kaplan (1881-1984) COURTESY
THE JACOB RADER MARCUS CENTER OF THE AMERICAN
JEWISH ARCHIVES

Trude Weiss-Rosmarin (1908-1989)
COURTESY THE JACOB RADER MARCUS CENTER OF
THE AMERICAN JEWISH ARCHIVES

Henrietta Szold (1860-1945) COURTESY OF HADASSAH, THE WOMEN'S ZIONIST ORGANIZATION OF AMERICA, INC.

Abraham Joshua Heschel (1907–1972)
COURTESY THE JACOB RADER MARCUS CENTER OF THE
AMERICAN JEWISH ARCHIVES

Menachem Mendel Schneerson (1902-1993) MIKE ALBANS/AP PHOTO

CHAPTER SIX

The Future of American Judaism

If I were writing about the future of American Catholicism in 2002 I would, of course, have to start with the fact that "there will be a new pope."[1] But there is nothing comparable in American Judaism; it will make little difference who heads the rabbinic organization of each of the branches or who assumes the leadership of the national synagogue organizations. For sure, someone could push Orthodox synagogues and Orthodox rabbis toward greater ecumenical activity with their non-Orthodox fellow Jews, and a different Reform or Conservative leader could initiate discussions that might one day merge the two movements. But none of these is on the horizon, and the future will depend much less on the leadership of synagogue organizations or rabbinical associations and far more on what the laity does, for Judaism is as much (if not more) a religion of individual Jews as it is of institutions and leaders.

A case in point. A quite traditional rabbi took over the leadership of the Reform rabbinical association in the late 1990s, and though the version he wanted was largely scuttled, he did provide leadership in what became the 1999 Statement of Principles of Reform Judaism. This was more traditional than any of the previous three platforms (1885, 1937, 1976) of American Reform Judaism, but not only do most Reform Jews have no idea of its contents but whatever moves toward tradition now characterize Reform Judaism (and they are many), they were unfolding for three decades prior to 1999. And they had little to do with the national leader of any Reform institution and a great deal to do with the local rabbi and his or her congregants.

In this chapter I will look at areas of the contemporary Judaic community—renewal, Jews who come to Judaism through conversion, homosexual congregations, learning, synagogue design, and the role of Israel—that are widely discussed in the publications and in the synagogue reception halls of each sector. They are not in their order of importance (who could really measure this anyway?) but rather the order in which I believe this changing landscape will be best understood.

Spirituality

There is little doubt that a pervasive trend in American religious life at the beginning of the new millennium is the search for "spirituality," and though classical Hebrew has no word for "spirituality" and the modern Hebrew word (*ruchaneeyut*) comes from the English word, this trend is true in Judaism too.[2] All the available information suggests that this quest is likely to continue for some time. Unlike the so-called religious revival of the 1950s—when "never before in national history had as many Americans belonged to, attended, or associated themselves with religious institutions"[3]—the revival at the turn of the millenium is about involvement, not just joining. Perhaps as many as 60 percent of American Jews belonged to synagogues in the 1950s and early 1960s (in contrast to 10 percent in 1950[4] and 35–40 percent in 2000), but most were joiners, not what one Orthodox rabbi has called "involvers."[5] Jews may have joined in large numbers, but they didn't attend much, and the youth and adult education programs were, in the famous phrase, a mile wide and an inch deep.

Spirituality was absent in the 1950s, as social, political (especially the cold war and civil rights), and ethical concerns in the secular world dominated. The so-called return was neither to attendance at religious worship services or to personal observance, as Marshall Sklare and Joseph Greenblum so thoroughly documented in their comprehensive study of a suburban Chicago Jewish community.[6]

The agitation in synagogues everywhere at the start of the new millenium is about the creation of the universe, the meaning of life, the search for beauty, purpose, inner peace, wisdom, or, in a phrase, worthwhile spiritual styles.[7] It began in the 1990s (perhaps as early as the late 1980s in some synagogues), intensifying at the end of that decade into a search for new depths of meaning in Judaism. When rabbis announced a class in Jewish thought, modest numbers attended; when they used the word *spirituality* in the title, the course was packed. It is the cry of our age.[8]

Rabbis and other Jewish professionals use spirituality in the manner Wade Clark Roof described in *Spiritual Marketplace*: the search for internal, experiential expressions of religiosity ("nourishing the human soul or inner life") as well as external or institutional modes of relating to the sacred.[9] High Holiday sermon titles everywhere are filled with first-person confessions of exploring possibilities of belief, and the sermons themselves frequently offer congregants Jewish resources and Jewish opportunities beyond the institution for pursuing the quest for meaning. Not only in sermons but in adult education classes, congregational workshops, religious school programs, and synagogue bulletins—spirituality is everywhere. In the 1980s this movement was known as "renewal,"[10] today, it is spirituality through worship, spirituality through meditation, spirituality through the study of texts, spirituality through nature,[11] and spirituality through good deeds.[12] *Religion* suggests boring; *spirituality* suggests "impulse[s] of the heart" or "inner connections."[13]

At one synagogue in suburban Chicago, where "spirituality" has dominated the *Bulletin* for several years, the congregation has moved Sabbath evening worship services from 8:15 to 6:30. In addition, the oneg, or food and beverages, which nearly everywhere follow prayer, precede the service, as the worshippers welcome the Sabbath not just with prayer but with refreshments and conversation, moving from the week of work to the holy time of the Sabbath.

The Sabbath worship begins with community singing (*nigunim*), and from joyful rounds of Hebrew music the cantor consciously moves toward softer, slower, more contemplative melodies. The worshippers are encouraged to feel they are leaving the world of work behind and entering the peace and rest of the Sabbath. The sanctuary features pews that break down the rigid straight rows that yield only the backs of heads, as worshippers seem to prefer to engage other worshippers visually during prayer.

During one Sabbath worship service the rabbi introduced and commented on three familiar prayers in the liturgy, giving each of them an interpretation that suggested ways in which the worshippers could use these liturgical selections to find their own path to "greater spirituality," to "draw water from one's own inner well." And her sermon that same Sabbath explained two paths by which an individual might "approach spirituality," "how to come closer to God and *kedushah*, holiness." In brief, these involved the study of sacred Jewish texts (especially Torah) and the possible awareness—through this study—that God addresses a Jew in Torah through relationship (spirituality), but that connecting with God is also about building a "spiritual community" and participating in a "shared quest" with other Jews (religiosity). So, the rabbi continued, spirituality involves "personal seeking" and "true community," the "interrelationship of the spiritual and the religious." And her conclusion, a Hasidic story, summed up the constant exhortation of rabbis who write and talk about spirituality: each Jew must find her own way to come closer to God.

Rabbi Baer once said to his teacher, the Seer of Lublin, "Show me one general way to the service of God." The tzaddik [leader] replied: "It is impossible to tell a person what way to take. For one way to serve God is through learning, another through prayer, another through fasting, and still another through eating. We should carefully observe what way our heart draws us to, and then choose this way with all our strength."

The congregations that have been exploring spirituality seem to this observer much more interested in the inner life of the worshipper than synagogues where a standard liturgy is utilized. The rabbi, cantor, or service leader wants to explore what happens internally when worshippers pray, whether in petitionary prayer or prayers that praise and/or thank God. They emphasize inner spiritual practice, the need to savor and relish each word, the connections between the interaction of words and images, or the external and internal aspects of the worship experience.

One way this is done is to ask the worshippers from time to time during the service to think about the words they are saying or singing as they say them or sing them. Some service leaders even try to probe within the words, exploring, as a mystic might do, the individual letters. At one service in Michigan, the leader discussed the Shema prayer, the prayer we have mentioned many times as one of the fundamental declarations of Jewish theology ("Hear O Israel, Adonai is our God, Adonai is one"). It has been said of this prayer, whose "very syllables are filled with spiritual meaning for worshippers,"[14] that throughout the entire realm of literature, secular or sacred, there is probably no utterance to be found that can be compared to its intrinsic intellectual and spiritual force, or in the influence it exerted upon the whole thinking and feeling of civilized mankind, to the six words of the Deuteronomic verse (6:4) which have become the battle-cry of the Jewish people for more than twenty-five centuries.[15]

The service leader urged the worshippers to think about the word *one*, the oneness in the universe (if not beyond), and each worshipper's search for the underlying unity or oneness of the world, the oneness that perhaps unifies all creation. And this was followed by some exercises in which the congregants were encouraged to ponder the three letters of the word *shema*, the first word of this Deuteronomic verse: the *shin*, the *mem*, and the *ayin*. If they could hold each letter for ten seconds (almost impossible, it seemed, for those not experienced in either Buddhist meditative practices or Hasidic mystical exercises), they might have some part of the insight of the medieval mystic who wrote *Sefer Yetzirah* (*The Book of Creation*).[16]

The author of this book emphasized that the *shin* represents the king of fire, or a hot state of consciousness, the *mem* represents the king of water, or a cool harmonic state,[17] and the third letter, which is a silent letter in modern Hebrew, represents the unity of the two states, the movement from fire to water or from the anxieties of the weekdays to the peace and harmony of the Sabbath. As the sanctuary filled with strange (perhaps "awesome") sounds ("shhhh" and "mmmmm"), the worshippers tried to say the words very slowly, seeking their own spiritual journey from the profane to the holy.

Finally, there is an increasing insistence on the part of rabbis to convince their congregants that spirituality is not only for the Sabbath and the synagogue but something to be vigilant about at the weekday workplace as well. Take the biblical (and greatly expanded over the centuries) prohibition not to steal; rabbis frequently try to convey a sense of how to observe this commandment on the job, not just avoiding taking something from a store. They urge their congregants not to "steal" their employers' time, not to steal company paper, pens, and other supplies for their personal use, not to use business phones for personal calls, and, of course, they preach on the need not to steal in another

way, by not overcharging, overbilling, or overinflating anything related to one's livelihood.

A Changing Landscape: Jews by Choice

In sermons everywhere this rabbi hears discussions of how Judaism is an
inward and outward spiritual path that offers guidance throughout life,
and of course these rabbis have a plate (if not a table) full of beliefs, foods,
holidays, home occasions, and rituals to draw upon. For most the term
spirituality is a synonym for sacred or deeply held values—what Kerry
Olitzky has defined simply as the "process through which the individual
strives to meet God"[18]—and the American Jewish community is filled
with professionals and laypeople offering to help Jews find what is sacred
to them, what they hold deeply, what that sense of higher purpose in their
daily lives might be.

In a Southern California synagogue this author was struck by the new
faces and new names that sounded "less Jewish" than in the previous generation. Through most of the twentieth century one could generally identify American Jews as overwhelmingly of central and east European
background and find names and faces that reflected this ancestry. But like
so much of the United States, where in the 1990s the growth of a city's
Asian American and Hispanic communities outpaced the increase in the
black population, American Judaism is becoming much more polyglot.

The author watched recently (2001) as parents picked up children
from a large, affluent Los Angeles synagogue Sunday morning religious
education program, and he attended other events at the same congregation that weekend. A generous number of black, Asian, and Latina/o
Jewish mothers and/or fathers picked up their children; a Jewish mother
who teaches at a Jewish day school and her Jewish husband, active at the
synagogue, celebrated the naming of their daughter, Chloe Tamar, at the
Sabbath worship service; and the two b'nai mitzvah on Saturday were
Miguel and Chad.

Some of this is a result of Latino Jewish emigration to the United
States, but much of this change has to do with a growing interest in Judaism among non-Jews, an effort by several branches of Judaism to develop strategies for reaching both the unaffiliated and what one scholar of

outreach programs calls the "unchurched,"[19] and a dramatic rise in conversions and in intermarriages.[20] A generation ago the Reform movement had hardly made a dent on the mass of unaffiliated Jews, and the other branches did even less.[21] In almost every region of the country organizers of Conservative and Reform conversion courses (usually six months to a year in length) report dramatic enrollment increases in the past decade or so, primarily among dual religion couples. In nine of the eleven regions of the Reform movement in 2001, the instructors reported a Latino and/or black enrollment of at least 10 percent. *Mikveh* managers—a brief immersion in a mikveh, or ritual bath, is required for converts—report unprecedented numbers using the facilities. Rabbis everywhere describe increasing numbers of adults who are studying with them toward the putative goal of conversion.[22] In the Sun Belt bar and bat mitzvah receptions, not to mention weddings, are frequently filled with salsa as well as Israeli dancing, and not just because these are popular but rather because there is a Latino family member in the celebration. So it appears a much greater multi-ethnic and multicultural Judaism is steadily emerging.

This influx of Jews by choice is part of the explanation for the dramatic increase in adult b'not mitzvah (plural of bat mitzvah) ceremonies, described earlier, at Conservative and Reform congregations everywhere. A group of women commit themselves to a course of study (usually weekly for two years, alternating the study of Hebrew with Jewish studies) with the rabbi and cantor, which culminates in a public ceremony where the women chant from the Torah and the supplemental scriptural reading (haftarah) and conduct the worship service. The classes consist of women who did not have a chance to be called to the Torah at age thirteen, either because bat mitzvah was uncommon in their community or because they were not Jewish at that time.

A Changing Landscape: Gay and Lesbian Congregations

An equally dramatic change in the life of the American Jewish religious community is the increasing number of lesbian and gay congregations as well as the rise in "commitment" ceremonies for gay and lesbian couples, specifically, and the institutionalization of lesbian and gay life-cycle events generally. The author recently attended a GLBTQ congregation in California—lesbian, gay, bisexual, transgendered, and questioning Jews—members of the World Congress of Gay, Lesbian, Bisexual, and Transgendered Jewish Organizations (Keshet Ga'avah), and where the rabbi castigated heterocentric, mainstream Judaism as being insensitive to GLBTQ needs, especially in the area of life-cycle events. One of the prayers asked the "Creator of the Universe that our hiding draw to an end, and that achieving our fullest creative expression as queers, as Jews, and as humans be among the blessings You bestow on us." While Orthodox Judaism continues to call homosexual behavior abnormal and points to the unanimous condemnation of homosexual behavior by the Jewish tradition, and Conservative Judaism continues to deny admission to rabbinical school to openly homosexual individuals, the other two streams of American Judaism have been attempting to come to terms with this relatively recent phenomenon of openly gay and lesbian religious Jews.

Reconstructionist and Reform rabbis (and then laypeople) began studying and discussing homosexuality in the 1970s, and little by little (not without considerable emotional debate in Reform Judaism in the 1980s) heterosexual rabbis and laypersons came to terms with lesbian and gay rabbis, congregations, and commitment ceremonies. First the Reconstructionist Rabbinical College (1980s) and then the Hebrew Union College–Jewish Institute of Religion, began accepting openly homosexual students ("Sexual orientation is irrelevant to the human worth of a person"). This was followed by rabbinic resolutions supporting rabbinic participation in gay and lesbian commitment ceremonies.[23] With the start of the new millennium, "straight" congregations have even begun to discuss the possibility of hiring a homosexual rabbi (so that "all rabbis, regardless of sexual orientation, be accorded the opportunity to fulfill the sacred vocation that they have chosen"). Such discussions, intensely emotional and potentially divisive, have begun to take place, notwithstanding the presumed tension between a homosexual rabbi and the traditional notion of a rabbi as role model.[24]

Less frequent discussions, but even more emotional and divisive, have begun to take place in Orthodox synaogues, but especially in informal conversations among Orthodox Jews at meals, after worship, and in social gatherings. Just as nearly every Orthodox Jew has someone in their extended family who has intermarried, so too do these same Jews hear about Orthodox friends, if not family, who are secretly gay or lesbian.

Stimulated by Sandi Simcha DuBowski's documentary *Trembling Before G-d*—a film about gay Orthodox Jews who are rejected by their communities, parents, and rabbis, as they struggle to reconcile the conflicting parts of their identities (homosexual and Judaic)—a few Orthodox congregations have found ways to open dialogue about this troubling subject. Most congregations have refused to screen the film (released in a number of large cities in 2002 after opening in New York City on 24 October 2001). They have cited Orthodox Judaism's general opposition to homosexuality, and the fierce opposition of some Orthodox rabbis to the film (Avi Shafran called it "distorted," though he did note a "stern and stubborn cadre of rabbis" who cause Orthodox gay and lesbian Jews deep anguish and pain).[25] A few synagogues in places such as Chicago, Los Angeles, New York, San Francisco, and Washington have initiated dialogue about this dilemma. Indeed, at least a dozen Orthodox synagogues hosted postscreening dialogues after the New York City opening. These are, for the most part, the same congregations willing to explore dialogue with Conservative and Reform Judaism and creative ways to involve women in the male-dominated Orthodox synagogue.

Those Orthodox rabbis who have commented upon the film in their synagoue bulletins, in sermons the author has heard, or in the media, have generally reiterated the Orthodox view that homosexuality is a choice, and that Orthdox gay or lesbian Jews should work hard to "overcome their stigma," to become "cured" of their "illness." For those who have seen this film, and listened to its real-life subjects, they understand that these Jews want to find an Orthodox synagogue and community (not Reform or Reconstructionist) that affirms their sexuality, as they seem unable to make a choice in either their sexuality or their spirituality. They seek to live as observant lesbian and gay Orthodox Jews.

A Changing Landscape: Education

The face of Jewish education is also changing dramatically. The number of children in Jewish education programs may have nearly doubled between 1946 and 1954,[26] but more than 90 percent were enrolled in congregational or "supplemental" schools (weekday afternoon, Saturday or Sunday morning), which children typically begin at age seven or eight and continue until confirmation in the ninth or tenth grade.[27] As late as 1958 there were less than 250 (and mostly Orthodox) day schools in the United States, and these were overwhelmingly located in the New York metropolitan area.[28] By the (late) 1990s, however, one estimate suggested that at least 40 percent of the students in programs of Jewish education were enrolled in Jewish day schools.[29]

There are at least five hundred Orthodox (Torah Umesorah), seventy Conservative (Solomon Schechter), twenty Reform (Progressive Association of Reform Day Schools), and fifty transdenominational Jewish day schools enrolling more than two hundred thousand students in 2001, and the biggest gain has been in schools outside the Orthodox community.[30] Everywhere there are congregations, whose members rejected day schools one or two generations ago as "too parochial" or "un-American," in which discussions are taking place about the possibility of establishing a Jewish primary (if not secondary) school. And while synagogue supplemental schools no longer occupy the dominant place in Jewish communal education priorities, they enroll at least a quarter-million young Jews. As a result, they are still the primary source of Judaica knowledge for a large percentage of the Jewish population.

There is every reason to believe that the surge in Jewish day schools will continue. Among Reform and Conservative Jews, interest has been expanding tremendously in the past decade or two, and the second generation of graduates of non-Orthodox schools is beginning to emerge. With the continued loss of enthusiasm for American public schools, combined with a positive feeling about Judaic identity, the Progressive Association of Reform Day Schools and the Solomon Schechter Day School assocation should continue to expand.

An interesting dilemma faces day schools in smaller Jewish communities, towns where there are only a few thousand Jews and perhaps 150 students in the K-8 school. In many cases these schols are administered by Orthodox leaders, and an Orthodox rabbi often teaches the Jewish studies component of the curriculum. In such cases the school will observe Jewish ceremonies, customs, and rituals in a traditional manner, including the dietary laws, with little compromise. But since the Orthodox community is rarely large enough to support the school on its own, it must draw families affiliated with the Conservative and (less so) Reform synagogue.

This has one great advantage, unavailable to supplementary schools tied to a particular wing of American Judaism, ecumenism. As two graduates of a day school in Charleston, South Carolina, explained, "Our school was composed of Orthodox, Conservative, Reform and 'nothing' [i.e., unaffiliated] Jews, so the standards of religiosity were different." Such schools, all over the country, must balance their Orthodox environment ("The school kept kosher and required the boys to wear *kipot* [head covering]") with the awareness that a significant proportion of the students are not from Orthodox homes. The most common way of handling this is for the school to insist upon traditional observance in the school but resist trying to make the children Orthodox outside of the school ("Outside of the school was not their business").[31] As the principal of the Addlestone Hebrew Academy in Charleston put it, "Our goal is not to make the children *shomer shabbat* [Sabbath observers] or observant outside the school, but to give them the best possible Jewish education."[32]

Since the majority of Jewish students receiving a Jewish education will continue to be in synagogue supplemental schools, considerable efforts have been underway to make this experience more positive, despite its "supplemental" and thus low priority interest for chldren and parents. Educators have also worked hard to prevent, to the extent it is possible, a division between the "elite" who attend day school and the "mass" who attend supplemental school. Most common among Reform and Conservative synagogues, where the majority of these supplemental schools exist, is the attempt to integrate home and synagogue, to make the educational experience in school carry over more directly to the home. There are experimental programs everywhere, as educators attempt to counter the lack of quantity (hours of instruction) with greater quality (relevance to the lives of parents and children).[33]

When one looks at the curriculum of supplemental schools, it is obvious that Jewish education has become much more family oriented in the past decade or so. In previous decades parents dropped off their children at the synagogue, and while some congregations provided a lecture series during the hours of children's religious education, most parents left the synagogue and returned a few hours later to retrieve their children. Now, increasingly, where space permits, parents and children study together, or at least concomitantly.

At a variety of Conservative synagogues in different parts of the country, periodic Sabbath afternoon family programs have replaced the traditional Sunday morning religious education program. These are usually not scheduled every week, but biweekly, or less often; parents and children come to the synagogue together for programs that involve both, separately or together. And, frequently, at least in the months when the Sabbath ends early, families come together from their separate programs to join in havdalah, a ritual with candle, spices, and wine that says a bittersweet goodbye to the Sabbath and welcomes the ordinary days of the week.

Other congregations, Conservative, Reconstructionist, and Reform, have substituted periodic daylong and weekend overnight programs for the weekly Sabbath or Sunday religious education classes. Trying to give the students a taste of the richness and joy of the Jewish, overnight summer camp experience, these programs hope to substitute intensity for less regularity.

And everywhere Jewish education is linked to technology. At Baltimore's Conservative Chizuk Amuno Congregation, online discussions of the Talmud engage high school teens. They commit themselves to study Talmud online every Sunday morning for one hour, combining individual work at a terminal with small group analysis and discussion of the text, and follow this with a live "chat" session with a rabbi. Computer terminals dominate not only the day schools but the supplemental programs as well.

A Changing Landscape: Architecture

The majority of American Jews attend worship services in synaogues that are at least forty-five years old. The (late) 1940s and 1950s witnessed the greatest church and synagogue building boom in history, and the latter was dominated by one architect, Percival Goodman (1904–1989). New York–based as a private architect since 1936, after studies at the École des Beaux Arts in Paris, and a professor at Columbia University since 1946, Goodman was the coauthor (with his brother) of *Communitas: Means of Livelihood and Ways of Life* (1947). He would design about fifty synagogues in the first decade after World War II, distinguished by the use of light, the integration of sculpture, painting, and stained glass into the design, an elevated pulpit that delineated the rabbi as the authority and the worshippers as (to lesser or greater extents) watchers and listeners, and, most of all, the concept of a multi-use foyer and social hall opening into the sanctuary.[34] These sanctuaries were about their ability to expand; they were sociofugal and they discouraged interaction.

Goodman, and most synagogue architects of the postwar decade as well as all other periods of American Jewish history, designed churches and synagogues in similar styles. In fact, at least since the centuries during which Jews lived in medieval Spain, Jews have imitated their environment in their sacred architecture. One scholar of medieval Judaism and Islam noted that "the great synagogues of Bagdad and Toledo were certainly inspired by the examples of Muslim public places of worship."[35] In Muslim Spain synagogues were built in the style of mosques; the sanctuary would resemble the Arabic *liwan*, or hall; sanctuary walls were adorned with verses from the Bible in elegant Spanish characters, just as their Muslim neighbors filled their mosques with verses from the Quran. And in Christian Europe Jews imitated churches and monasteries instead of mosques, often hiring distinguished church architects to design their synagogues. In fact, after some years would pass, non-Jewish styles of architecture became known among Jews as "traditionally Jewish."

This acculturation has continued to characterize synagogue architecture in the United States. The architect of the oldest (1763) synagogue building in the United States—the Newport, Rhode Island Touro Synagogue—used a chapel from London's Whitehall Palace as his model.[36] The popular Greek Revival style of synagogue architecture was chosen by the traditional Jews of Charleston, South Carolina for Kahal Kodesh Beth Elohim, dedicated in 1841. The "basic shape of the Greek temple was the rectangular cella, with a colonnaded portico extending over the entire width and height of the structure." The synagogue has (I use the present tense intentionally; tours in Charleston continue to include this on nearly every itinerary of the downtown area) ten Corinthian columns adorning the ark, and a six-column Theseum portico, in "imitation of a Greek Doric temple."[37] It not only imitated a Greek temple but Greek Revival churches, private buildings, and homes in downtown Charleston.[38]

The Egyptian Revival Style of Philadelphia's Mikve Israel's second synagogue building (1825) included columns copied from an ancient

Egyptian temple as well as other buildings in Philadelphia.[39] The English Gothic style of synagogue architecture, favored by at least a dozen traditional congregations in the late nineteenth century—including Cincinnati's Mound Street Temple (1869)—imitated (especially) American and European churches of the period. The best extant example of this style is the magnificent Mickve Israel in Savannah—resplendent with arches, spires, and colored, stain-glass windows—only one of the many public and private Gothic buildings in late nineteenth-century Savannah.[40]

Moorish or Oriental Revival synagogues were constructed in the nineteenth and early twentieth centuries from coast to coast. Among the most celebrated are Cincinnati's Temple B'nai Jeshurun (dedicated in 1866 and called an "Alhambra temple"),[41] New York's Emanu-El (1868), Philadelphia's Rodeph Shalom (1870), the Temple in Cleveland (1924), and Los Angeles's Wilshire Boulevard Temple (1926). Not every synagogue was pure Gothic or any other style; Moorish, Gothic, Italian Renaissance (Detroit's Shaarey Zedek's 1915 synagogue), Romanesque Revival (also called neo-Romanesque by Rochester's Temple B'rith Kodesh congregants when describing their 1894 building with its pitched roof, rusticated stonewalk, high arched windows, and corner tower), Romantic Revival often were combined in a single large structure, just as architects did in churches everywhere.[42]

One striking distinction between European and American synagogues is their use of "urban space." In pre-Emancipation Europe (circa pre-nineteenth century), synagogues were frequently hidden, or built (e.g., in a courtyard) so that non-Jews would not see them when they walked down the main streets of the town or city. In contrast, from the beginning, American Jews frequently built their synagogues on the main streets of towns and cities, often adjacent to or in clear sight of churches.

The current synagogue construction (and renovation) explosion is about making Judaism more intimate and meaningful, not about size. Sanctuaries and chapels have movable chairs, either arranged in semicircles or in an "antiphonal" form, so that worshippers have a sense of participation with other worshippers. At B'nai Shalom in Westborough, Massachusetts, the movable seats in the sanctuary are arranged into a semicircular shape for Friday evening worship (about 175 chairs in three front sections) and converted to auditorium style with a middle aisle with four hundred chairs for b'nai mitzvah on Saturday mornings. At such congregations the *bima* is rarely elevated, as the rabbi and cantor stand at the same level as the worshippers. The style is sociopetal, as the rabbi and cantor are facilitators, participating in prayer with (rather than to) the congregation.

A Changing Landscape: Zion

As worship patterns have changed dramatically in the past decade or so, one wonders about the role of Israel in American Judaism of the future. There is an axiom among some of those who study American Judaism, especially sociologists, that Israel was a minor component in the religious life of American Jewry in the 1950s and the (early) 1960s, and that only with the Six Day War of 1967 did Israel become a major component. Two scholars have recently summed up this position nicely: "Prior to the time [1967], neither Israel nor the Holocaust were major components in American Jewish identity. It has been regularly observed that analysts of American Jewish life . . . had little to say about either subject."[43] They may be right with respect to "analysts," but they certainly are wrong in the area of the synagogue.

Of course, not every synagogue in the two decades prior to 1967 was sympathetic to Zionism, but overwhelmingly this was the case. Even the most superficial inspection of synagogue bulletins in these years reveals that rabbis regularly delivered sermons on the subject of Israel, religious schools made Israel—its history and its people—a major part of the curriculum, and synagogues celebrated Israel in numerous programs. Whether, as Nathan Glazer has argued, this had "remarkably slight effect on the inner life of American Jewry,"[44] is hard to prove or disprove, but the evidence for its omnipresence is great.

In Conservative and Reform synagogues all over the country, and in numerous Orthodox congregations as well, rabbis spoke about the War of Independence, the massive migration of Jews from Arab lands after this war, the Suez Crisis, and, regularly, the social, economic, political, and religious situation in Israel. In Baltimore, Chicago, Cleveland, Los Angeles, Miami, New York, Philadelphia, St. Louis, and Washington, D.C.,[45] printed collections of High Holiday sermons and sermon titles listed in synagogue bulletins indicate that it was commonplace for one of the four or five holyday sermons rabbis delivered (some preached during the Memorial Service on Yom Kippur, some did not) to dwell on the topic of Israel. And nearly every synagogue in the United States supported an appeal for Israel Bonds in the middle of a High Holiday worship service.

In the religious education programs at synagogues in these same nine cities, textbooks on Israel were widely utilized in the junior high and high school classes. It did not matter whether the rabbi was a committed American Zionist or whether the leaders of the congregation were active in Zionist organizations; indeed, some curricula in the 1950s and 1960s may even be said to have been built so much around Israel that Judaic life in the diaspora received less attention than did Israeli society. At one "model seder" I attended in the late 1950s in Los Angeles—albeit at a Reform congregation where the rabbi was a leading Zionist—the Passover food served to the religious school children consisted of hummus, pita, and felafel. At congregations as far apart as Miami and Los Angeles, religious school children adopted Israeli pen pals, and the students enjoyed the fruits of correspondence back and forth from these cities to the Israeli schools with which they were linked.

Israeli dancing, Israeli Independence Day celebrations, and performances of Israeli music fill the synagogue bulletins from these two decades. Of course there were some Reform congregations where the members were "reared in an atmosphere of virulent anti-Zionism,"[46] but this was more often than not a phenomenon of the 1930s and 1940s, and, even then, it was a feature of only a minority of American synagogues. While it is true that the Six Day War "catapulted Israel into the center of America Jewish concerns,"[47] Israel was hardly on the periphery of synagogue life between 1948 and 1967.

A study of these same synagogue bulletins (and, when available, High Holiday sermons) at the turn of the millennium reveals that Israel is far less a part of synagogue life today than in the past fifty or so years. It has been clearly replaced by an emphasis on ceremonies, events, ideas, and rituals with which American Jews have, seemingly, more direct contact.

With modest historical perspective, scholars now realize that the "impact of the Six Day War is actually significantly less than a look at American Jewish communal life might indicate,"[48] and there is abundant evidence to suggest that Israel is less in the consciousness of synagogue Jews than it was fifty years or so earlier. Of course, even if sukkah building has

replaced Israeli pen pals and the study of liturgy has replaced Israeli dancing, most synagogue Jews (as most churched Americans) are highly pro-
Israel, notwithstanding concomitant support for Palestinian nationalism.[49] But synagogues have turned inward in the past decade or so, and
diaspora Jewish life has become a higher priority than Israel.

One can find entire synagogue bulletins with no mention of Israel in
a list of weekly or monthly activities and rabbis who go weeks without
delivering a talk on Israel, not because the synagogue lay and professional leadership, as well as the members, are not enthusiastic about the Jewish state (they are), but because other topics seem more relevant for day-
to-day Judaic life in the United States. Israel is simply no longer (leaving
aside the question if it ever was) the center of Jewish life—and certainly
not central to American Jewish life—whether (in fact) we look at the 35
to 40 percent of American Jews who belong to synagogues or even the
rest of American Jewry.

Israel's legal rulings matter less and less to American Jews; Israeli
dancing has lost its appeal; the content of Jewish summer camp programs
is less and less Israel-centered and more and more Judaism-centered; Israeli lecturers have been replaced in synagoues by American Jewish
scholars; the Jewish enrollment in college-level Hebrew language courses (now more frequently biblical Hebrew rather than modern Hebrew)
peaked in an earlier period; and synagogue school curricula are less oriented around Israeli politics and society than in the days of David Ben-
Gurion and Golda Meir. The head of the publishing house that supplies
more textbooks to synagogue and day school programs than any other,
David Behrman, noted that curricular emphases have shifted to the "three
H's": history, Hebrew, and Holocaust, and one historian of contemporary American Judaism, Jack Wertheimer, has concluded that "judging
by the interest in curricular materials, ethics and Jewish vaues are replac-
ing Israel as key subjects in the supplemental school."[50] In one Seattle Reform congregation the curriculum of the 1960s and 1970s had an Israel
component in the fourth through sixth grades, an Israel component in the
seventh through eighth grades, and an Israel component in the preconfir-
mation and confirmation year. The 2000–2001 curriculum did not have
an Israel unit in any of those years, substituting in its place American Jewish community, ethics, holidays, prayer and (especially) prayer book, and
the principles of Reform Judaism. Israel seemingly offered American

Jews a strong sense of pride and identity in the 1950s and 1960s, but the ingredients of Judaic identity today come from sources other than the holy land. Although nearly every synagogue takes pride in nurturing an intimate connection to Israel, "Making a Jewish Home" is a much more likely program than "Our Relationship to the State of Israel."

The exception to this generalization about the priority of domestic, life-cycle, and festival events over Israel is when Israel was at war or during the intense intifadas. At those times, American Jews have felt that Israel's very existence was threatened, and synagogue activities reflected a fervent concern with the horror, tragedy, and violence in Israel. Synagogue members organized fund-raising drives for social services, relief efforts, education, and advocacy: the Reform rabbis of America sponsored a drive in 2002 to purchase a fully equipped ambulance for Magen David Adom, the Israel emergency medical response organization; Young Israel adopted Israeli families through a program called Project Embrace and One Family, an Israeli organization that helps victims of terror; and one synagogue in New York City put up-to-the-minute reports of events in Israel, and the most recent Israeli casualities of war, as well as pictures of individual terror victims, on their web site. Rabbis delivered continual sermons on the Middle East crisis; it was especially common to hear sermons illuminating the true dimensions of the long and complex Israeli-Palestinian conflict as well as sermons that probed the relationship between survival of diaspora Jewish communities and their understanding of Israel. Congregational leaders organized local rallies—joining the sectors—in support of Israel, programs with speakers from Israel, and trips to Israel to show their backing. Discussions and debates were plentiful, generally without a strong political agenda but with the goal of educating congregants and guests. And there was no lack of fasting and praying, including a proclamation by the Union of Orthodox Jewish Congregations of America and the (Orthodox) Rabbinical Council of America for a Yom Kippur Katan, a day of fasting, prayer, and repentance to enable American Jews to feel connected to what was happening in Israel and to overcome despair and hopelessness as suicide bombings continued without cessation. Perhaps most interesting, congregations of all branches found ways to insist that Israel fulfill its vision as a country that exemplifies the moral values of Judaism, including efforts to end the Israeli occupation of the West Bank while concomitantly guaranteeing Israel's security.

Thus, among the topics for discussion in synagogues around the country during the spring and summer of 2002 were the need to protect the human rights of foreign workers in Tel Aviv, programs for poor Jews in poverty-stricken neighborhoods of Jerusalem, for Bedouin nomads in the Negev who have been moved around continually as new development towns replace their primitive homes, and for Palestinians in West Bank villages. Synagogue programs certainly dramatized the need to protect the body of the Jewish state, but so many of them brought to the attention of American Jews the soul of the state as well—the need to be fierce defenders of human rights for all the inhabitants of the land of Israel/Palestine.

Earlier I mentioned a program title, "Making a Jewish Home." Such topics are also more likely to be present in the increasingly affluent Orthodox neighborhoods or communities that thrive in numerous American cities. These centers, in places such as Beachwood, Cleveland Heights, and University Heights, Ohio (suburbs of Cleveland), though ostensibly "Orthodox" to an outsider, are of three types: Modern Orthodox, right-wing Orthodox, or Hasidic. And each of them lays claim to the term *Orthodox*, although they differ significantly. Each of these neighborhoods is filled with small (and large) synagogues, kosher bakeries, restaurants, bagel shops, Jewish gift and bookshops. Sabbath afternoons find families walking with and among other Jewish families, visiting other Orthodox families, and engaging in programs of Torah study.

Torah study dominates all the Orthodox neighborhoods, and there are abundant programs for Jewish men, Jewish women, and youth. They take place in homes, learning centers (*kollels*), and synagogues. At the kollel the community pays a living-wage fellowship to men who study Talmud full-time; the Los Angeles Kollel supports twelve men and their families at about $36,000 per year.[51] The Modern Orthodox and right-wing Orthodox, while not Jewish "pluralists" in any sense, do welcome Reform and Conservative Jews who wish to study in their centers. Whatever they might think about Conservative and Reform Judaism is kept private and the emphasis is on textual study. In the Hasidic environment the *rebbes* who vigorously proselytize among the unaffiliated quickly make it clear that both Reform and Conservative Judaism (though not Reform and Conservative *Jews*)—not to mention Modern Orthodox Judaism—are illegitimate and inauthentic.

The Modern Orthodox centers and communities emphasize *Torah Umadah*, living a Torah lifestyle while accumulating secular education and participating in the larger society. Modern Orthodox young men and women will usually attend Jewish day schools, separated commonly by sex, but they will continue their education in colleges and universities, public and private, where Jews are in a minority and women and men attend classes together. The right-wing Orthodox will also attend Jewish day schools, but they reject secular colleges and universities, continuing their education under Jewish auspices. The Modern Orthodox usually dress like any Americans of a similar class; right-wing Orthodox men commonly wear head covering all the time and married women wear long dresses, wigs, and scarves over their wigs; [52] Hasidic men usually wear full beards, hats, and dark clothes.

Lubavticher, one of the many branches of Hasidism (other brances include Belzer, Breslover, Chernobyler, Satmar, and Skvirer), is especially active in missionary activities. Through their Habad Houses all over the country, even in places that seem as if they would not have a Hasidic community (Memphis, Tennessee, Alexandria, Virginia, Toledo, Ohio, Phoenix, Arizona), the Lubavtich Hasidim bring the Hasidic doctrine to all who step into their territory. They do not mention pluralism, presenting one way, and only one way, to observe Judaic ritual and ceremony. Hasidic rebbes, who may or may not also be rabbis, are spiritual masters, men who provide guidance, usually with mystical overtones, for matters of Jewish ritual as well as for the spiritual life.

Hasidism is no more homogeneous than are the Orthodox. Some Lubavitchers believed that their late rebbe, Menachem M. Schneersohn, may have been the Messiah; other Lubavitchers deny this. Some Lubavitchers believe a rebbe has a soul that is higher than other humans; others (and Breslover Hasidim) do not. Some Hasids believe in angels, migration of souls, and petitionary prayer to (rather than through) a rebbe; others do not. The range of dress, ritual, and belief among the Hasidim is certainly as varied as among any other group of Jews.

CHAPTER SEVEN

Select Profiles of Judaic
Thinkers in America

It is not easy to choose eight women and men who are representative of the many thinkers that have made significant contributions to Judaism in America, as there are obviously a large number who might have been included. Having discussed briefly two seminal Modern Orthodox thinkers in chapter 3 (Rabbi Leo Jung and the Rav, Rabbi Joseph Soloveitchik), I thus chose two persons from Conservative Judaism (Abraham Joshua Heschel and Solomon Schechter), arguably the branch that has made the most profound contributions to Judaic thought in America; one each from Reconstructionist (Mordecai M. Kaplan), Reform (Isaac Mayer Wise), and ultra-Orthodox Judaism (Menachem Mendel Schneerson); one from American Zionism's religious stream (Henrietta Szold); one who dominated the early nineteenth-century Judaic community (Rebecca Gratz); and one who had a pivotal influence on Judaic thinking in the third quarter of the twentieth century (Trude Weiss-Rosmarin). There is no objective measure for such choices, and surely a different historian of Judaism would make different choices, but I hope that I explicate (however briefly) the thinking of each of these individuals and make clear why I consider them notable and vital.

Rebecca Gratz (1781–1869)

Philadelphia-born Gratz was one of the most influential Jewish women of the antebellum era. Unmarried, like a great many middle- and upper-class antebellum Philadelphians, Gratz's closest ties were with her unmarried brothers, with whom she lived throughout her life, and the greatest fulfillment in her life seemed to come from her more than sixty years of communal service. Her institutions were her legacy—Female Hebrew Benevolent Society, Hebrew Sunday School, Jewish Foster Home—and they thrived, in great part because of her extraordinary organizational abilities, long after her death.

Rebecca Gratz was a member of the emerging leisure class; this intellectual woman made a career of managing organizations, and she convinced two or three generations of Jewish women that they, too, could manage institutions and make a place for themselves (and for Judaism) within American culture. Shut out of the family business by American law and circumscribed in her religious activities by a patriarchal Jewish tradition, Gratz found a rewarding life in benevolent societies.

She worked at being fully Jewish (an implacable foe of reform in Judaism and a model of women's piety, today we would call her an Orthodox Jew) and fully American (she was from an upper-class family that intermarried in large numbers and included many family members who embraced Christianity) in every decade of her life. She demonstrated with clarity how "her values and attitudes toward philanthropy and domesticity blended Judaism with popular American ideas shared by gentile women of her class."[1] Her sense of religious duty was as deep as it was simple, confidently believing that her treatment of the poor would be discussed with her at the judgment seat of God, and it paralleled the desire of similar Protestant women of her age to be models and teachers of religious virtue within their families and communities. She spent abundant time in religious activities, and the regimen of her philanthropic organizations followed the descriptions of piety in Victorian culture and the regimen of Christian institutions (discipline, prayer, study).

It is a truism that for three centuries men have dominated American Judaism. They have founded the synagogues, they have initiated the call for, and almost exclusively been the ones to hire, rabbis, and they have dominated the religious activities of the synagogues. On the other hand, the religious education of children in the home has been the task of women and, beginning with Rebecca Gratz, so has (to a large extent) the establishment of religious education programs in the synagogue. Synagogue minutes attest to the significant role of women not only in establishing but maintaining religious education programs. Indeed, it is virtually the only area of synagogue life in which women early emerged as administrators—religious school principals.

The Hebrew Sunday School that she founded was her greatest commitment in time and energy; she personally evaluated each student, assigned them to the appropriate class, and graded all weekly assignments. Here too Victorian culture was the model, as she emphasized domestic piety and devotion to God. It was the emerging women's culture that had the greatest impact on Gratz, and Jewish organizations gave her a public, institutionalized role in Jewish life—it was perhaps the first time in Jewish history that a woman taught religion publicly. The women's culture also helped her resolve some of the conflicts in Jewish women's religious identities, for Gratz, without formal religious education, showed Jewish women how to keep Judaism in their homes and Christianity out (e.g., how to respond to evangelists), and, in the case of the many intermarriages within her family, how to maintain one's Judaism in spite of a Christian spouse.

She found intimacy largely through correspondence, and her closest ties, after her unmarried brothers, were to her sister Rachel's children, the nieces and nephews whom she raised after Rachel's death, and to the children of a dear friend, Maria Fenno Hoffman. Gratz deeply believed in the class and social distinctions that placed her among Philadephia's elite and agreed with non-Jewish upper-class women that philanthropy offered wealthy women a way to eradicate poverty, but she did not, for the most part, display her status. She did stack the management of the philanthropic organizations she managed with family members and close friends from her synagogue, Mikveh Israel, but she spent far more time among the poor than among the balls and gala events of the rich. She also spent more time reading and discussing classical and English fiction and poetry, as well as the Bible, than in frivolous social activities, continually searching for stimulating intellectual contacts among people such as Washington Irving, Grace Aguilar, and Catherine Sedgwick.

Abraham Joshua Heschel (1907–1972)

Born in eastern Europe, Heschel was a descendant of Hasidic masters Dov Baer of Mezhrich and (the Apter rebbe) Abraham Joshua Heschel of

Apt on his father's side, and Levi Isaac of Berdichev on his mother's side. He left the world of Polish Hasidism (Talmud and kabbalah) for secular studies in Vilna and Germany (including a Ph.D. in philosophy from the University of Berlin) and a teaching position at the German Liberal Jewish seminary, the Hochschule fuer die Wissenschaft des Judentums—all of which contributed to his deep learning in traditional Jewish sources (as well as Hasidism and mysticism) and his comfort in an academic setting. The Nazis deported him, together with all the Polish Jews, in 1938, and he was rescued from the fate of most of Polish Jewry (including his family) by the Hebrew Union College (Reform) in Cincinnati where he taught rabbinics and philosophy for a few years. In 1946 he moved to New York and the faculty of the Jewish Theological Seminary (Conservative) where he taught Jewish ethics, mysticism, and philosophy until his death. He was never really at home in either institution: the college feared his piety and the seminary his social activism.

He greatly influenced two or three generations of Conservative rabbis as a teacher and a Jew, and through his writing and his activism had an enormous influence among American Jews and Christians beyond the seminary. For Heschel, the question for modern men and women (he uses this term despite sustained critiques of "modernity" in his writings) is how to "think, feel, act and live" in a way that recognizes that we are created in the image of God. [2] At the foundation of Heschel's understanding of acting and living is his study of prophetic consciousness—on which he wrote his dissertation, published years later in English—he often left his study to participate in civil rights marches and antiwar protests, combining thought and action in his life. [3]

Heschel's elegant prose writings, suffused with piety and mysticism, attempt to offer modern religious believers a traditional interpretation of Judaism couched in modern idioms (e.g., "meaningfulness," ineffable, wonder, radical amazement), a reconciliation of personal religious experience, and a traditional conceptualization of the commandments. The experience of God becomes the experience of a sense of infinite, or spiritual, meaningfulness; meaningfulness is the authority for belief and practice. "Awe is the awareness of *transcendent meaning*, of a spiritual suggestiveness of reality, an allusiveness to transcendent meaning." [4] Heschel is continually trying to move his readers beyond reason to the ineffable area of faith, to a religious context where words indicate a reality that is not directly visible, where religious statements point toward rather than describe reality.

Thus Heschel integrates popular modern language and individual experience into a traditional religious framework, trying to convince readers that though they may not have perceived the divine in their own profound experiences of meaningfulness, they nevertheless have encountered the divine presence. "There is a transcendent meaning to the universe independent of our comprehension."[5] Wonder, too, may be the "starting point of religion," and frequently there are experiences to which "we respond with *radical amazement*" (sometimes, "radical astonishment") and "there are mysteries of reality to which we respond with awe."[6] For him a sense of personal meaningfulness functions as a primary means of authority for modern American Jews.

In *God in Search of Man: A Philosophy of Judaism* he raises two fundamental questions: what have we done to make possible "a civilization where factories were established in order to exterminate millions of men, women, and children," where "soap was made of human flesh," and what are we doing "to make such crimes impossible?"[7] The problem for Heschel is the person, or the person in relation to God, and it arises out of a dynamic relationship between situation, insight, and response. These terms come from his analysis of biblical prophetic consciousness (*The Prophets*), as their consciousness is archetypal of all open-minded human consciousness; the insights and challenge of the prophets are compared to human consciousness as it moves from situation to insight and to response. Once one grasps Heschel's primary insight of revelation (a quite traditional understanding not agreeable to many modern Jews), one is then able to grasp Heschel's understanding of faith, history, prayer, and time.

For Heschel, the Hebrew Bible, and particularly the prophets, offers a primary model for the authentic spiritual life. Through the Bible we grasp not so much truths about God or values that are being transmitted but the divine pathos, God's outraged response to human suffering and anguish, God's feelings (joy, pleasure, sorrow, wrath) about human action. God is "moved and affected by what happens in the world"; for Heschel, "God is interested in human history," and "every deed and event in the world concerns Him and arouses His reaction." This is the fundamental basis of the relation between God and us, the starting point for understanding the events of our life, for God can "be experienced by us only if and when we are aware of His attention to us, of His being concerned with us."[8]

Heschel's popularity among non-Jews probably comes from his accessible phenomenology of religion in *Man's Quest for God: Studies in Prayer and Symbolism* (1954), *God in Search of Man* (1955), *Who is Man?* (1966), and *Man Is Not Alone: A Philosophy of Religion* (1951), as well as his popular study, *The Prophets* (1962). His most acclaimed book, *The Sabbath: Its Meaning for Modern Man* (1951), is a meditation one reads with radical amazement, noting the achievement of someone who ten years earlier knew almost no English. In addition to its elegance and power, it subtly delineates a persuasive rationale for the meaning of ritual in one's life.[9]

Mordecai M. Kaplan (1881–1984)

When the Reconstructionist Rabbinical College opened its doors to students in 1968, the Reconstructionist "movement," founded by Mordecai M. Kaplan, once "American Orthodoxy's most accommodating and widely cultured rabbi,"[10] officially became a denomination like Conservative, Orthodox, and Reform Judaism. Before Kaplan had insisted congregations that joined his movement (the Federation of Reconstructionist Congregations and Fellowships) belong to one of the three existing branches or denominations, and they did so.

Thirty-four years before the college opened, Kaplan's *Judaism as a Civlization: Toward the Reconstruction of American-Jewish Life* (1934) and his *Reconstructionist* journal (1934) officially launched the movement with a sustained critique of the existing branches of American Judaism and a detailed plan for reconstructing Judaism in the United States. By "reconstructing Judaism" he meant to bring it in consonance with what modern Jews could believe and what Jews as Americans could affirm. He had no special interest in a new denomination, seeing the existing divisions in American Judaism as divisive if not destructive, but rather in a new school of thought or philosophy of Judaism.

Following his theological break with Orthodoxy,[11] and drawing upon such disparate fields as anthropology, ethics, history, philosophy, sociology, and theology, the essential argument in his new philosophy emerged: that Judaism is not a religion but a civilization—an evolving civilization of the Jewish people in which faith is but one element—and that this redefinition would unify a diverse American Jewry.[12] Even more: "the spiritual regeneration of the Jewish people demands that religion cease to be its sole preoccupation."[13] Kaplan would make the synagogue a center of art, ethics, language (Hebrew), music, recreation, religion, and Zionism—rather than mainly rituals and prayer—and the sanctuary of the synagogue would be joined (better, ringed) by ancillary areas (equally "sacred") where drama, folk dancing, painting, singing, study, volleyball, and the like would feed into the worship environment.

Kaplan developed this conception of an organic Jewish community while a professor at the Conservative Jewish Theological Seminary for over fifty years. He would eventually retire from the seminary to advance reconstructionism as a movement and move it from a philosophy to a program of action. Long opposing the Conservative seminary's ideology and policies (he viewed the seminary as Orthodox in praxis and Reform in theology), he nevertheless deeply appreciated that the seminary provided him with a forum with which to teach and write about what was wrong with Conservative Judaism (and the other branches, of course).

This theology began with a rejection of a supernatural deity, as Kaplan frequently referred to himself as a naturalist and spoke of God as immanent, as present within humanity and society, as the apotheosis of human creativity. God, for Kaplan, is the force or power we recognize throughout the world of nature, the force that is responsible for the amazing design, harmony, order, plan, and purpose we discover everywhere.[14]

The Jewish people were the highest *sanctum* (value) for Kaplan, and their spirit provided individual Jews with a way to transcend their concerns and link themselves to an ultimate concern. Drawing generously upon the new science of sociology, and especially Émile Durkheim and his study of people and peoplehood, Kaplan suggested that modern Jews might find in the unity of their people what a Jew had traditionally found in a supernatural God. The Jewish people articulate and establish their values, and they are not just the sum total of the values of their members, but they are the character, essence, and unity of the Jewish people. These ultimate values, constructed by the people, are called God. "God," he wrote in 1937, "is what the world means to the man who believes in the possibility of maximum life and strives for it."[15] And each Jew ought to stand before God and find sustenance and life in this presence.

Judaic rituals and practices (he called them "folkways") provide the Jewish people the way to feel God's presence and to maintain their identity as a people. Religion springs out of the life of this people ("The group shapes its values" he would say frequently) and fortifies the events, institutions, memories, and things that the Jewish people (or any people) require for their collective existence. Although holidays and observances have been created by the Jewish people (revelation is only a metaphor), they assume a sacred significance for Kaplan; they serve as symbols that link the people one to another and offer a source of inspiration and meaning for the Jews' lives.

Kaplan's concept of civilization offered, in the words of Eugene B. Borowitz, "Jewish identity through culture," and "in place of supernaturalistic Jewish faith, [he] projected a humanist conception of God." Although the Reconstructionist denomination had barely one hundred congregations at the turn of the millennium, Kaplan's thought deeply influenced hundreds of Reform and Conservative rabbis as well as Jews everywhere.

Solomon Schechter (1847–1915)

Born in Romania, Schechter received a traditional Jewish education in his native land and in Poland and continued with advanced Jewish studies in Vienna. He came to England in 1882, and eventually became university lecturer (later, reader) in Talmudics at Cambridge University (1890–1902). There, in the 1890s, he achieved international scholarly fame with his rediscovery and manuscript identification of fragments in the Cairo *Genizah*. These included the Hebrew original of Ecclesiasticus (Ben Sirah) and the "Sectarian Document," [16] but other discoveries "revolutionized our views concerning the history of the *geonic* [post-Talmudic] times in a way undreamed of before." [17]

When the reorganized ("new") Jewish Theological Seminary in New York convinced Schechter (and his wife, Mathilde) to leave Cambridge for its presidency, he was arguably the most famous Jewish scholar in the world. Scholarship remained his central focus and highest priority, and he hired a core faculty of distinguished scholars upon his arrival. The seminary received generous funding from wealthy Reform Jews who were committed to establishing a modern *and* a traditionally Judaic institution that would produce English-speaking rabbis, with college degrees, for the immigrant masses, and Schechter was a perfect choice.[18]

While Schechter may not have clearly constructed a new Conservative Judaism, as distinct from an Orthodox Judaism,[19] he did exactly what he was hired to do—create a modern seminary that could claim to be deeply traditional *and* American. He was committed to the scientific study of Judaism and was punctilious in his observance of Jewish law. He insisted that a student who entered the seminary "should know everything Jewish— Bible, Talmud, Midrash, Liturgy, Jewish ethics and Jewish philosophy, Jewish history and Jewish mysticism, and even Jewish folklore." For "none of these subjects, with its various ramifications, should be entirely strange to him."[20]

Schechter's blend of the modern and the traditional rejected both Reform ("Lord, forgive them, for they know nothing") and Orthodoxy ("a return to Mosaism would be illegal, pernicious and indeed impossible"), and he affirmed, as the central thrust of Conservative Judaism, an emphasis on the "Tradition." This emphasis meant, for Schechter, a far greater appreciation of, and commitment to, the beliefs, customs, laws, observances, and rituals in the Jewish past, as understood by the Jewish people (the "people's will," he called it), while at the same time using science and history to probe, challenge, and uncover the past.[21]

Unlike his Orthodox opponents, Schechter respected much of modern, scientific biblical criticism, including the conclusions that Solomon did not write Ecclesiastes, that David did not author the entire Psalter, and that Isaiah 1–40 is not by the same author as Second (Deutero-) Isaiah—all of which, incidentally, had already been suggested or hinted at by the ancient rabbis. He even raised the question of whether Moses actually existed and if he had any connection with the Pentateuch! But most of all, he rejected (or at least minimized) the notion of a divine revelation and emphasized instead the need for constant reinterpretation of the tradition by "catholic Israel"— the totality (or at least the vast majority) of the Jewish people: "The Torah is not in heaven; its interpretation is left to the conscience of catholic Israel." Hence Schechter spoke of "development, progress, and retrogression" and of the "subjective notions of successive generations regarding religion" in order to emphasize not only the evolutionary character of Judaism but the obligation of each generation of Jews—rabbis and laypeople—to change (albeit slowly and deliberately) the revered tradition in "accordance with its own spiritual needs."[22]

With this commitment to "change," Schechter emphasized that the seminary would not be a yeshiva, where Talmud was the overwhelming subject of study, nor a college, where Jewish law was not held sacred, but a Jewish seminary where ordination of rabbis, not just study for study's sake, would be a high priority; where the Bible, as "it is interpreted by Tradition," would be primary; where "the centre of authority is . . . placed in some *living body*"—the Conservative Jewish movement; and where every student was "expected to observe the Jewish Sabbath and to conform to the Jewish dietary laws."[23] There was no institution like it at the time, and even a century after Schechter arrived in America, none had emerged.

Menachem Mendel Schneerson (1902–1993)

The seventh in the line of *rebbes* (a Yiddish term or dynastic title for the chief rabbi or leader) of the Lubavitch sect of Hasidism, and the great-great grandson of the third Lubavitcher rebbe, his namesake, Rabbi Menachem Mendel of Lubavitch, this late Lubavitcher rebbe was the head of the Habad movement and a direct descendant of the founder of the movement, Rabbi Schneur Zalman (1745–1813). In addition to intensive Torah and Talmud learning, he spent the 1930s in Berlin (like Joseph Soloveitchik and Abraham Joshua Heschel) and Paris studying math and engineering before coming to the United States in 1941.

He and his wife Chaya Moussia, the second daughter of the sixth Lubavitcher rebbe, had no children, but succession was not a public problem, as Rabbi Schneerson did little to negate the claim of his followers that he was the Messiah. Although his sect of Hasidism had traditionally avoided explicit messianic speculation, Rabbi Schneerson preached the imminence of the messianic era. He had explained that "all the signs [including the "miracle" 1991 Gulf War] regarding the end of exile and the time of Redemption" had been fulfilled,[24] that this would be the last generation of Jews in exile, that the prophet Elijah was coming daily to

Tiberias and would soon proclaim the Messiah, that his followers should announce that the Messiah was on his way ("Demand the coming of [the Messiah], talk [continually] about [the Messiah's] coming")[25] and prepare themselves to return to the Land of Israel, led by the Messiah, where they would build the third Temple in Jerusalem and fulfill all the commandments in the most perfect manner.

When the Messiah did not arrive as Schneerson expected, he found it "incomprehensible," while his followers interpreted their rebbe's words to mean that the rebbe was the Messiah. For weeks and even months after his death, in cities such as Baltimore, Los Angeles, and New York, Lubavitcher Hasidim distributed flyers declaring that the rebbe would be resurrected and usher in the messianic era. While awaiting a miracle, they have not crowned a successor.

Rabbi Scheneerson would deliver long lectures at Sabbath afternoon synagogue *fabrengen,* or gatherings, and the Lubavitcher sect would frequently publish essays derived from the lectures. In addition to the coming of the Messiah who will rebuild the Temple in Jerusalem, he believed quite literally in the direct revelation of the entire Torah to Moses at Mount Sinai and thus its perfection, in the Jews' obligation to observe all its commandments, in the return of the Jews of the diaspora ("the darkness of exile") to the Land of Israel, and in an eternal reward for observing the commandments—resurrection—that would join body and soul once again.

In addition to theological discourses on messianic and redemption themes, the Lubavitcher rebbe spoke frequently about more mundane, but equally serious, subjects such as *tznius,* or modesty. Modesty of dress (skirts that cover a woman's knees), modesty of conversation, modesty of appetites, modesty of person (self-assurance and confidence but not arrogance or boastful pride)—all sanctified God.[26] This is why all rigorously observant married women wear a *sheitel,* or wig, to cover their hair, and, according to Rabbi Schneerson, such modesty "has a beneficial impact on children and grandchildren, sustenance and health."[27]

The rebbe rarely lectured without discussing the central core of Lubavitcher Hasidism: joy. The Torah, properly interpreted, combines the supreme wisdom of all sciences and systems of knowledge, and a Hasid must observe its ceremonies, customs, and rituals with enthusiasm, never mechanically, and this is true of the most elevated as well as the simplest of deeds.

This perfect Torah is the gift of God, but as the leader of a mystical movement, Rabbi Schneerson would speak of God in the language of the *Zohar* and Kabbalah. The Torah came from "the Infinite Light of the *Ein-Sof*"[28] or (though words are inadequate as God is totally beyond knowledge or comprehension) the most absolute, infinite force of God. When his discourses turned to the language of mysticism and obscure symbolism, it is not at all clear to the uninitiated what he is saying.

Henrietta Szold (1860–1945)

One of the eight daughters of Rabbi Benjamin (1829–1902) and Sophie (1839–1916) Szold, Henrietta Szold grew up in a rich intellectual and Jewishly observant home in Baltimore, Maryland, whose gracious Southern hospitality would influence her throughout her life. Her father, Hungarian-born and educated, came to a Baltimore synagogue one year before Henrietta's birth, and her parents made a determined effort to provide Henrietta with extensive learning opportunities. She taught for fifteen years at the same private school from which she graduated, but it was the opportunity to teach English to east European Jewish immigrants in night school (the Russian School) that made her determined to spend her life working in the field of Jewish education. While serving as superintendent she also became a correspondent ("Shulamith") for an Anglo-Jewish newspaper, and then, for twenty-three years (1893–1916), the secretary to the Publication Committee and (in everything but name) editor for the newly formed Jewish Publication Society in Philadelphia. She edited the *American Jewish Year Book* and compiled the index (volume six) to the English edition of Heinrich Graetz's important and popular *History of the Jews*, translated two volumes of Louis Ginsberg's monumental *Legends of the Jews*, oversaw the 1917 JPS Bible translation, leaving the society only after it published its one-hundredth volume.

Henrietta Szold's work with Russian Jews led her to join the Zionist Association of Baltimore in 1893, and eventually she became president of her local chapter (Daughters of Zion-Hadassah) and then national president of Hadassah. Busy lecturing, fund-raising, and organizing chapters outside New York and Philadelphia (by 1917 Hadassah had forty-seven chapters and four thousand members), she achieved her first success in

January of 1913 when Hadassah raised sufficient funds to send two nurses to Palestine. She then created and developed the Zionist Organization of America's Department of Education (1918–1920) before moving (at the age of sixty) to Palestine, remaining there until her death.

It was a 1909 visit to Palestine with her widowed mother that left her determined to devote her life to Zionist causes. Not just the absence of education programs in American Zionism but the sickness she witnessed in the colonies and cities she visited in Palestine spurred her to build a national Jewish women's organization (Hadassah) that would work to ameliorate disease in Palestine, create a network of prenatal, postnatal, dental, and X-ray clinics and medical services, and, eventually, a hospital in Jerusalem, establish study circles in the United States, and articulate an ideology that championed a strong American and Jewish cultural identity, a deep commitment to contributing time and money to Palestinian causes, and a careful businesslike (i.e., American) approach to the upbuilding of Palestine.

By the time of Szold's death Hadassah was a household word in American Jewry with several hundred thousand Jewish women as members. It became so omnipresent that Brenda Patimkin's mother, in response to a question to Neil Klugman, Brenda's boyfriend, in Philip Roth's 1950s novella *Goodbye Columbus* ("Is your mother in Hadassah?") could respond to Neil's question ("She's in Arizona now. Do they have Hadassah there?"), "Wherever there are Jewish women," and the matter was closed.[29]

Trude Weiss-Rosmarin (1908–1989)

A rigorously observant and fiercely independent Orthodox Jewish intellectual, deeply grounded in Jewish and general literature in a number of languages, and just as deeply committed to Jewish pluralism, Weiss-Rosmarin was one of the most important American Jewish intellectuals in the middle of the twentieth century and an important influence on one or two generations of American Jews.

Born in Germany, she followed a rebellious adolescence[30] by achieving her Ph.D. at the age of twenty-two from the University of Würzburg in Semitics, archeology, and philosophy,[31] and completed considerable study at the Freie Juedische Lehrhaus (established by Franz Rosenzweig) and other Jewish institutions of higher learning. She left Nazi Germany and came to the United States, but the 1930s (not to mention several subsequent decades) was not a propitious time for a female, Jewish academic, fresh off the boat, to find an academic appointment. Undeterred, she carved out a career as an "independent intellectual,"[32] author of numerous books, founder of the School of the Jewish Woman (1933–1939) in New York City, editor of the *Jewish Spectator*—a serious, influential, and independent monthly which she held together on a shoestring budget—and, most of all, a passionate proselytizer for all things Jewish.

She was a feminist long before the second wave of feminism brought young Jews into the movement, anxious to "inspire the Jewish women of this generation" to action and, especially, leadership in Jewish communal organizations and institutions.[33] And perhaps, in part, because of this overt "feminist impulse" she has been mostly marginalized by subsequent male writers. And yet countless American Jews read her *Jewish Spectator* editorials for half a century and learned from her books.[34]

Weiss-Rosmarin spoke unhesitatingly in editorials and books about the "Jewish genius,"[35] and it encompassed a variety of special achievements. The pursuit of learning was part of this genius, and she insisted on regular study of Torah, Talmud, and world literature. Deeply read in Bible, Jewish philosophy, midrash, Mishnah, and Talmud (as well as the literature of Christian origins),[36] she insisted that Jews had an unbroken cultural tradition of uninterrupted creativeness, and she championed Jewish artistic expression of every kind. She affirmed Judaic ritual and ceremony, pushing Conservative, Reconstructionist, and Reform Jews to see its group and individual benefits, but she also had a passion for uprooting suffering and evil and an uncompromising and unwavering insistence on ethical behavior. A disciple of the Polish Jewish historian Simon Dubnow and the Russian Zionist Ahad Ha-am, she attacked the attempts to have Judaism qualify for admission in the diaspora by relinquishing its uniqueness (e.g., Hebrew cultural expressions). This continual emphasis on Jewish "distinctiveness" led her to maximize "the eternal and fundamental differences between Judaism and Christianity," to reject terms such as "Judeo-Christian," and to continually remind Jews that the New Testament, notwithstanding the warm words of liberal Christians, "represents

Jews as a stunted, backward and obsolete religion."[37] She warned Jews not to minimize the importance of the diaspora, where the majority of world Jewry will try to construct a Judaic life. In this diaspora she championed Jewish day schools (the 1940s), long before they were popular, and every effort to publish Judaica for children and teens. And while championing the scientific achievements of the century, she wrote incessantly about the need for spiritual and ethical progress.

A fervent but critical Zionist, strongly committed to Hebrew culture and a Jewish nation, she was an early (and heavily criticized) advocate of dialogue with Palestinian Arabs and recognition of Palestinian nationalism and of a binational state. She criticized Israel for a lack of humility and for "waving the flag of 'western civilization' " in its encounter with Muslim civilization, pleading for "cross-fertilization and symbiosis" with a "kindred religious civilization." She never doubted that "every foot of Palestinian earth is holy to the Jew," and that "Jerusalem belongs to the Jewish people by sacred, sanctified and inalienable rights," but, more sigificant, she understood that there were two equally valid nationalisms in conflict, Jewish *and* Arab, and urged that Jewish-Muslim dialogue replace the "great Jewish delusion"—Jewish-Christian dialogue.[38]

In her earliest books she was quite traditional, determined to use archeology to "confirm" the historical truth of one hundred passages in the Bible so that what some call legends might be seen as history: "The walls and fortifications of Beth-Shan have been excavated and substantiate the correctness of the Biblical narrative."[39] In a similar vein, she vigorously attacked Freud's thesis, in *Moses and Monotheism*, that Moses had Egyptian origins and that monotheism came from Egyptian religion, although her strong traditionalism did not prevent her from also arguing that circumcision has its origins in Egypt, not in the Patriarchs.[40] At the same time, she could write a book that offered numerous programmatic ideas (poems, quizzes, readings, songs, stories) to Jews who chose to celebrate the Sabbath not in the synagogue but at home or at "assemblies."[41]

Later in her life she ceased defending traditional or Orthodox positions on the Bible, and became a rather liberal biblical critic. She rejected divine revelation, affirming multiple authors of the biblical text; she wondered about the historical value of the "historical" books of the Bible; and she concluded that there was "no historical Moses."[42]

But more than anything else—even her passionate Zionism and her deep support for Jewish religious pluralism—was her celebration of Jewish women. "ALL DEPENDS UPON THE WOMAN!" she wrote in 1940, eager to highlight the Jewish achievements of Jewish women (from the Bible to synagogue sisterhoods), and "inspire the Jewish women of this generation with pride in the Jewish past and confidence for the Jewish future."[43] She undertook this mandate in her editorials and the articles she featured in the *Jewish Spectator*, anticipating Betty Friedan's denunciation of the "feminine mystique" that identified womanhood with the role of wife and mother by several decades.

Isaac Mayer Wise (1819–1900)

The leader of the moderate wing of Reform Judaism, and, to a large extent, the architect of the central institutions of Reform (the Union of American Hebrew Congregations, 1873, the Hebrew Union College, 1875, and the Central Conference of American Rabbis, 1889), Wise delineated the basic theology and practise of Reform Judaism for the first century or so of its life in the United States. He also formulated with clarity a program of Americanization for Reform, arguing that the Declaration of Independence and the Constitution were the fulfillment of God's revelation to Moses, that the liberty and independence achieved by the Hebrews who left Egypt paralleled the "democratic liberty" of the United States. Indeed, "Moses formed one pole and the American revolution the other," wrote Wise, and the God of the Hebrews was the "national Deity" of both ancient Israel and the United States. [44]

A Bohemian immigrant, he came first to Albany's traditional Beth El in 1846 but was forced to resign in 1850 because of his reforms. He introduced an organ and retained the family pews (men and women had never prayed together in Albany) at Anshe Emeth (his new synagogue) when the congregation took over a church in 1851. In 1854 he went to B'nai Jeshurun in Cincinnati, where he served for the rest of his career; there he excised the traditional prayers he did not find meaningful or relevant, eliminated the 2,500-year-old celebration of the second day of all holidays (that made certain the simultaneous celebration with Jews in Jerusalem), save Rosh Hashanah, forbade the wearing of the tallith or prayer shawl (except when called to the Torah), and made numerous other changes in ceremony, custom, and ritual. Because he and his colleagues denied the authority of Jewish law, all these changes were permissible to the rabbis of the Reform movement.

In the area of theology Wise was more moderate, and his doctrines remained an essential part of Reform prayer books until the last decades of the following century. He insisted that Judaism was a revealed religion, that the one, invisible, just, merciful and good God[45]—the "Creator, Preserver and Ruler"—gave the Hebrews a Bible of "immediate divine origin."[46] As a national figure in Jewish circles who received and accepted invitations to speak all over the United States, it is possible to find, in endless sermons and addresses, inconsistencies in Wise's theology (was the entire Bible divine revelation? was the Decalogue alone and not all the Torah's commandments divinely revealed?), he battled against what he called Modern Biblical Criticism, and never stopped affirming that divine revelation to Moses at Mount Sinai was basic to his system of ethical monotheism and the foundation of all biblical truth.

Although he would often note that "dogmas have no place in our system," he would concomitantly insist that there were "three theological dogmas" in Judaism: "the Covenant, the Revelation, and the Promise."[47] By no dogmas he meant, like Jewish philosophers before him, that his fundamentals of Judaism were demonstrated not just by reason but nature and history as well. And nothing was more repeated by him than the affirmation (dogma?) that "the whole Torah is one in spirit, in principle, in doctrine, in precept and in law" because "it stems from one author," God.[48]

His writings fundamentally shaped the prayer book theology of Reform Judaism, but, even more, his rejection of the authority of Jewish law (despite his affirmation of the divine revelation of these same commandments) dominated subsequent Reform theology. Some took it to an extreme, arguing that since the hundreds of ceremonies, customs, observances, and rituals in Judaism lacked divine authority, Reform Jews should discard them all. Others found a few to observe, citing "relevance" or "spirituality" as their authority for observance. But all Reform Jews, and this flowed from Wise's thinking, acknowledged the right of each individual Reform Jew (or each Reform Jewish congregation) to choose those that resonated within her or him. And each Reform Jew affirmed the right of all other Reform Jews to make their own informed choice, whether that resulted in considerable or negligible observance. In this, perhaps, even more than in the institutions and organizations he helped design and build, he may well be the "Father of Reform Judaism."[49]

CHAPTER EIGHT

The Retrieval of Tradition

It is axiomatic among students of American religion to note that increased amounts of tradition have found their way into Christianity in the past three decades. In some churches there has been a developing liturgical interest or liturgical revival; the Catholic Church has even moved vigorously to halt experimental liturgical practices.[1] With the accession of John Paul II to the papacy (1979)—and his insistence on priestly celibacy, refusal to consider the ordaining of women, vigorous rejection of birth control and homosexual relations, and rebuking or censuring of liberal theologians—numerous Catholic churches restored the Holy Week Liturgy, encouraged daily attendance at Mass, and returned to other traditions. Protestant churches that previously interpreted the Eucharist symbolically, or interpreted it not at all, have been emphasizing the real presence of Christ in the Eucharist. Others have introduced incense, rejected revised prayer books, organized substantial lay Bible study groups, and, generally, affirmed a theological traditionalism and rituals that emphasize continuity with the past. And conservative Protestant churches, Holiness churches, Pentecostal bodies, and Fundamentalist denominations (there is an important distinction in Protestantism between Pentecostal and Fundamentalist that is usually lost on American Jews)[2] have all grown significantly in this period. It is also axiomatic among Jews to note that as the whole complexion of America has shifted rightward, increased amounts of traditional ceremony, customs, observances, and ritual have found their way into all the branches of American Judaism in the past three decades.

Reform Judaism

In New Brunswick, New Jersey, in February of 1999, at an old and "classical" Reform congregation,[3] 80 percent of the males and 20 percent of the women wore head covering at Sabbath services.[4] At a Reform congregation in Southern California in March of 2000, the rabbi continuously bowed her head and bent her knees in an exaggerated fashion, virtually davening—so unusual at a Reform service—hoping, so she explained later, to experience God directly. In a Reform congregation in Santa Fe, New Mexico, in June of 1999, the cantor chanted the *avot* prayer while facing the ark and (seemingly) the entire congregation (many wearing jeans, string ties, boots, and head covering) bowed their collective heads at "Baruch atah adonai."

In the 1950s and even the 1960s, Reform congregations everywhere in America continued the nearly century-old pattern of distancing themselves from traditional observances. At Reform worship services rabbis, cantors, and laypeople rarely wore head covering, nor would a visitor to the Reform rabbinical seminary in Cincinnati be likely to find *kippot* on rabbinic students in the chapel services. When the Torah was removed from the ark, it was held by the rabbi and then promptly placed down on the reading lectern without much fanfare. It was extremely rare to find a Reform household in which a sukkah was erected, in which even part of the dietary laws were observed or even discussed. A musical instrument that was also found in concert orchestras often served as a shofar for the High Holidays; dancing with the Torah scrolls on the holiday of Simchat Torah was unseemly; and the reading of sizable portions of the weekly scriptural portion from the Torah virtually nowhere to be found.

All this began to change by the mid-1970s, as the striking increase in ritual (of course, to a greater or lesser extent) in nearly every Reform congregation was a conscious reaction to the decades in which Reform Judaism had divested itself of ceremonies and observances and placed most of its emphasis on affirmations of ethical monotheism and programs for social justice. By 1975 more and more Reform rabbis and cantors, even if raised in hatless congregations, began to wear head covering and tallith at worship services, and steadily introduced greater amounts of tradition into the life of the home, the sanctuary, and the synagogue. A former president of Rochester's Reform Temple B'rith Kodesh, unhappily observing what he called "creeping Orthodoxy," reacted by describing the rabbi as "Orthodox Hasidic."[5]

In theological terms Reform Judaism moved from the transcendent view of God that characterized this branch of Judaism for fifty years, to an immanent view of God that has been increasingly the language of worship since the 1970s. Choirs hidden by screens and organs even more remote dominated Reform worship, as did a God more akin to that of the biblical prophet Ezekiel than that of the eighteenth-century Hasidic master Nachman of Bratslav. For Rabbi Nachman, and increasingly for Reform Jewish thinkers of this generation, God is present in the here and now, permeating all creation, and Reform worship began to look everywhere, including the tradition, for rituals that might add meaning to worshipper's spiritual lives.[6]

There is no single reason for this,[7] but most rabbis that I have interviewed attribute it to the increase in personal levels of rabbinic and cantorial observance that resulted from a compulsory year of seminary study in Israel. Reform cantors and rabbis seem to have concluded that they could not speak of a religious group ("Jews") if there were (virtually) no rituals that distinguished that group from non-Jews. To connect to other Jews—in time and space—they began to participate in common activities (rituals) with members of a common religious group (Jews), although they had rarely encountered traditional Jews previously.[8]

Scores of rabbinical and cantorial students returned to the United States to continue their studies at the Hebrew Union College–Jewish Institute of Religion in Cincinnati or New York with a level of observance rejected by earlier generations of their peers. When they began to serve congregations, these rabbis became models of increased levels of personal ritual within the congregations they served. And the subsequent rabbinic classes, for the past twenty-five years, have adopted more and more ceremonies, customs, and rituals; so much so that the quandary of a small number of Reform Jewish congregations (who represent the last vestige of "classical Reform" and bemoan what they call "Reform orthodoxy") is how to retain a sense of being an authentic Reform Jew if they do not wear a kippah or bow their head and bend their knee at this or that point in the liturgy.

The drive toward greater observance unleashed a countermovement within the Reform rabbinical association in the 1970s—the American Association for Progressive Reform Judaism (AAPR). Led by two professors from the Reform rabbinic seminary, it gathered few followers and quickly dissipated. Not just Reform rabbis, but members of Reform congregations from coast to coast and border to border have enthusiastically embraced traditions that were seen as anathema to their Reform parents and grandparents. When the Torah is removed from the ark, the rabbi or carrier more often than not parades the Torah in and out of the congregation, and the worshippers touch it with their prayer books, their tallith, or their fingers and bring whatever they touch it with to their lips as a sign of respect for and excitement over the Torah. Synagogue bulletins now routinely list homes in which sukkot have been constructed, and members of the congregations eat some meals in them during the weeklong celebration of Sukkot. Abundant amounts of Hebrew now replace English in the reading and chanting of the liturgy; nearly every rabbi and cantor and a majority of worshippers in Reform synagogues all over the country will be found wearing head covering; and it is not at all unusual to find rabbis who observe the dietary laws serving Reform congregations.

By the early 1980s, as national Reform Jewish lay leaders, many of whom were still comfortable in classical congregations, increasingly observed (often negatively) these changes, they responded with a common Reform Jewish procedure—a survey. The chairman of the board of the Union of American Hebrew Congregations proposed that the Joint Commission on Worship of the American Conference of Cantors, Central Conference of American Rabbis, and the UAHC (all Reform) study "the evolving trends of worship within our movement." Calling the more observant rabbis, and their followers, neotraditionalists, and contrasting them to the classical reformers (essentially ignoring the middle of the road or majority of Reform synagogues), the authors of the survey, Ronald N. Ashkenas and Todd D. Jick, themselves Reform Jews, identifed "a wide array of new worship modes, messages, styles and symbols." In fact, they went so far as to claim that "in some congregations . . . clear cut distinctions between Reform . . . and Orthodox modes of worship were disappearing."[9]

Ashkenas and Jick took note of the "much greater use of the *kippa*,"[10] and twenty years later it is quite rare to find a rabbi who does not wear head covering during services; to visit a congregation where there is no *hakafah* (procession) around the sanctuary when the Torah is removed from the ark; to find *treyf* (foods that violate the dietary laws) at the oneg reception after Friday evening or at a lunch following Saturday morning prayers; to find a cantor who does not face the ark during prayers such as the Amidah or, as it is popularly known, the avot, even when there is no such instruction in the prayer book; or to see congregants who do not touch the Torah as it passes by and bring either their (increasingly worn) tallith or prayer book to their lips. "Fifty years ago Reform Jews knew nothing about *Havdalah*," noted Arnold Jacob Wolf in 1993, "and little about *kashrut*."[11] Congregants who do not participate in these rituals—and numerous others "borrowed" from Conservative and Orthodox worship—are increasingly feeling uncomfortable, just as those who practiced such customs, two generations ago, would have been viewed as quite strange or, negatively, as "orthodox."

The steady and even dramatic increase of personal observance by newly graduating rabbis has had ramifications in virtually every congregation in the Reform movement. In Savannah Betsy Klein explained that her husband "can't stand to see the rabbi with a *tallis*. He can't stand to see the rabbi with a *yarmulke*." In Jacksonville, Florida, Georgia Rosen noted that when her father was president of Ahavath Chesed, the family never lit candles for Hanukkah or the Sabbath, never held a seder for Passover, and never celebrated any Jewish holidays.[12] At one large, classical Reform congregation, where rabbis had never worn head covering on the pulpit, where "a *kippah* was not a welcome sight in our sanctuary," and where it "was openly expressed that those wanting to wear a *kippah* should join a different congregation," the leadership realized that the "best and brightest" (as a recent congregational president put it) rabbinic graduates would not even interview for assistantships.

The president who served in 1998 and 1999 told the congregation that "a very significant majority of new Reform Jewish [*sic*] rabbis embrace a return to . . . tradition. As we recruit rabbis in the future, we will find that most recently ordained rabbis share this philosophy." The senior rabbi was well aware that although "classic Reform Judaism" had disappeared nearly everywhere, it remained a powerful memory and "emotional issue" among many members of the congregation he served.[13] In February 1998 this same senior rabbi tried to explain, at great length, why he, for the first time, would wear head covering at religious services. Claiming that "some" Reform congregations prohibited worshippers from ascending the pulpit with head covering, he declared that the congregation would remain committed to what he (correctly) believed was the essence of Reform Judaism: "Every individual is free to do as he or she pleases."[14]

Although doing as one pleases, or "informed choice," has long been a hallmark of Reform Judaism, Reform rabbis have continually felt the need to offer a platform for their congregants. In 1885 (Pittsburgh), 1937 (Columbus), 1976 (San Francisco), and 1999 (Pittsburgh), rabbis gathered at their annual convention and issued a platform or principles. Of course, in a movement characterized by "informed choice," none of these credal affirmations could be binding, only guidelines, and most members of Reform congregations never even saw the platforms. But they remain the closest the movement ever came to an official statement of belief, even if this tells us something about the rabbis and their doctrinal attitudes and little about what Reform congregants actually believe.

The most recent platform, the 1999 Statement of Principles of Reform Judaism,[15] enables us to note that not only have Reform Jews adopted an abundance of ceremonies, customs, and rituals previously found unappealing but there has been an ideological move toward a more traditional position as well. The preamble claims (quite inaccurately) that "throughout our history" Reform Jews have "remained firmly rooted in Jewish tradition." While in actuality this rootedness is no more than thirty years old, Reform rabbis now wish to present themselves as "preserving tradition" and encouraging their members to "engage in a dialogue with the sources of our tradition." Reform rabbis had previously wished to preserve little of the past and had emphasized not a dialogue with tradition but "our encounters with other cultures." Today, however, Reform is embarked on a mission to have both: embrace the past and participate fully in the present.

Unlike previous platforms, the Statement of Principles is filled with Hebrew words and phrases (b'rit, "covenant"; b'tzelem Elohim, "in the image of God"; tikkun olam, "repairing the world"; tzedek, "justice/righteousness"; mitzvah, "commandment"; and many more). It affirms a covenantal relationship between Reform Jews and God, and is even so bold as to suggest that Reform Jews—who reject any authority, whether that of the commandments or their rabbis—ought to not only "study" but consider "the performance of" some of the 613 mitzvot that lie at the heart of more traditional expressions of Judaism. The platform softens this suggestion by calling the mitzvot not commandments but "sacred obligations," yet the intent is clear: those hundreds of ceremonies, obligations, and rituals that sustained Jews for two thousand years *might* provide Reform Jews with "meaning and purpose" in their lives.[16]

While it would be far too traditional for Reform rabbis to speak of these mitzvot, even if they are not called commandments, as divinely revealed (see the earlier discussion of revelation in chapter 2), the platform does affirm "the truths revealed in Torah," and not just the ethical and moral "sacred obligations" but "the whole array of *mitzvot*." Of special note are those that have been ignored by Reform Jews for the two hundred years of its existence and that "demand renewed attention." And the Statement of Principles does "call [Reform Jews] to *mitzvot*" and maintains, with the Judaic tradition, that observing these mitzvot is the "means by which we make our lives holy."

In addition, the rabbis assembled in Pittsburgh "affirm the importance of studying Hebrew" and advocate "regular home and congregational observance." Each of these reflects changing realities in the movement; Reform worship services everywhere utilize more and more Hebrew readings and singing, and Reform Jews, as individuals and/or families at home and in their synagogues, are observing more and more festivals and life-cycle events. There is even a modest movement in the direction of *adding* days of celebration and observance, as congregations in many diverse parts of the country are finding their members expressing a desire to worship on the second day of Rosh Hashanah.

And not only is "tradition" a healthy word in Reform today (one congregation outside Baltimore defines itself, in its constitution and its publicity, as a "traditional Reform" synagogue) but lay leaders are turning to the traditional textual sources of Judaism in ways absent a few decades earlier. It is standard to find these leaders beginning their meetings with a *dvar Torah*, brief Torah study, and for them to participate in programs—often of several days—where they engage in the study of Judaic texts. While there is little evidence that "adult education" programs have returned to their peak in the 1960s and 1970s, everywhere it is evident that the current generation of leaders is far more knowledgeable in Hebrew and in Judaism than Reform leaders of earlier generations. Whereas these leaders once shunned aspects of "tradition," today they embrace the movement's opportunities to learn from this same tradition.

Finally, just as Reform Jews have given considerable thought to those rituals and ceremonies they wish to add, not subtract, in the past three decades, so they have broadened their embracing of diverse members of the Jewish community. Gay and lesbian Reform rabbinical students study openly at all four branches of the seminary, Latino and Hispanic Jews seem well-integrated into congregations in Arizona (especially), California, Florida, New Mexico, and Texas, and women rabbis and cantors are no longer a topic of discussion.

Orthodox Judaism

At an Orthodox congegation in Los Angeles in September of 1997 I witnessed a congregational celebration commemorating the completion of the study of an entire tractate (volume) of the Talmud. What was unusual about this event was not only such a celebration, but one's awareness that the members of the congregation had studied the Talmud volume in an English translation. The increasing availability of Orthodox-sponsored English translations of traditional texts such as the Talmud has meant that thousands of Orthodox Jews, previously unable to study these texts for lack of a sufficient linguistic background, have engaged in such text study, and—more significantly—it is a sign that such study of traditional Hebrew and Aramaic texts in English is not only permissible but encouraged. A generation ago Orthodox congregants laughed at people who suggested such study in English, and the result was a generation of American Orthodox Jews far less learned in traditional texts. Today there is a positive attitude toward such text study in the vernacular, and the availability of traditional texts of all kinds in English translation.

An ultra-Orthodox (*haredi*) Jewish press produces Artscroll publications, popular, uncritical volumes of Judaica for Jewish fundamentalists (and anyone else). Largely defensive in nature, the translators and editors of these volumes attempt to bolster traditional claims for authenticity and reliability in the face of two centuries or more of modern, critical scholarship, and to serve as proselytizing tools for members of the haredi community seeking to win nonharedi Jews to Torah as interpreted in the funamentalist community. Without much subtlety, many of these publications target the nonharedi potential recruit and introduce the correct (i.e., traditional) practices of the past.[17]

The abundance of available texts has dramatically increased Orthodox adult learning. "Torah"[18] study classes may be found in Orthodox synagogues everywhere; there are easily accessible programs to load a daily study calendar into one's Palm Pilot; a "travel edition" of the Art Scroll Schottenstein Talmud is available; and everywhere an expectation exists in the Orthodox community of far more knowledge of traditional texts among average members of the congregation.

In individual congregations as well as nationally the Orthodox movement celebrated the accomplishment of those who had committed to study one page every day (*daf yomi*) of the Talmud, whether in English or the original Hebrew/Aramaic. Begun in 1923 with the suggestion, by Rabbi Meir Shapiro of Lublin at the First International Congress of the Agudat Israel movement, that Orthodox Jews around the world could be united by studying the same page of Tamud every day, the program of daf yomi is now (2002) in its eleventh cycle of study, covering the entire Talmud in seven years at the one-page daily pace. And sophisticated electronic hardware and software is utilized everywhere for this study, ranging from chat rooms to discuss the daf yomi to Palm Pilot programs that contain the daily text.

Not only did a standing-room-only crowd of more than twenty-five thousand Orthodox Jews gather at New York's Madison Square Garden to celebrate the completion of the tenth cycle of daf yomi in late September of 1997—and another ten to fifteen thousand at the Long Island Nassau Coliseum at the same time—it was unimaginable in the Orthodox world that earlier cycle completions would have drawn such an enthusiastic response. But in the late 1990s and early 2000s daf yomi classes and increased Torah learning characterize Orthodox communities everywhere. Indeed, where once it mattered little, synagogue leaders are increasingly embarrassed to be ignorant of Jewish texts, and adult study is probably more widespread today in this community—reversing the trend of an earlier generation—than in any of the other branches of American Judaism.

In addition, study of traditional texts is but one of many areas in which the Orthodox, especially those labeled haredi, have become more aggressive in using sophisticated means of communication (especially print media) for outreach efforts. Nonharedi Jews are exhorted to cultivate greater identification with their Jewish heritage by becoming observant members of the haredi community. A plethora of traditional print media actively proselytize nonharedi Jews, urging them to "return" to the Torah and a traditional Jewish life of observance.

There has been a massive upsurge not only in the study of traditional texts within the American Orthodox community but in clothing as well. Paralleling the curious phenomenon of country music, there has been a huge increase in "black-hattedness" for men and head covering for women. Although Jewish law, as understood by the Orthodox community, requires the hair of a married woman to be covered (although how is up to her), this was rarely observed except in the most punctilious community. As late as 1990, Orthodox rabbis, and even students at (Orthodox) Yeshiva University, were rarely seen in black hats, and many did not have beards. By the end of the decade beards became de rigueur for Orthodox rabbis; a sizable portion of Yeshiva male undergraduate students wear black hats during the week, and an even larger percentage on the Sabbath; it is the same at Stern College, the Yeshiva undergraduate college for women, as in walking the campus one finds more and more married women students with hat or scarf; and in many Orthodox communities Orthodox laypeople expect their rabbi to wear a fedora. This phenomenon was reflected, albeit absurdly, even in the intermarriage-condoning movie, *Keeping the Faith*, where the older Conservative rabbi (played by Eli Wallach) wore a fedora.

Although the younger rabbi in the film was not Orthodox, he wore head covering while walking on the streets of New York City. While this is still rare among non-Orthodox rabbis and laymen, it has become increasingly common among the Orthodox, including professionals. Orthodox men everywhere wear kippot in public and at the workplace, including the United States capital. Indeed, the author recently wore a kippah to a major league baseball game and discovered that while fans heckled his neighbor, who wore a cap of the opposing team, not one fan commented on the kippah. While those who feel that a kippah might interfere with their livelihood are excused by the community from donning head covering, fewer and fewer Orthodox men in recent years have taken advantage of this "exemption."

The percentage of Orthodox girls and boys receiving a full-time primary and secondary Jewish education has continued to grow by leaps and bounds. According to the New York State report on nonpublic school enrollment, Jewish day school enrollment in New York grew from 77,746 in 1990 to 97,185 in 1998, an increase of almost twenty-thousand children or 25 percent in eight years.[19] There has also been a striking expansion in graduates from Jewish day schools, and with this increase another turn to "tradition." A very large percentage of Orthodox high school graduates spend at least one year of study in Israel immediately after high school. While this is virtually automatic for those planning to attend Yeshiva University, it is also increasingly true of Orthodox Jewish students in every American city who are not planning to attend a sectarian or Jewish (there are no non-Jewish undergraduates at Yeshiva University) university. And most of these spend their year in Israel in programs organized or sponsored by Orthodoxy.

Paralleling this has been the dramatic growth in the number of married Orthodox women who cover their heads in public, in the number of Orthodox who will not eat anything at restaurants that are not kosher, even if they are vegetarian, and in the requirements for declaring meat kosher. When the author was growing up, even the most traditionally observant or strictly Orthodox attended American public schools and after-school Hebrew programs; mixed dancing at Orthodox synagogues was frequent and enjoyed without comment; today, a generation of children of the dancers of the 1940s and 1950s has graduated from Jewish day schools and refuses to engage in mixed dancing. In those same decades observant Orthodox Jews looked quickly at labels to decide whether something treyf was included; today those who observe kashrut are very punctilious about studying labels. The ante has been upped so high that only *really* kosher (*glatt*) will satisfy significant quantities of Orthodox housewives. Tova Mirvis sums up the changes well in her novel about Orthodox Jews in Memphis, Tennessee: "The Orthodox world wasn't as strict as it was now. Candy bars that we used to think were kosher were no longer considered so, the synagogue dances we used to hold were now considered scandalous . . . the whole Orthodox world had taken a giant step to the right."[20]

One Orthodox rabbi, David J. Radinsky of Charleston, South Carolina, told the author that the level of observance in his congregation (Brith Sholom Beth Israel) has increased significantly in the past decade or so. While it is still true that not more than ten percent of the three-hundred-member "families" walk rather than drive to Sabbath services, this is not the result of nonobservance, he explained, but the distance so many suburban members live from the downtown synagogue. More women use the mikveh (ritual bath) each month, more congregants observe the Sabbath than previously, more families buy lulavim for Sukkot each year, and more give mishloach manot (presents) on Purim. When he first came to Charleston thirty years earlier, he concluded that "only a handful of our members even knew what *mishloach manot* was." This is another reminder that affiliation is not the same as observance in every sector of American Judaism—or that the level of observance is in the eye of the beholder. As the principal of the Maimonides Hebrew Day School in Savannah explained in commenting upon the majority of members of the Orthodox synagogue in her city, "They belong to the Orthodox synagogue but they are not Orthodox."[21]

But it is not just in areas of ceremony, observance, and ritual that tradition has been energized in all shades of Orthodoxy, but in ethical observances as well. For example, it is commonplace in the last few years for rabbis to preach on the intricate laws of gossip and slander (*lashon harah*), and to remind their listeners that God explicitly forbade this in the Torah (Leviticus 19:16). Thus this commandment about what one Philadelphia Orthodox rabbi called in a sermon "discretion of the mouth" is as important as any of the other more than six hundred observances God authored. The rabbi went on to cite the great rabbinic ethicist Yisrael Meir Kagan (the Chofetz Chayim) and his writing on "the evil tongue." He said, according to the rabbi, that a Jew who finds himself or herself in a group of people who are gossiping about others, and cannot leave, is forbidden to speak lashon harah even if he or she may feel awkward as the only silent person. The truth, of course, is that everyone sometimes commits sins involving lashon harah.[22] In *The Ladies Auxiliary*, the fictional Memphis Orthodox Jewish women tried "our best" not to talk about Batsheva, the new woman in town, and to avoid "needless gossip," especially during Sabath dinner. So, instead of gossiping about Batsheva, "we talked about Shira Feldman, Becky Feldman's seventeen-year-old daugther, who had once again been spotted wearing a scandously short-skirt."[23] But it is increasingly "out" to speak (or to listen to) lashon harah, even if one doesn't explicitly mention names, in an Orthodox community, whether in the business world, the synagogue, or the home.[24]

In the area of business ethics there is an increasing use of the *heter* (permission) as Orthodox Jews have continually expanded the areas in which tradition may be observed. In one community an Orthodox rabbi granted a heter to a kosher pizza shop owner after carefully considering whether his establishment would significantly reduce the income of an already existing pizza restaurant in the same neighborhood. In another city a particular kind of heter was granted by a rabbi so that one man might "loan" another man money for a business despite the prohibition against paying and receiving interest. He wrote this *heter iska*, or partnership agreement, so that the "loan" would be a return on investment rather than interest on a loan, thus permitted according to halacha, or Jewish law. More and more Orthodox Jews are seeking a traditional imprimator for their actions in every area of their life, making no distinction between religious and secular.

Conservative Judaism

Among the three large branches of American Judaism, the Conservative movement has undergone the least movement in the area of ceremony, custom, liturgy, observance, ritual, and theology. Worn out by the radical and often traumatic decision in the 1980s to ordain women as rabbis, Conservative congregations moved little in the 1990s. But the discernible movement was usually in the direction of tradition or, at the very least, a reaffirmation of existing tradition.

Every Conservative rabbi at the turn of the millennium reports a modest number of (mostly) young families who were keeping kosher or considering a switch to kashrut and tells of annually participating in the kashering of several homes. These rabbis tell of growing numbers of congregants erecting sukkot and purchasing lulavim to use in the Sukkot ritual. One Conservative rabbi in 2001 claimed that Conservative Judaism shifted "so far to the right in the past 20 years that there is not much room to shift right,"[25] and there is considerable truth to this. Conservative Judaism, as a movement, embraced so much ritual and observance in the second half of the twentieth century that there is little latitude for more tradition without becoming Orthodox. Unlike Reform Judaism, where it is still hard to find Jews who take kashrut and Shabbat seriously, and unlike Orthodox Judaism, where all the commandments are affirmed as divine revelation, Conservative Judaism continues to attempt to share a theology of questioning and doubt about revelation and thus authority along with Reform Judaism while trying to maximize traditional ritual and observance without the aid of the authority of halachah that charaterizes Orthodox Judaism.

The past decade or so has seen a flourishing of *hevra kadisha* (sacred burial) societies in Conservative congregations, groups of Jews who prepare the deceased for burial and tend to the needs of the bereaved. It is becoming increasingly common in the Conservative movement to honor the two-thousand-year-old tradition of burying the dead in clean, white linen, cotton, or muslin shrouds, a practice that emphasizes the equality of death. And the physical washing of the body by members (separated by sex) of the Conservative congregations is a traditional religious requirement mostly ignored by Reform Jews but increasingly observed by congregations in this movement.

Another tradition, rapidly becoming popular in the movement, is the *t'naim* (stipulations) or engagement document. Somewhat akin to a prenuptial agreement, the stipulations are put into a document that formalizes the agreement, or engagement, between the future bride and groom as well as between their families. Unlike the generally standard form of the document used in many Orthodox circles, these documents are frequently constructed from a basic text (promising that the marriage will take place under a *huppah* or canopy), but provisions are added by individuals or couples to make the t'naim, and the ceremony built around them, quite diverse.

In the area of liturgy the movement resisted further moves to the "left" and reaffirmed its traditional basis. When the relatively new prayer book of 1985, *Siddur Sim Shalom: A Prayerbook for Shabbat, Festival, and Weekdays*, was modestly revised in 1998, the movement was not ready for another radical change and the accompanying traumas within congregations. Although alternative versions of the Amidah—invoking the partriachs Abraham, Isaac, and Jacob as well as the matriarchs Sarah, Rebecca,

Rachel, and Leah—were included, they were put on a separate page in order that congregations that wished to retain the traditional exclusive patriarchal invocation could do so. Not only were Conservative Jews not ready for a standard Amidah with the matriarchs included but the movement was still not completely ready for gender-neutral language (the editor called the compromise "gender-sensitive"),[26] though the 1998 edition did eliminate *He, Him, Father,* and *King,* and left the Hebrew word *Adonai* in Hebrew in English passages rather than use the English equivalent, "Lord." Likewise, those who were uncomfortable with the Hebrew *m'chayeh ha'meyteem* (resurrects the dead) in the Amidah and pushed for a less literal phrase were defeated, and the 1998 edition continues to use the traditional Hebrew and English ("gives life to the dead") words whose literal meaning most Conservative Jews reject.

Theology is probably the area in which the most fundamental division between Conservative and Reform Jewish ideology—as well as between Conservative and Reform rabbis and laypeople—may be found. It is not, as many Conservative and Reform congregants to whom this author spoke think, the number of ceremonies, observances, and rituals one observes that distinguishes a Conservative from a Reform Jew. A Reform Jew may make an "informed choice" to observe kashrut (admittedly rare) and many other rituals and score higher (not so rare) on indexes of observance than some Conservative congregants. It is, rather, the position on Torah: for Reform Jews the Torah is entirely composed by men (and perhaps some women) in a manner similar to other great works of literature, whereas for Conservative Jews everywhere (and for Conservative philosophers, rabbis, and theologians) Torah is the intersection of the human *and* the divine. The Conservative prayer books reflect this, Conservative publications affirm this, and Conservative Jews are much more likely than Reform Jews to actually believe it.

Reconstructionist Judaism

One Sabbath evening in 2001 a guest at a Reconstructionist worship service in California noticed that when the rabbi asked how many of the approximately fifty adult worshippers had grown up in a Reconstructionist congregation, only one responded positively. This would never happen at a Conservative, Orthodox, or Reform synagogue service, where a majority (if not the large majority) is far more likely to have affiliated with the same branch of Judaism that they had attended during their bar or bat mitzvah.

Reconstructionism is the newest and—despite its statistical insignificance (3 percent) within American Judaism and the fact that most Jews are not able to locate a Reconstructionist synagogue—probably the fastest growing of the movements, the branch that attracts the largest number of previously unaffiliated, disaffected, and even militantly secular Jews. These are the Jews of whom a *Los Angeles Times* 1988 survey might have been speaking when it found that almost one-half the respondents cited a "commitment to social justice" as the most important characteristic of their Jewishness. Many once secular Jews, who now seek some kind of spiritual connection to Judaism and the Jewish community, have joined Reconstructionist congregations. Reconstructionist rabbis everywhere note their congregants seem comfortable with the increasing amounts of tradition that have characterized the past couple decades. This branch of Judaism may be the first to have a laity that is more observant and more Jewishly educated than their parents. A generation or so ago the members of the synagogues of this small, self-selecting branch were Red Diaper babies (children of ex-Communists) or the children of Jewishly estranged parents. Today, they are Jews—judging from the bulletins of several dozen congregations—who consume Judaism, in all its manifestations, in large amounts, exploring and experimenting with traditions (e.g., kashrut, building a sukkah, partially observing the Sabbath, studying sacred Jewish texts) their parents never imagined.

This sets off Reconstructionism from its closest "competitor," Reform Judaism. Whereas individual Jews may observe kashrut, there is no discussion of such a ritual as a movement. If there were, hundreds of thousands of Reform Jews would be uncomfortable. But such a discussion, even if some Reconstructionist rabbis speak of this sector as "posthalachic," would raise few eyebrows among the "new kids on the block," the Reconstructionists.

When the author attended Sabbath worship at three Reconstructionist synagogues in the late 1960s, counterculture and renewal activities dominated the services. Some thirty years later Reconstructionist synagogues have incorporated an abundance of traditions into a Sabbath service with a formal liturgy (*Shabbat VeHagim*). There is still a strong likelihood that an occasional prayer sung by the worshippers will be accompanied by some congrregants dancing on the pulpit with movements seeking to interpret the liturgical message. It is likely that the rabbi will pause at some point in the liturgy and ask newcomers to the synagogue to say a few words about themselves. The rabbi will usually lead a wide-ranging Torah discussion on Saturday mornings rather than deliver a sermon. The oneg following services is not likely to include treyf foods. But the rituals of the service—especially the Torah service—will (generally) parallel a service at most any Conservative synagogue.

Reonstructionists are also the Jews who are on the cutting edge of new ceremonies and rituals. They include mikveh (ritual bath) ceremonies for miscarriage and chemotherapy, covenantal (as opposed to naming) rituals for baby girls, ecological seders on Tu B'shevat (Jewish Arbor Day), and numerous new customs incorporated into the Sabbath service.

The major exception to the earlier generalization (that Reconstructionism includes the largest percentage of members not raised exclusively and consistently as Jews) is the Reconstructionist Jews who were raised in a Conservative congregation, the most common denomination for those Reconstructionists who did have a bat or bar mitzvah. And yet there is impressionistic evidence that Reconstructionist synagogue members may be more observant, at least in some areas such as kashrut, than members of Conservative synagogues. While this may be disputed, there is a sizable percentage of Reconstructionist Jews who did grow up in a Conservative home and were already exposed to a modest amount of ceremony, custom, and observance.

It will not surprise this author if the growth of Reconstructionist Judaism continues, at least in the first decade of the new millennium, to outpace that of the major branches. Since predictions of the future, in the Judaic tradition, are reserved for children and fools, let this guarded prophecy be my first—and last.

NOTES

1. What Is American Judaism?

1. Sergio DellaPergola et al., "Prospecting the Jewish Future: Population Projections, 2000–2080," *American Jewish Year Book 2000*, vol. 100 (New York, 2000), especially 118–24.

2. Of course, this is not an inevitable result of intermarriage. It is in theory possible that every marriage of a Jew and a non-Jew would produce Jewish children, and the Jewish population would, by this means, actually increase. But because America is, more or less, a Christian land, most marriages of Jews and non-Jews produce children who are not raised as Jews.

3. In 2002–2003 the family "membership fee schedule" or "dues" at Congregation Adat Rayim (Conservative) in Springfield, Virginia, is $1,490 yearly (billed at ca. $125 a month) or $745 yearly for an individual. These dues do not include the Building Fund. Nearly every synagogue I visited has a similar dues plan, whether paid monthly, quarterly, or on some other schedule.

4. For example, see Howard M. Sachar, *A History of the Jews in America* (New York, 1992).

5. The Saturday religion columnist of the *New York Times*, during 2002 alone, noted once that there were about 750 synagogues in the Union of Orthodox Jewish Congregations of America and, on another occasion, that there were 2,500.

2. Beliefs, Festivals, and Life-cycle Events

1. Emanuel Rackman, "Symposium Response," *Tradition* 20:1 (Spring, 1982): 58.

2. In interviews with worshippers, there are numerous explanations provided for this, including the attractiveness of the cantor's music and/or rabbi's sermon, the fellowship of other congregants, or the food served after worship.

3. Samuel Belkin, *In His Image: The Jewish Philosophy of Man as Expressed in Rabbinic Tradition* (Westport, Conn., 1960, 1979), 30, 32–33. The lengthy quote is from Midrash Tehillim 24:3.

4. *Emet Ve'emunah—Statement of Principles of Conservative Judaism* (New York, 1988), 17.

5. Norman Lamm, *Faith and Doubt: Studies in Traditional Jewish Thought* (New York, 1971), 5–6.

6. Levi A. Olan, "On Being Displeased with God" (11 April 1965) and "Life with or Without God" (15 October 1967)—addresses delivered on KRLD and WFAA radio and found in the archives of Temple Emanu-El, Dallas, Texas.

7. "Guiding Principles of Reform Judaism," *Yearbook of the Central Conference of American Rabbis* 47 (1937): 97–100.

8. The conclusion about "myth" comes from a survey of twenty Mid-Atlantic states Conservative and Reform congregations completed by the author in 2000. Membership lists were used to choose a random sample of congregants to complete a survey and mail it to the author. No membership lists were available to the author from Orthodox or Reconstructionist congregations.

9. Eugene B. Borowitz, *Renewing the Covenant: A Theology for the Post-Modern Jew* (Philadelphia, 1991), 152.

10. Shalom Rosenberg, "Revelation," in *Contemporary Jewish Religious Thought: Original Essays on Critical Concepts, Movements, and Beliefs*, Arthur A. Cohen and Paul Mendes-Flohr, eds. (New York, 1987), 825.

11. Samuel S. Cohon, *Jewish Theology: A Historical and Systematic Interpretation of Judaism and Its Foundations* (Aasen, The Netherlands, 1971), 128.

12. Abraham Joshua Heschel, *Moral Grandeur and Spiritual Audacity: Essays*, Susannah Heschel, ed. (New York, 1996), 13.

13. Eliezer Berkovits, *God, Man and History: A Jewish Interpretation* (Middle Village, N.Y., 1959, 1965), 16.

14. W. Gunther Plaut, *The Case for the Chosen People* (New York, 1965), 163.

15. Emanuel Rackman, *One Man's Judaism* (Tel Aviv, n.d.), 3, 5, and 351–52.

16. Byron L. Sherwin, *Toward a Jewish Theology: Methods, Problems, and Possibilities* (Lewiston, N.Y., 1991), 33.

17. Hayim Halevy Donin, *To Be a Jew: A Guide to Jewish Observance in Contemporary Life* (New York, 1972), 25.

18. *Emet Ve'emunah*, 20.

19. "Guiding Principles of Reform Judaism."

20. Plaut, *Chosen People*, 89–90.

21. Samuel Belkin, *Essays in Traditional Jewish Thought* (New York, 1956), 36.

22. Samuel S. Cohon, *Judaism: A Way of Life* (Cincinnati, 1948), 247–49, 251.

23. Israel I. Mattuck, *The Essentials of Liberal Judaism* (London, 1947), 129.

24. "San Francisco Platform: Reform Judaism—A Centenary Perspective," *Yearbook of the Central Conference of American Rabbis* 86 (1976): 174–78.

25. A concise statement of the relationship between the mitzvot and the legal system called halachah is in David Novak, "Mitsvah," in Tikva Frymer-Kensky, David Novak et al., *Christianity in Jewish Terms* (Boulder, 2000), 115–26.

26. Belkin, *In His Image*, 22.

27. Lamm, *Faith and Doubt*, 18 and 21.

28. *Yearbook of the Central Conference of American Rabbis* 86 (1976): 174–78.

29. *Emet Ve-emunah*, 23–24.

30. Increasingly, for Reform Jews, this means, as Arnold Jacob Wolf puts it in describing himself as neo-Hasidic, "accept[ing] unconditionally for ourselves traditional areas of obedience." *Yearbook of the Central Conference of American Rabbis* 100 (1991): 34.

31. K. Kohler, *Studies, Addresses and Personal Papers* (New York, 1931), 209.

32. David Novak, *The Election of Israel* (New York, 1995), 115–38.

33. Jacob Petuchowski, *Ever Since Sinai: A Modern View of Torah* (New York, 1961), 56.

34. Belkin, *Essays*, 123.

35. Novak, *Election of Israel*, 132.

36. Plaut, *Chosen People*, 86–87.

37. Byron L. Sherwin, *Toward a Jewish Theology: Methods, Problems and Possibilities* (Lewiston, N.Y., 1991), 35.

38. Michael Wyschograd, *The Body of Faith: Judaism as Corporeal Election* (Minneapolis, 1983), 173–223.

39. *Unfinished Business: Selected Writings of Arnold Jacob Wolf*, Jonathan S. Wolf, ed. (Chicago, 1998), 233.

40. Plaut, *Chosen People*, 81.

41. Cohon, *Jewish Theology*, 128.

42. For an example of such deletion, see *On Wings of Light: The Hillel Siddur for Kabbalat Shabbat and Shabbat Evenings*, Richard N. Levy, ed. (Hoboken, N.J., 2000), 134–35.

43. *Gates of Prayer for Shabbat and Weekdays: A Gender Sensitive Prayerbook*, Chaim Stern, ed. (New York, 1994), 75.

44. Mordecai M. Kaplan, *The Purpose and Meaning of Jewish Existence: A People in the Image of God* (Philadelphia, 1971), 290.

45. Mordecai M. Kaplan, *The Meaning of God in Modern Jewish Religion* (Detroit, 1937, 1994), 94.

46. *Siddur Sim Shalom: For Shabbat and Festivals* (New York, 1998), xiii.

47. Ibid., xx.

48. Abba Hillel Silver, *A History of Messianic Speculation in Israel from the First through the Seventeenth Centuries* (Boston, 1927, 1959), ix. For the variety of messianic calculations, see 243–59.

49. Baruch M. Bokser, "Messianism, the Exodus Pattern, and Early Rabbinic Judaism," in *The Messiah: Developments in Earliest Judaism and Christianity*, James H. Charlesworth, ed. (Minneapolis, 1992), 239–41.

50. Messianism was mostly "passive" in the past few centuries—waiting for God to transform the world—but messianic activists have constantly been ready and willing to "force the end" with concrete actions.

51. The important medieval philosopher Moses Maimonides emphasized the nonmiraculous nature of the messianic era; see Melachim 12:1. He reminds us that there were plenty of messianic visions that did not include a radical transformation of time and history but did include the ingathering of the diaspora Jews, deliverance from bondage, restoration of the davidic monarchy, and rebuilding the Temple.

52. Raphael Patai, *The Messiah Texts* (Detroit, 1979), 65–80.

53. *Kol Haneshamah: Shabbat Eve*, 2d ed. (Wyncote, Pa., 1993), 136–7.

54. Joseph A. Lookstein, "A Nation in a State of Shock," a sermon delivered on Saturday, 20 April 1968 (Congregation Kehilath Jeshurun).

55. Milton Steinberg, *Anatomy of Faith*, Arthur A. Cohen, ed. (New York, 1960), 273–4.

56. Ibid., 275.

57. Milton Steinberg, *A Believing Jew: The Selected Writings of Milton Steinberg*, Maurice Samuel, ed. (New York, 1951), 25–29.

58. Babylonian Talmud, Rosh Hashanah 11a.

59. A shofar is a curved or bent ram's horn. Its blowing occupies the central place in the arrangement of the Rosh Hashanah liturgy, and its sound calls the Jew to earnest reflection and sincere improvement during this season.

60. Mishnah Yoma 8:9.

61. Ibid.

62. Exodus 23:16, 34:22; Leviticus 23:39; Deuteronomy 16:13.

63. For a powerful and insightful non-Jew's response to Simchat Torah, see Harvey Cox, *Common Prayers: Faith, Family, and a Christian's Journey Through the Jewish Year* (Boston, 2001), chapter 5 ("Gamboling with God: Simhat Torah," 70–80).

64. I and II Maccabees.

65. Babylonian Talmud, Shabbat 21b.

66. Mishnah Rosh Hashanah 1:1 Babylonian Talmud, Rosh Hashanah 14a-b.

67. Leviticus 19:23

68. Esther 9:17.

69. The method of counting is to mention both the days and the weeks, e.g., "This day completes sixteen days, which are two weeks and two days."

70. The term *Pentecost*, by which Christians know this festival, is the Greek word for "fiftieth," signifying that it is the festival that Jews celebrate on the fiftieth day after the first day of Passover.

71. Abraham Joshua Heschel, *The Sabbath: Its Meaning for Modern Man* (New York, 1951, 1990), 18.

72. The origins of this ceremony are in Genesis 17:11–14 and Leviticus 12:3.

73. In most Orthodox congregations, which prohibit the Torah from being read by women in a mixed gathering, the young woman has a special ceremony on Sunday when there is no Torah reading. In some Orthodox congregations she becomes a bat mitzvah at the women's prayer service where she leads the service and reads the Torah and haftarah for the first time.

74. Although each wing or sector of American Judaism interprets the tradition differently, no weddings are conducted on the Sabbath or festivals, and (for some) on other "intermediate days" during (Passover and Sukkot) and between (Passover and Shavuot) festivals.

75. Deuteronomy 21:23 commands that the deceased shall be buried on the day they die.

76. The yahrzeit light practice is linked to the thought expressed in Proverbs 20:27: "The spirit of man is the lamp of the Lord."

77. This custom is linked to Genesis 35:20: "And Jacob set up a pillar upon [Rachel's] grave."

3. A History of Judaism in America

1. Herbert I. Bloom, *The Economic Activity of the Jews of Amsterdam in the Seventeenth and Eighteenth Centuries* (Williamsport, 1937), 115–71; Stephen Alexander Fortune, *Merchants and Jews: The Struggle for British West Indian Commerce, 1650–1750* (Gainesville, 1984), 1–98 and 130–50.

2. Arnold Wiznitzer discusses the issue of the name of the ship in "The Exodus from Brazil, and Arrival in New Amsterdam of the Jewish Pilgrim Fathers, 1654," *American Jewish Historical Quarterly* 44.2 (December, 1954): 80–97.

3. Morris U. Schappes, *A Documentary History of the Jews of the United States, 1654–1875*, 3d ed. (New York, 1971), 1–13.

4. As Stephen J. Whitfield once pointed out, when the president of the Southern Baptist Convention, Reverend Bailey Smith, asserted in 1980 that God did not hear the prayers of Jews, it was the Southern Baptists who took the lead in repudiating his statement.

5. Those "Jews" who left Spain or Portugal after 1500 had remained behind only by converting to Catholicism and practicing Judaism in secret.

6. "The Earliest Extant Minute Books of the Spanish and Portuguese Congregation Shearith Israel in New York, 1728–1786," *Publications of the American Jewish Historical Society* 21 (1913): 73.

7. Edwin Wolf II and Maxwell Whiteman, *The History of the Jews of Philadelphia from Colonial Times to the Age of Jackson* (Philadelphia, 1957), 116.

8. Called *junta, adjunta, junto,* or *mahamad.*

9. Wolf and Whiteman, *History of the Jews of Philadelphia,* 125.

10. Selig Adler and Thomas E. Connolly, *From Ararat to Suburbia: The History of the Jewish Community of Buffalo* (Philadelphia, 1960), 70.

11. Stuart E. Rosenberg, *The Jewish Community in Rochester, 1843–1925* (New York, 1954), 21–22.

12. Isaac Mayer Wise, *Reminiscences* (Cincinnati, 1901), 45–46.

13. *"Earliest Extant Minute Books,"* 74 (14 September 1757). Congregations were also sensitive to the need for decorum in the synagogue; one common example was levying fines on congregants who acted as "barbarians" during the reading of the book of Esther on Purim by hooting and hissing too raucously when the name of Haman was mentioned.

14. Israel Goldstein, *A Century of Judaism in New York: B'nai Jeshurun, 1825–1925, New York's Oldest Ashkenazic Congregation* (New York, 1930), 51–52.

15. Israel Tabak, "Rabbi Abraham Rice of Baltimore: Pioneer of Orthodox Judaism in America," *Tradition* 7 (Summer, 1965): 102.

16. Wolf and Whiteman, *History of the Jews of Philadelphia,* 234; Adler and Connolly, *From Ararat to Suburbia,* 60 and 70; Goldstein, *Century of Judaism in New York,* 81–85; Isaac M. Fein, *The Making of an American Jewish Community: The History of Baltimore Jewry from 1773 to 1920* (Philadelphia, 1971), 50.

17. *American Jewry and the Civil War* (Philadelphia, 1951), 1 and 247, n.1.

18. Oral interview with Gus Bernd Kaufman, Macon, Ga., 9 June 2002.

19. Naomi W. Cohen, *Encounter with Emancipation: The German Jews in the United States, 1830–1914* (Philadephia, 1984), 185.

20. The *Occident* was the first Anglo-Jewish journal of national significance.

21. On Leeser see Lance J. Sussman, *Isaac Leeser and the Making of American Judaism* (Detroit, 1995).

22. See www.kkbe.org/. KKBE's Coming Street cemetery is probably the oldest surviving Jewish cemetery in the South. Ten members of the congrega-

3. A HISTORY OF JUDAISM IN AMERICA

tion who fought in the American Revolution are buried there, as well as the important nineteenth-century Charleston Jewish poet Penina Moïse.

23. *The Constitution of the Reformed Society of Israelites for Promoting True Principles of Judaism According to Its Purity and Spirit* (Charleston, 1825); Barnett Elzas, *The Jews of South Carolina from the Earliest Times to the Present Day* (Philadelphia, 1905), 151–64; L. C. Moïse, *Biography of Isaac Harby* (Macon, Ga., 1931), 52–59; David Philipson, *The Reform Movement in Judaism* (New York, 1931), 329–34; Charles Reznikoff and Uriah Z. Engelman, *The Jews of Charleston* (Philadelphia, 1950), 115–26; Robert Liberles, "Conflict Over Reform: The Case of Congregation Beth Elohim, Charleston, South Carolina," in *The American Synagogue: A Sanctuary Transformed*, Jack Wertheimer, ed. (Cambridge and New York, 1987), 274–96; Jacob Rader Marcus, *United States Jewry, 1776–1985*, vol. 1 (Detroit, 1989), 623–37; Michael A. Meyer, *Response to Modernity: A History of the Reform Movement in Judaism* (New York, 1988), 228–31.

24. James G. Heller, *Isaac Mayer Wise: His Life, Work, and Thought* (New York, 1965), 565.

25. Isaac Leeser, "Synagogue Reforms," *Occident* 6.3 (June, 1848), 112, quoted in Karla Goldman, *Beyond the Gallery: Finding a Place for Women in American Judaism* (Cambridge, 2000), 109.

26. Marsha L. Rozenblit, "Choosing a Synagogue: The Social Composition of Two German Congregations in Nineteenth-Century Baltimore," in *The American Synagogue*, Wertheimer, ed., 341.

27. For a fuller discussion of this difficulty, see Marc Lee Raphael, "'Our Treasury is Empty and our Bank Account is Overdrawn': Washington Hebrew Congregation, 1855–1872," *American Jewish History* 84.2 (June, 1996): 81–98.

28. Reports of the Immigration Commission, III, Statistical Review of Immigration, 1820–1910, Distribution of Immigrants 1850–1960, 61st Congress, 3rd Session, Senate Document No. 756, Washington D.C. (1911), Table 39.

29. John S. Billings, *Vital Statistics of the Jews in the United States*, United States Census Bulletin No. 19 (Washington, DC, 1890), 5.

30. Ernest Poole, "Task Work Bowing to Factory System," *Outlook*, 21 November 1903; Melech Epstein, *Jewish Labor in U.S.A.: An Industrial, Political and Cultural History of the Jewish Labor Movement, 1882–1914* (New York, 1950).

31. *Jewish Communal Survey of Greater New York* (New York, 1928), 1–12. In Philadelphia, for example, immigrant Jews moved from the slum area of Society Hill to Logan, Parkside, South Philly, Strawberry Mansion, and West Philly.

32. Mark Zborowski and Elizabeth Herzog, *Life Is with People: the Jewish Little Town of Eastern Europe* (New York, 1952). For a trenchant critique of this study, see Barbara Kirshenblatt-Gimblett's introduction to the 1995 edition,

ix–xlvii. I have also drawn upon Lucy Dawidowicz, *Golden Tradition: Jewish Life and Thought in Eastern Europe* (Boston, 1968).

33. Irving Howe, *The World of Our Fathers: The Journey of the East European Jews to America and the Life They Found and Made* (New York, 1976).

34. Mark H. Elovitz, *A Century of Jewish Life in Dixie: The Birmingham Experience* (University, Ala., 1974), 64–65.

35. Marc Lee Raphael, "Babin's Kosher Restaurant: A Los Angeles Odyssey," *Western States Jewish Historical Quarterly* 1.4 (July, 1969): 174–81.

36. "History of Our Congregation," Congregation Sha'arey Israel, 2001–2002 Calendar and Directory, 3—in the synagogue archives.

37. Marc Lee Raphael, *Jews and Judaism in a Midwestern Community: Columbus, Ohio, 1840–1975* (Columbus, 1979), 182–83.

38. On *lansmanschaften*, see Daniel Soyer, *Jewish Immigrant Associations and American Identity in New York, 1880–1939* (Cambridge, 1997).

39. Jeffrey S. Gurock, "Resistors and Accommodators: Varieties of Orthodox Rabbis in America, 1883–1983," in *The American Rabbinate: A Century of Continuity and Change, 1883–1983*, Jacob Rader Marcus and Abraham J. Peck, eds. (Hoboken, N.J., 1985), 10–97.

40. Jeffrey S. Gurock and Jacob J. Schacter, *A Modern Heretic and a Traditional Community: Mordecai M. Kaplan, Orthodoxy, and American Judaism* (New York, 1997), 31–54; and Jacob David Willowski, *She-elot u-Teshuvot Ridbaz* (Jerusalem, 1908), 11, quoted in Aaron Rothkoff, "The American Sojourns of Ridvaz: Religious Problems within the Immigrant Community," *American Jewish Historical Quarterly* 57.4 (June, 1968): 557–72.

41. Abraham J. Karp, "New York Chooses a Rabbi," *Publications of the American Jewish Historical Society* 44.3 (March, 1955): 129–98.

42. Judah Isaacs, "Abraham J. G. Lesser," in *Guardians of Our Heritage*, Leo Jung, ed. (New York, 1958), 352; Moshe Davis, "Jewish Religious Life and Institutions in America," in *The Jews: Their History, Culture, and Religion*, 3d ed., vol. 1, Louis Finkelstein, ed. (Philadelphia, 1960), 539.

43. Jenna Weissman Joselit, *New York's Jewish Jews: The Orthodox Community in the Interwar Years* (Bloomington, 1990), 36–37 and 69. Joselit also noted that Jung's East Side Orthodox contemporary, Rabbi Joseph Lookstein—who served the "grandfather of modern Orthodox synagogues," Kehilath Jeshurun—shared his congregants' "interest in the opera and theatre, European travel, fine food, and beautifully designed clothes" (67). On Lookstein, see also Moshe D. Sherman, *Orthodox Judaism in America: A Biographical Dictionary and Sourcebook* (Westport, Conn., 1996), 139–41.

44. Marc Lee Raphael, "Rabbi Leo Jung and the Americanization of Orthodox Judaism: A Biographical Essay," in *Reverence, Righteousness, and Ra-*

hamanut: Essays in Memory of Rabbi Dr. Leo Jung, Jacob J. Schacter, ed. (Northvale, N.J., 1992), 21–91. Rabbi Jung's sermons remind one of Italian rabbis of the late Renaissance and early modern Europe who regularly quote Aristotle, Dante, Copernicus, and Galileo (not without great sensitivity to Church censors) as well as rabbinic sources.

45. Joseph B. Soloveitchik, *The Halachic Mind* (New York, 1986), written in 1944 but not published until 1986; Pinchas Hacohen Peli, "Hermeneutics in the Thought of Rabbi Soloveitchik—Medium or Messsage?" *Tradition* 23.3 (Spring 1988): 9–31; Alan T. Levenson, "Joseph Soloveitchik's *The Halachic Mind*: A Liberal Critique," *CCAR Journal: A Reform Jewish Quarterly* (Winter 1993): 55–64; Seth Farber, "Reproach, Recognition, and Respect: Rabbi Joseph B. Soloveitchik and Orthodoxy's Mid-Century Attitude Toward Non-Orthodox Denominations," *American Jewish History* 89.2 (June, 2001): 193–214.

46. Bela Fischer, "A History of the Nashua Jewish Community," typescript, 19 and 23, Beth Abraham Temple, Nashua, N.H.; Rosenberg, *Jewish Community*, 176–77.

47. Charlton W. Tebeau, *Synagogue in the Central City: Temple Israel of Greater Miami, 1922–1972* (Coral Gables, 1972), 46.

48. Judith E. Endelman, *The Jewish Community of Indianapolis, 1849 to the Present* (Bloomington, 1984), 142–44.

49. The Rabbinical Assembly (Conservative rabbis) published this in 1946 and nearly every Conservative congregation in America adopted it.

50. The Ahavath Achim constitution (1936) and the Shearith Israel minutes are in each synagogue's archives in Atlanta.

51. Michael J. Safra, "America's Challenge to Traditional Jewish Worship: Changes in Atlanta's Synagogues, 1867–1972" (master's thesis, University of Michigan, 1997), 84. Mr. Safra's thesis also led me to numerous sources in Atlanta synagogue archives.

52. Jeffrey S. Gurock, "Consensus Building and Conflict Over Creating the Young People's Synagogue of the Lower East Side," in *The Americanization of the Synagogue*, Norman J. Cohen and Robert Seltzer, eds. (New York, 1995), 230–46.

53. Shearith Israel Minutes, 12 December 1960, at Shearith Israel, Atlanta.

54. Nathan Glazer, *American Judaism* (Chicago, 1957), 59.

55. *Atlanta Georgian*, 18 October 1905. An example of the "middle ground" is that while Congregation Beth Israel of Atlanta rejected the Reform *Union Prayer Book* and the Hebrew-only prayerbooks in use at the two Orthodox synagogues in Atlanta, it used Marcus Jastrow's *Abodath Israel*, a "traditional" prayerbook with lots of English and an abbreviated liturgy. (Whether a prayerbook may be both abbreviated *and* traditional depends on one's understanding of "traditional.")

56. Berel Wein, "New World Jews," *Jewish Action* 58.4 (Summer 1998): 29–30.

57. Kenneth T. Jackson, *Crabgrass Frontier: The Suburbanization of the United States* (New York, 1985), 238.

58. See Joseph Krauskopf, *Our Pulpit: Sunday Discourses* (Philadelphia, 1906).

59. "Rabbi Max Landsberg and the Triumph of Radical Reform, 1865–1894," in Peter Eisenstadt, *Affirming the Covenant: A History of Temple B'rith Kodesh—Rochester, New York, 1848–1998* (Rochester, 1999), 37–77.

60. See Leon Harrison, *The Religion of a Modern Liberal: The Selected Sermons of Thirty-five Years in the Jewish Ministry* (New York, 1931).

61. See Marc Lee Raphael, "Rabbi Jacob Voorsanger of San Francisco on Jews and Judaism: The Implications of the Pittsburgh Platform," *American Jewish Historical Quarterly* 63.2 (December 1973): 185–203.

62. [Edith Lindeman Calisch], *Three Score and Twenty: A Brief Biography of Edward Nathan Calisch, Selected Addresses and Sermons* (Richmond, 1945).

63. Eisenstadt, *Affirming the Covenant*, 58 and 103.

64. Myron Berman, *Richmond Jewry, 1769–1976: Shabbat in Shockoe* (Charlottesville, 1979), 250.

65. Edward Leigh Pell to Edward Nathan Calisch, 22 May 1916, Calisch Papers, Beth Ahabah Archives, Richmond.

66. *Richmond Times Dispatch*, 8 April 1908, cited in Catherine Anne Wilkinson, "To Live and Die in Dixie: German Reform Jews in the Southern United States," chapter 3 (senior thesis, Princeton University, 1990), 11. I am grateful to Stephen J. Whitfield for enabling me to find this thesis.

67. As late as the 1950s most Reform Jewish worshippers ended their fasting when the services broke for two to three hours in mid-day on Yom Kippur.

68. Jeffrey S. Gurock, "'Different Streams Into a River Yet to Be'": Movement Towards an All-Inclusive American Judaism, 1920–1945," in *The Margins of Jewish History*, Marc Lee Raphael, ed. (Williamsburg, 2000), 23–40.

69. Haym Soloveitchik, "Rupture and Reconstruction: The Transformation of Contemporary Orthodoxy," *Tradition* 28.4 (Summer, 1994): 99.

70. Mordecai Kaplan, *The Reconstructionist Papers* (New York, 1936), v.

71. One study of congregations over more than two years found that 60 percent of the adult respondents had very few friends, if any, in the synagogue. See Leonard Fein et al., *Reform Is a Verb: Notes on Reform and Reforming Jews* (New York, 1972), 140.

72. Gerald B. Bubis and Harry Wasserman, *Synagogue Havurot: A Comparative Study* (Washington, D.C., 1983), 8–11; Harold Schulweis, "Restructuring the Synagogue," *Conservative Judaism* 27.4 (Summer 1973): 13–23.

73. The best study of these rabbis is Pamela S. Nadell, *Women Who Would Be Rabbis: A History of Women's Ordination, 1889–1985* (Boston, 1998).

74. Norman R. Mirsky, "A Rabbi Named Sally," in *Unorthodox Judaism* (Columbus, 1978), 65–79.

75. Janet Marder, "How Women are Changing the Rabbinate," *Reform Judaism* 19.4 (Summer 1991): 5–8 and 41.

76. The latest versions of the Conservative, Reconstructionist, and Reform prayer books include a prayer for the matriarchs (Sarah, Rebecca, Rachel, and Leah) in the midst of the traditional exclusively partriarchal Amidah prayer. They also introduce inclusive language in many English translations of gendered Hebrew texts.

77. Laura Geller, "From Equality to Transformation: The Challenge of Women's Rabbinic Leadership," in *Women Rabbis: Exploration and Celebration*, Gary P. Zola, ed. (Cincinnati, 1996), 69–80; Nina Beth Cardin, "The First Generation of Women's Rabbinate," *Conservative Judaism* 48.1 (Fall 1995): 15–20.

78. On women presidents in American synagogues, see Beth Moskowitz, "Lay Leaders in the Synagogue: An American Response," in *A Leadership Dialogue: Voices of British and American Jewish Women Community Leaders*, Sarah Silberstein Swartz, ed. (Waltham, Mass., 2001), 69–70.

4. Institutions, Organizations, and American Jewish Religious Activity

1. Howard R. Greenstein, *Turning Point: Zionism and Reform Judaism* (Chico, Cal., 1981), 51–71. Greenstein was not aware that congregations in Georgia, Michigan, and Nebraska attempted similar anti-Zionist member pledges.

2. Allan Tarshish, "The Board of Delegates of American Israelites (1859–1878)," *American Jewish Historical Quarterly* 49.1–4 (September 1959–June 1960): 19–20.

3. For its many programs, see www.huc.edu/. For interesting reflections on Jewish seminary education across the branches of American Judaism, see "The Future of Rabbinic Training in Amerca: A Symposium," *Judaism* 18.4 (Fall 1969): 387–420 (especially, the exchange between Arnold Jacob Wolf and Charles S. Liebman).

4. *American Judaism* 6.1 (1956): 20; 6.2 (1956): 13; 9.3 (1960): 4; 4.4 (1961): 8; 15.2 (1965–66): 8; *Year Book of the Central Conference of American Rabbis* 71 (1961): 143–44.

5. Maurice N. Eisendrath, "The State of Our Union," 15 November 1959, 14, at UAHC (New York City).

6. Fred R. Kogen, "Have Clamp, Will Travel: Adventures of a Reform Mohel," *Reform Judaism* 21.1 (Fall 1992): 16–9. The first group of physicians,

twenty in number, were certified as Reform *mohalim* by the Brith Milah Board of Reform Judaism in 1987.

7. Maurice Eisendrath, "The Case for a Missionary Judaism," in *Great Jewish Speeches Throughout History*, Steve Israel and Seth Forman, eds. (Northvale, N.J., 1994), 248. On p. 249 the date is incorrectly identified as 1979.

8. See http://uahc.org/growth/.

9. For a history of a representative Reform sisterhood, see "'This Faithful Band of Workers in Israel,' the Sisterhood," in Charlton W. Tebeau, *Synagogue in the Central City: Temple Israel of Greater Miami, 1922–1972* (Coral Gables, Fla., 1972), 133–47.

10. The platform may be found on http://www.ccarnet.org/platforms/.

11. The United Synagogue of America, Report, 1913 [5673], 9–13.

12. As early as 1921 the Committee on the Interpretation of Jewish Law (chaired by the legal authority Louis Ginzberg) gave strong support to family pews. *United Synagogue Recorder* 1.3 (July 1921), 8.

13. Ahavat Achim Constitution, 1936, and Ahavat Achim Minutes, 24 April 1952, at Ahavat Achim, Atlanta, Ga.

14. Herbert Rosenblum, "The Founding of the United Synagogue of America, 1913," Ph.D. diss., Brandeis University, 1970; Abraham J. Karp, *A History of the United Synagogue of America, 1913–1963* (New York, 1964).

15. "Responsum on the Sabbath," Rabbinical Assembly, *Proceedings* 14 (1950): 112–88.

16. For a brief history of USY, see Anne Levenson, "USY at 50," *United Synagogue Review* 53.2 (Spring 2001): 23–26.

17. United Synagogue of America, National Women's League, *They Dared to Dream: A History of National Women's League, 1918–1968* (New York, 1967).

18. Nearly every Conservative, Orthodox, and Reform congregation I visited had a sisterhood and brotherhood (or men's club) in the middle decades of the twentieth century. For a study of three denominationally distinct, affluent, and well-acculturated New York City sisterhoods (Conservative, Orthodox, Reform), see Jenna Weissman Joselit, "The Special Sphere of the Middle-Class American Jewish Woman: The Synagogue Sisterhood, 1890–1940," in *The American Synagogue: A Sanctuary Transformed*, Jack Wertheimer, ed. (New York, 1987), 206–30. Joselit concluded that these sisterhoods were "strikingly similar; differences between the three were few" (229, n.99).

19. Jewish Theological Seminary Association, *Proceedings of the First Biennial Convention 1888* (New York, 1888), 3–12; and *American Hebrew*, 25 March 1898, 612.

20. For its many programs, see http://www.jtsa.edu/.

21. Emil Lehman, Report—National Survey on Synagogue Attendance, in

Proceedings of the 1950 Biennial Convention, The United Synagogue of America (Washington, 1950), 58.

22. *United Synagogue Review* 49.2 (Spring 1997).

23. Union of Orthodox Jewish Congregations of America, *Second Biennial Convention*, 21 June 1903 (Philadelphia, 1903), 34. A copy of the founding principles (first convention) and the constitution is available from the office of the UOJCA in New York City.

24. The most reliable figures come from two UOJCA publications, *The Orthodox Union* and *Jewish Action*. But unlike the United Synagogue and the UAHC, no directory of member congregations is available to a researcher who wishes to count the synagogues that have joined. Jeffrey S. Gurock estimated in the mid-1980s that there were about one thousand synagogues affiliated with the Union of Orthodox Jewish Congregations of America. "The Orthodox Synagogue," in *American Synagogue*, Wertheimer, ed., 67.

25. Berel Wein, "New World Jews," *Jewish Action* 58.4 (Summer 1998): 28–30; Judith Bleich, "Orthodox Union Centennial Symposium," *Jewish Action* 59.1 (Fall 1998).

26. UOJCA, *1947 Year Book*, 14–22.

27. http://www.ou.org/kosher/. The website even has introductions to kashrut (beginning and advanced) for the nonobservant. The union added 5,565 new products and 268 new companies in 2000 alone.

28. Union of Orthodox Jewish Congregations of America, Leadership Briefing (April 2001): 5.

29. Jeffrey S. Gurock, *The Men and Women of Yeshiva: Higher Education, Orthodoxy, and American Judaism* (New York, 1988). For its many programs, see http://www.yu.edu/riets/.

30. For a halachic defense of single-sex (women) prayer groups, see Avraham Weiss, *Women at Prayer: A Halakhic Analysis of Women's Prayer Groups* (Hoboken, N.J., 1990). And see the Jewish Orthodox Feminist Alliance *Journal* as well as http://www.jofa.org/. One Orthodox congregation struggling with how to reconcile Jewish law and gender equality (women are separated from men in prayer but participate fully in the Torah service) is the D.C. Minyan; see www.dcminyan.com/, a "traditional, egalitarian minyan."

31. Joel B. Wolowelsky, *Women, Jewish Law, and Modernity: New Opportunities in a Post-Feminist Age* (Hoboken, N.J., 1997), 84.

32. See Tamar Frankel, *The Voice of Sarah: Feminine Spirituality and Traditional Judaism* (San Francisco, 1990).

33. For a typical (and bitter) objection to Orthodox feminism, in a Modern Orthodox publication, see Emanuel Feldman, "Orthodox Feminism and Feminist Orthodoxy," *Jewish Action* 60.2 (Winter 1999): 12–17.

34. Mordecai M. Kaplan, "Reconstructionism as Both a Challenging and Unifying Influence," *Reconstructionist* 10.11 (6 October 1944): 16–21, 11.6 (11 May 1945): 8, 21.9 (10 June 1955): 3, and 26.14 (18 November 1960): 3.

35. Federation of Reconstructionist Congregations and Havurot, *A History of Congregations and Havurot* (New York, 1983).

36. For its many programs, see http://www.rrc.edu/.

5. The Synagogue

1. At the turn of the millennium the tension over "boundaries" was reflected in the constant acrimony between Conservative, Orthodox, Reconstructionist, and Reform synagogues, on the one hand, and "Messianic Jewish" congregations on the other. The latter argued that one could be Jewish and at the same time affirm a belief in the risen Christ, while all four sectors of American Judaism rejected the resurrection, declaring it incompatible with a Judaic faith.

2. One observer, who studied two suburban Minneapolis Conservative synagogues for a year, concluded that their "shabbat morning services are virtually identical liturgically." Riv-Ellen Prell, "Late Twentieth Century Conservative Synagogues: An Ethnographic View," in *Jewish Identity and Religious Commitment: The North American Study of Conservative Synagogues and Their Members, 1995–96*, Jack Wertheimer, ed. (New York, n.d.), 39; and Riv-Ellen Prell, "Choice and Memory: Conservative Synagogue Cultures and the Rabbinical Role," *Proceedings of the Rabbinical Assembly* 59 (1998): 51–57.

3. Erving Goffman, *The Presentation of Self in Everyday Life* (New York, 1959), 22.

4. Harvey J. Fields, "*Gates of Prayer*: Ten Years Later—A Symposium," *Journal of Reform Judaism* 32.4 (Fall, 1985): 21.

5. Marc P. Lalonde et al, "Ritual Performance in a Reform Sabbath Service," in *Ritual and Ethnic Identity: A Comparative Study of the Social Meaning of Liturgical Ritual in Synagogues*, Jack N. Lightstone and Frederick B. Bird, eds. (Waterloo, Ontario, 1995), 89–108.

6. My experience confirms the observation of Ronald L. Grimes that someone dressed casually is likely to be "ignored, snubbed, gossiped about, or frowned at"; *Beginnings in Ritual Studies* (Washington, D.C., 1982), 40.

7. In the 1940s, Rabbi Reuben J. Magil of Harrisburg, Pennsylvania, would "greet each member as he goes out" at the "entrance door of the Temple." "The Rabbi in a Small Community," *Proceedings of the Rabbinical Assembly* 49 (1949): 171.

8. Although I have never witnessed any rabbi wearing something analogous to the priest who wears "a sweatsuit instead of a robe when saying Mass"

(Grimes, *Beginnings*, 40), many rabbis conduct Sabbath eve services without a tie, especially in the Sun Belt and during the summer months.

9. Even with movable chairs, most regular worshippers sit in the same spot each week. Even in synagogues with separate seating for women, there are designated spots for the regulars; as Tova Mirvis puts it in her novel about Orthodox Jewish women in Memphis, Tennessee: "Mrs. Levy . . . always sat one row behind Helen Shayowitz with Bessie Kimmel, her first cousin, on one side and Edith Shapiro on the other, and some traditions were not meant to be broken." *The Ladies Auxiliary* (New York, 1999), 29.

10. In a study of worship and ritual practices conducted in the early 1980s, two researches already noted that the "central, fixed pulpit has been replaced or modified by more flexible arrangements." They made a connection between "fixed central pulpits" and the absence of "warm, communal feeling." Ronald N. Ashkenas and Todd D. Jick, *Coping with Change: The Reform Synagogue and Trends in Worship* (New York, 1984), 10 and 14.

11. These ingredients of "setting" are taken from the perceptive analysis of the relationship between performance and/or presentation and the surroundings in Goffman, *Presentation of Self*. Following Goffman, it is obvious that worshippers may feel "highly sacred" moments in a plain room with folding chairs.

12. *Yearbook of the Central Conference of American Rabbis* 16 (1906): 62.

13. From a survey of twenty Mid-Atlantic states Conservative and Reform congregations completed by the author in 2000. Membership lists were used to choose a random sample of congregants to complete a survey and mail it to the author. No membership lists were available to the author from Orthodox congregations.

14. One rabbi, Seymour Prystowsky of Lafayette Hill, Pennsylvania, indicated to the author (March 1999) that he never speaks for more than five minutes at the early service.

15. One rabbi in New York City, Judith Lewis, told the author (December 2000) that she loves the "early" service because in Manhattan she feels it maximizes congregational attendance and also allows her to enjoy Sabbath dinner with her children. It even provides her with sufficient time, should she wish, to prepare the dinner.

16. At numerous Orthodox synagogues where multiple books are in use, there will be multiple numbered signs posted, from time to time, on the pulpit indicating the page in two or three of the most commonly used books.

17. Marshall Sklare expressed disappointment over Sabbath worship attendance in Providence and Philadelphia in the early 1970s, but his criticism was whether Conservative Jews attended services "once a week or more." "Recent Developments in Conservative Judaism," *Midstream* 18.1 (January 1972): 13–14.

A survey, twenty years earlier, found attendance at Friday evening services (then the "main service of the week") at Conservative synagogues "at an appalling disproportion with the congregational membership." *National Survey, United Synagogue of America* (1950): 10.

18. For an extended argument that concludes that my 10 percent is an inflated figure, see Lawrence A. Hoffman, "From Common Cold to Uncommon Healing," *Central Conference of American Rabbis Journal: A Reform Jewish Quarterly* 41.2 (Spring 1994): 27–28, n.13.

19. George Gallup Jr. and Jim Castelli, *The People's Religion: American Faith in the 90s* (New York, 1989), 16, 30, and 34.

20. This does not mean that a quarter of the members attend Conservative services each Sabbath morning, but rather that the adults present equal about 25 percent of the membership. Even if every person present were different for one month, it would still leave us with a congregation in which members feel a sense of "regular" (once a month) attendance at Sabbath morning services.

21. It is a sufficiently serious problem in Conservative Judaism for the national magazine of the movement to feature an essay in which Judith Davis, a Conservative Jew, "demonstrates deliberately and explicitly that bar/bat mitzvah" is "not the family's private service." *United Synagogue Review* 53.2 (Spring 2001): 14–15.

22. Hoffman, "Common Cold," 5.

23. Cathy L. Felix, a rabbi in New Jersey, noted that her regular Sabbath evening worshippers don't attend on Sabbath morning because "they don't want to feel they are crashing anybody's [bar/bat mitzvah] party." "Building Temple by Creating Choices," *CCARJ: RJQ* 43.1 (Winter 1996): 37. See also Michael A. Signer, "The Context of Community: A Response to Lawrence Hoffman," *JRJ* 39.1 (Winter 1991): 82–83. Most Reconstructionist congregations whose services I have attended try to alleviate this problem by announcing during the worship service that all worshippers, not just friends and relatives of the b'nai mitzvah, are invited to the luncheon that follows the service.

24. *The American Reform Rabbi: A Profile of a Profession* (New York, 1965), 9.

25. In Murray Polner, *Rabbi: The American Experience* (New York, 1977), 56–57.

26. Samuel E. Karff, "The Rabbi as Religious Figure," in *Tanu Rabbanan: Our Rabbis Taught: Essays on the Occasion of the Centennial of the Central Conference of American Rabbis,* Joseph B. Glaser, ed. (New York, 1990), 82–83.

27. Thoughtful reflections on the decline of preaching, trial sermons, and the listing of sermon titles are in Harry Essrig, "Impressions of Preaching Today," *JRJ* 35.1 (Winter 1988): 1–3.

28. Gilbert S. Rosenthal, "Jewish Preaching Today," *JRJ* 35.4 (Fall 1988): 75.

29. Ibid., 74.

30. On the rabbi as manager, see Daniel F. Polish's conference paper in *Yearbook of the Central Conference of American Rabbis* 90 (1980): 127–43.

31. Karff, "The Rabbi as Religious Figure," 72.

32. For reflections on boundaries in groups, see Kenwyn K. Smith and David N. Berg, *Paradoxes of Group Life: Understanding Conflict, Paralysis, and Movement in Group Dynamics* (San Francisco, 1987).

33. These are the words used in the Jewish Reconstructionist Federation 1998 report, "Boundaries and Opportunities: The Role of Non-Jews in Jewish Reconstructionist Federation Congregations."

34. Hayim Herring, "The Conservative Movement: Whither or Wither?" *Conservative Judaism* 52.3 (Spring 2000): 18.

35. Sidney Goldstein and Alice Goldstein, "Conservative Jewry: A Sociodemographic Overview," in *Jews in the Center: Conservative Synagogues and Their Members*, Jack Wertheimer, ed. (New Brunswick, N.Y., 2000), 86. It is well-established that large numbers of those dual religion couples who approach Reconstructionist and Reform rabbis to discuss an interfaith wedding consist of a Jewish man or woman raised as an Orthodox or Conservative Jew.

36. Barry Kosmin, "Coming of Age in the Conservative Synagogue: The Bar/Bat Mitzvah Class of 5755," in *Jews in the Center*, Wertheimer, ed., 232–68; and Sidney Goldstein and Alice Goldstein, "Conservative Jewry: An Ambivalent Profile—How Behavior Reflects Identity," *Proceedings of the Rabbinical Assembly* 59 (1998): 61–62.

37. Arguably, the most radical statement in the 1999 Reform "platform" is that Reform Judaism is to "actively encourage those who are seeking a spiritual home to find it in Judaism." Central Conference of American Rabbis, A Statement of Principles for Reform Judaism, May 1999. See http://www.ccarnet.org/platforms/principles/.

38. Typical of Reform synagogue policies is the Role of the Non-Jew in the Synagogue, Adopted by the Board of Trustees of Temple Israel, February 16, 1999, and available from Temple Israel of Omaha, Nebraska, 68132.

39. Smith and Berg, *Paradoxes of Group Life*, 107.

40. This strategy makes good sense from the perspective of group dynamics, for those who are delineated as "outside" the group will, fairly quickly, either decide they do not care about the group or they will join other groups. Neither response would be supportive of Jewish family identity in the synagogue.

41. Proceedings of the Fifty-fifth General Assembly, UAHC, December 7–11, 1979, Toronto, at UAHC (New York City). See also Schindler's call for a "clarification of Reform Judaism [*sic*] boundaries," *YCCAR* 103 (1994): 48.

42. CCAR, *Rabbi's Manual*, rev. ed. (New York, 1961), 112.

43. The Status of Children of Mixed Marriages was adoped by the Central Conference of American Rabbis on 15 March 1983. See http://www.ccarnet.org/.

44. I used the 1998 membership lists of ten Mid-Atlantic Reform congregations, of varying sizes, to conduct an extensive (twelve-page) random survey of 10 percent of each membership list.

45. United States Census Bureau data, March 1998.

46. These units, too, have considerably more women than men, probably because divorced Jewish men remarry at a much higher rate than divorced Jewish women. This is mostly the result of men marrying younger women, while women find it harder to marry younger men.

47. It is, of course, not inevitable that a correlation will exist between the age of marriage and intermarriage, but nearly every survey the author has seen points to such symmetry.

48. All students of intermarriage are in agreement that the rates of intermarriage, and the numbers of non-Jews who have not converted to Judaism, would be even higher if Jews who do not belong to synagogues were included in the survey. It is also certain that finding Jews who intermarried and converted to Christianity would be aided by surveying Jews who intermarried and did not subsequently join a synagogue.

49. For detailed statistics, see Marc Lee Raphael, "Reform Jewish Congregants and Intermarriage, 1998," *CCARJ: RJQ* 47.3 (Summer 2000): 49–55.

50. On the changing role of the rabbi, see the nine essays on "The Role of the Rabbi" in *Reconstructionist* 64.1 (Fall 1999): 7–65.

51. To emphasize this partnership, Cantor Michael A. Shochet of Falls Church, Virginia, recently delivered a sermon on the High Holidays.

52. For information on some of these professional groups, see http://www.rj.org/acc (American Conference of Cantors), www.cantors.org (Cantors Assembly), www.rj.org/nata (National Association of Temple Administrators), www.naase.org (North American Association of Synagogue Executives), www.rj.org/nate (National Association of Temple Educators), www.usa.org/jea (Jewish Educators Assembly), as well as the journals of the associations, e.g., the ACC monthly newsletter *Koleinu*, and the Cantors Assembly *Journal of Synagogue Music*.

53. It survives, mostly, in the "old-fashioned" and "formal" congregations described earlier in this chapter.

6. The Future of American Judaism

1. Chester Gillis, *Roman Catholicism in America* (New York, 1999), 272.

2. Neil Gillman argues convincingly that "spirituality" is more Platonic and Christian than biblical and rabbinic. "Judaism and the Search for Sprirituality,"

Conservative Judaism 38.2 (1985–86): 5. Among the professionals writing about spirituality, few are more insightful than Gillman. See also his "The Renewed Yearning and Search for God: A New Jewish Spirituality?" *Proceedings of the Rabbincal Assembly* 61 (2000): 20–42.

3. James Hudnut-Beumler, *Looking for God in the Suburbs: The Religion of the American Dream and Its Critics, 1945–1965* (New Brunswick, N.J., 1994), 1.

4. Prior to the "revival," not only were just 10 percent of American Jews affiliated, but only 10 percent of those Jews attended services outside of the High Holidays. Robert S. Ellwood, *1950: Crossroads of American Religious Life* (Louisville, 2000), 205.

5. Rabbi Abner Weiss of Los Angeles in February 2000, at a conference sponsored by the University of Southern California and the HUC-JIR.

6. Marshall Sklare and Joseph Greenblum, *Jewish Identity on the Suburban Frontier: A Study of Group Survival in the Open Society* (New York, 1967). An even earlier, and insightful, critique of the so-called religious revival, is in Stuart E. Rosenberg, "Religious Revival in America: Fact or Fancy?" *United Synagogue Review* (Winter, 1961): 14 and 16. [I am grateful to Riv-Ellen Prell for the Rosenberg citation.]

7. Karen D. Kedar, *God Whispers: Stories of the Soul, Lessons of the Heart* (Woodstock, Vt., 1999). She is a Reform rabbi at a synagogue in a Chicago suburb.

8. Steven A. Chester, "The Rabbi—The Nature of Religious Leadership Today," *Yearbook of the Central Conference of American Rabbis* 103 (1994): 52–9.

9. Wade Clark Roof, *Spiritual Marketplace: Baby Boomers and the Remaking of American Religion* (Princeton, 1999). A good Jewish example of this mix of internal and external is found in David S. Ariel, "The Inward and Outward Path," in *Spiritual Judaism: Restoring Heart and Soul to Jewish Life* (New York, 1998), 123–65.

10. Michael Lerner, *Jewish Renewal: A Path to Healing and Transformation* (New York, 1994). For a mix of the internal and external dimensions of spirituality, see his chapter "Making Judaism More Alive," 285–306.

11. Mark Verman, "The Role of Nature in Jewish Spirituality and Meditation," in *The History and Varieties of Jewish Meditation* (Northvale, N.J., 1996), 45–65.

12. See the bibliography in Verman, *Jewish Meditation,* 219–24.

13. Sara Isaacson, *Thorsons Principles of Jewish Spirituality* (London, 1999).

14. Rachel Adler, *Engendering Judaism: An Inclusive Theology and Ethics* (Boston, 1998), 78.

15. K. Kohler, *Studies, Addresses and Personal Papers* (New York, 1931).

16. For interesting reflections on the Shema, see *Ehad: The Many Meanings*

of God Is One, Shema booklet, 1988 (Library of Congress), and the presentation of the Shema in *Mishkan Tefillah: The New Reform Siddur for Shabbat Eve*.

17. On the *shin* and *mem* in *Sefer Yetzirah*, see Leonard R. Glotzer, *The Fundamentals of Jewish Mysticism: The Book of Creation and Its Commentaries* (Northvale, N.J., 1972), 114 and 116.

18. Kerry Olitzky, "Toward a Personal Definition of Jewish Spirituality," in *Paths of Faithfulness: Personal Essays on Jewish Sprituality*, Carol Ochs, Kerry Olitzky, and Joshua Saltzman, eds. (Hoboken, N.J., 1997), 113.

19. Egon Mayer, "Strategies for Taking Judaism Public," *Moment* (August 1992): 38–41.

20. Rabbi Alexander M. Schindler was right on target in 1995 when he said of outreach, "eveybody is doing it—the Conservatives, the Reconstructionists, liberal Orthodox groupings," and, of course, his own Reform movement. "Outreach Address," *Yearbook of the Central Conference of American Rabbis* 105–6 (1997): 294.

21. Joshua O. Haberman, "The New Exodus Out of Judaism," *Moment* (August 1992): 34–37 and 51–52.

22. Reform rabbis, energized by unprecedented numbers of earnest, religiously compelled, and communally alive non-Jews studying formally with colleagues and preparing for conversion, approved new guidelines in June 2001. They recommend that all Reform rabbis require a *bet din* (Jewish court), *mikveh* (ritual immersion in water), and symbolic circumcision for males after at least one year of active participation in a Jewish community and in Judaic rituals. See http://www.ccarnet.org/resolutions/.

23. The Reconstructionist rabbis approved their resolutions in 1993 and 1997; the Reform rabbis issued their resolution in 2000. For a detailed look at the controversy in the Reform movement, see Denise L. Eger, "Embracing Lesbians and Gay Men: A Reform Jewish Innovation," in *Contemporary Debates in American Reform Judaism: Conflicting Visions*, Dana E. Kaplan, ed. (New York, 2001), 180–92.

24. See Reconstructionist Rabbinical Association, "Fuller Acceptance of Gay and Lesbian Jews in Our Community, 1990"; Central Conference of American Rabbis, "Report of the Ad Hoc Committee on Homosexuality and the Rabbinate, 1990" and "Ad Hoc Committee on Human Sexuality, Report of the CCAR Convention, 1998," both on http://www.ccarnet.org/resolutions/; Resolutions, beginning in 1975, of the Union of American Hebrew Congregations, at http://www.uahc.org/resolutions/.

25. Avi Shafran, "Dissembling Before G-d," *Jewish Journal of Greater Los Angeles*, 22 February 2002.

26. Hudnut-Beumler, *Looking for God*, 37.

27. In the middle decades of the nineteenth century Sunday school programs concluded each academic year with examinations, and confirmations (often in German) took place only after students had demonstrated their knowledge of the fundamentals of Judaism in well-attended public examinations.

28. Since no census was taken in the 1990s, the number of day schools and the number of students enrolled in Jewish education programs of all kinds are, at best, estimates, and published figures vary greatly. Because he constantly reminds the reader that "it was estimated," useful statistics may be found in Jack Wertheimer, "Jewish Education in the United States: Recent Trends and Issues," in *American Jewish Year Book* 99 (1999): 3. Contrast these figures with, for example, Egon Mayer and Chaim I. Waxman, "Modern Jewish Orthodoxy in America: Toward the Year 2000," *Tradition* 16.3 (Spring 1977): 99.

29. Wertheimer, "Jewish Education," 52.

30. David Shluker, "The Impact of Jewish Day Schools," in United Jewish Communities and Jewish Educational Service of North America, *Jewish Day School Viability and Vitality* (New York, 1999), 30–31.

31. The quotes are from oral interviews with Jessica Levine and Emily Novitt, Charleston, S.C., 3 June 2002.

32. Oral interview with Rabbi Delouya, Charleston, S.C., 3 June 2002.

33. Linda Rabinowitch Thal, "Reimagining Congregational Education: A Case-Study of a Work-in-Progress," and "A Pilgrim's Progress: Educational Reform and Institutional Transformation at Congregation Beth Am," in *A Congregation of Learners: Transforming the Synagogue Into a Learning Community*, Isa Aron, Sara Lee, and Seymour Rossel, eds. (New York, 1995) 185–227 and 228–41.

34. Percival Goodman, "Synagogue Proposals in a New Traditional Light," *Architectural Record* 102 (September 1947): 100–1; Paul and Percival Goodman, "Jews in Modern Architecture: After a Late Start," *Commentary* 24.1 (July 1957): 34; "A Note on Architecture," in *Manual for the Synagogue Building Committee*, Stanley Rabinowitz, ed. (New York, [1946]), 6.

35. S. D. Goitein, *Jews and Arabs: Their Contacts Through the Ages* (New York, 1951), 182–84.

36. Rachel Wischnitzer, *Synagogue Architecture in the United States: History and Interpretation* (Philadephia, 1955), 13 and 16.

37. Ibid., 37.

38. Oral interview with Dale Rosengarten, Charleston, S.C., 4 June 2002. Baltimore Hebrew Congregation, with its four fluted, Greek Doric columns, was dedicated in 1845.

39. Wischnitzer, *Synagogue Architecture*, 27–32.

40. Mary L. Morrison, *Historic Savannah: Survey of Significant Buildings in*

the Historic and Victorian Districts of Savannah, Georgia, 2d ed. (Savannah, 1979), xxiv–xxv.

41. Wischnitzer, *Synagogue Architecture*, 72.

42. Most docents that I have listened to in historic synagogues, as well as synagogue histories, use the "architecture language" of Byzantine and Moorish interchangeably. In reality, though they share some elements, they are quite different styles.

43. Bernard Susser and Charles S. Liebman, *Choosing Survival: Strategies for a Jewish Future* (New York, 1999), 57.

44. Nathan Glazer, *American Judaism* (Chicago, 1957), 105.

45. The synagogue bulletins and sermon collections that I studied during the period 1948–1967 included Baltimore's Temple Oheb Shalom (Reform), Chizuk Amuno (Conservative), and Beth El (Conservative); Chicago's Anshe Emet (Conservative); Cleveland's Temple on the Heights (Conservative), Park Synagogue (Conservative), and Temple Emanu El (Reform); Los Angeles' Beth Jacob (Orthodox), Temple Beth Am (Conservative), Temple Isaiah (Reform), and Temple Israel (Reform); Miami's Temple Israel (Reform); New York's Kehilath Jeshurun (Orthodox), B'nai Jeshurun (Conservative), Shaare Zedek (Conservative), and Stephen Wise Free Synagogue (Reform); Philadelphia's Beth Sholom (Conservative); St. Louis's Shaare Zedek (Conservative); and Washington, D.C.'s Talmud Torah Congregation (Orthodox), Ohev Shalom (Orthodox), Washington Hebrew Congregation (Reform), and Adas Israel (Conservative).

46. Janice O. Rothschild, *As But a Day: The First Hundred Years, 1867–1967* (Atlanta, 1967), 100.

47. Susser and Liebman, *Choosing Survival*, 58.

48. Chaim I. Waxman, "Center and Periphery: Israel in American Jewish Life," in *Jews in America: A Contemporary Reader*, Roberta Rosenberg Farber and Chaim I. Waxman, eds. (Hanover, N.H., 1999), 214.

49. My survey of twenty Mid-Atlantic states Conservative and Reform congregations in 2000 revealed dramatic levels of support for the idea of a Palestinian state, though equally strong agreement that this putative state should not compromise the Jewish state. Of course, even the political leaders most committed to a peaceful solution of the Palestinian-Israeli problem remain unable to resolve the dilemma of two equally legitimate nationalisms.

50. Behrman is quoted in Wertheimer, "Jewish Education," *American Jewish Year Book* 99 (1999): 72.

51. Phone interview with Rabbi Chaim Fasman, July 2001.

52. Married women cover their hair, viewed as a sex symbol, as a sign of modesty, for only their husbands should see their real hair. For the same rea-

son, men and women refrain from shaking hands with members of the other sex in public.

7. Select Profiles of Judaic Thinkers in America

1. Dianne Ashton, *Rebecca Gratz: Women and Judaism in Antebellum America* (Detroit, 1997), 255.

2. For an example of his critique of modernity, see *The Insecurity of Freedom* (1966) or *Man is Not Alone* (1951).

3. Edward Kaplan, "The Spiritual Radicalism of Abraham Joshua Heschel," *Conservative Judaism* 28 (1973): 40–49, and Kaplan, "Spirituality and Social Action in the Writings of Abraham Joshua Heschel," *Proceedings of the Rabbinical Assembly* 59 (1998): 149–50. For the radical implications of faith, see Heschel's *A Passion for Truth* (New York, 1973), 149–80.

4. Abraham Joshua Heschel, *God in Search of Man: A Philosophy of Judaism* (New York, 1955), 106.

5. Ibid.

6. *Between God and Man: An Interpretation of Judaism, From the Writings of Abraham J. Heschel*, Fritz A. Rothschild, ed. (New York, 1959), 12. It seems as if Heschel sees awe/wonder as the starting point for all knowledge.

7. Heschel, *God in Search of Man*, 369.

8. *Between God and Man*, Rothschild, ed., 116–24.

9. *Abraham Joshua Heschel—Exploring his Life and Thought*, John C. Merkle, ed. (New York, 1985).

10. Jeffrey S. Gurock and Jacob J. Schacter, *A Modern Heretic and a Traditional Community: Mordecai M. Kaplan, Orthodoxy, and American Judaism* (New York, 1997), 148.

11. The best discussion of Kaplan's initial theological break is Gurock and Schacter, *Modern Heretic*, 31–37.

12. *The American Judaism of Mordecai M. Kaplan*, Emanuel S. Goldsmith, Mel Scult, and Robert Seltzer, eds. (New York, 1992).

13. Mordecai M. Kaplan, *Judaism as a Civilization: Toward the Reconstruction of American-Jewish Life* (New York, 1934), 345.

14. Eugene B. Borowitz, "Mordecai Kaplan: The Limits of Naturalism," in Borowitz, *A New Jewish Theology in the Making* (Philadelphia, 1968), 99–122.

15. Mordecai M. Kaplan, *The Meaning of God in Modern Jewish Religion* (Detroit, 1994 [1937]), 328.

16. *The Wisdom of Sirah* and *Documents of Jewish Sectaries, I, Fragments of a Zadokite Work*. Schechter also discovered important *midrashim* and edited a critical edition of one midrash collection, *Abot de Rabbi Nathan*.

17. Louis Ginzberg, "Solomon Schechter," in *Students, Scholars and Saints* (Philadelphia, 1928), 246.

18. Jewish Theological Seminary of America, *Proceedings of the Eighth Biennial Convention 1902* (New York, 1904), 9–28; JTSA, *Documents, Charter and By-Laws* (New York, 1903), 21.

19. Mel Scult, "Schechter's Seminary," in *Tradition Renewed: A History of the Jewish Theological Seminary*, vol. 1, Jack Wertheimer, ed. (New York, 1997), 85.

20. Solomon Schechter, "The Charter of the Seminary," in *Seminary Addresses and Other Papers by Solomon Schechter* (New York, 1959), 119.

21. "The Charter of the Seminary"; Solomon Schechter, *Studies in Judaism*, 1st series (Philadelphia, 1911), xix.

22. Solomon Schechter, "The Study of the Bible," in *Studies in Judaism*, 2d series (Philadelphia, 1908), 31–54; Solomon Schechter, "The History of Jewish Tradition," in *Studies in Judaism: A Selection* (New York and Philadelphia, 1960), 26; Schechter, *Studies*, 1st series, xviii; Schechter, *Studies*, 2d series, 116; Herert Parzen, "An Estimate of the Leadership of Dr. Solomon Schechter," *Conservative Judaism* 5.3 (April 1949): 16–27.

23. "Historical Judaism," in *Tradition and Change: The Development of Conservative Judaism*, Mordecai Waxman, ed. (New York, 1958), 94; JTSA, *Annual Register*, 1904.

24. Menachem Mendel Schneerson, *Besuras Hageulo: The Announcement of the Redemption*, translated by Yisroel H. Greenberg and Yisroel B. Kaufman (Brooklyn, 1998), 3–4.

25. *Anticipating the Redemption: Maamarim of the Lubavitcher Rebbe Rabbi Menachem M. Schneerson Concerning the Era of Redemption* (Brooklyn, 1994), 113.

26. *Beacons on the Talmud's Sea: Analyses of Passages from the Talmud and Issues in Halachah Adapted from the Works of the Lubavitcher Rebbe Rabbi Menachem M. Schneerson* (Brooklyn, 1997), 159.

27. *Beautiful Within: Modesty in Concept and Dress as Taught by the Lubavitcher Rebbe Rabbi Menachem Mendel Schneerson* (Brooklyn, 1995), 29.

28. *On the Essence of Chassidus: A Free Translation of an Essay by Rabbi Menachem M. Schneerson, The Lubavitcher Rebbe* (Brooklyn, 1978), 13.

29. For the most useful biographical accounts of Henrietta Szold, see Marvin Lowenthal, *Henrietta Szold: Life and Letters* (New York, 1942); Emma Ehrlich Levinger, *Fighting Angel: The Story of Henrietta Szold* (New York, 1946); Rose Zeitlin, *Henrietta Szold: Record of a Life* (New York, 1952); Alexandra Lee Levin, *The Szolds of Lombard Street: A Baltimore Family, 1859–1909* (Philadelphia, 1960); Michael Brown, "Henrietta Szold (1860–1945)," in *Encyclopedia of Jewish Women in America*, Paula E. Hyman and Deborah Dash

Moore, eds. (New York, 1997), 1368–73; Baila Round Shargel, *Lost Love: The Untold Story of Henrietta Szold* (Philadelphia, 1997).

30. For details of what Trude Weiss-Rosmarin described, with abundant examples, as a "black sheep," "dropout," "runaway," and "rebel," see Estelle Gilson, "Trude's a Holy Terror," *Jewish Spectator* 54.2 (Fall 1989): 6–10.

31. Her early interest in philosophy is evident in her *Religion of Reason: Hermann Cohen's System of Religious Philosophy* (New York, 1936).

32. Deborah Dash Moore, "Trude Weiss-Rosmarin and the *Jewish Spectator*," in *The "Other" New York Jewish Intellectuals*, Carole S. Kessner, ed. (New York, 1994), 101.

33. On Weiss-Rosmarin's "feminist impulses," see Pamela S. Nadell, "Women on the Margins of Jewish Historiography," in *The Margins of Jewish History*, Marc Lee Raphael, ed. (Williamsburg, 2000), 102–11.

34. Deborah Dash Moore notes that one thousand rabbis subscribed to the *Jewish Spectator* in the early 1950s. Moore, "Trude Weiss-Rosmarin," 117.

35. Trude Weiss-Rosmarin, *Jewish Survival: Essays and Studies* (New York, 1949), 108, 144, 150, and 270.

36. Her careful study of Christianity as well as classical Judaism led her to reject those who spoke of "Judeo-Christian culture," and to insist on the differences between the two "faith traditions." Trude Weiss-Rosmarin, *Judaism and Christianity: The Differences* (New York, 1943).

37. Weiss-Rosmarin, *Judaism and Christianity*, 7, 9, and 103.

38. Trude Weiss-Rosmarin, *Toward a Jewish-Muslim Dialogue* (New York, 1967), 9, 11, 15–16, 19–20, 23, 28, 29, 32, and 42–44; Trude Weiss-Rosmarin, *Jerusalem* (New York, 1950), 26 and 41.

39. Trude Weiss-Rosmarin, *New Light on the Bible* (New York, 1941), 67.

40. Trude Weiss-Rosmarin, *The Hebrew Moses: An Answer to Sigmund Freud* (New York, 1939). Sometimes she hyphenated her last name and at other times she did not.

41. Trude Weiss-Rosmarin, *The Oneg Shabbat Book* (New York, 1940).

42. *Jewish Expressions on Jesus: An Anthology*, Trude Weiss-Rosmarin, ed. (New York, 1977), especially xi.

43. Trude Weiss Rosmarin, *Jewish Women Through the Ages* (New York, 1940), 5 and 95.

44. Isaac Mayer Wise, *History of the Israelitish Nation from Abraham to the Present Times*, vol. 1 (Albany, 1854), iv and 80–81.

45. Following the tradition of medieval philosophy, Wise insisted that this "immutable essence of all substances" had "no corporeal form." *History of the Israelitish Nation*, 80.

46. *Occident*, January 1851, 494.

47. *American Israelite*, 4 November 1859, 22 June 1883, 30 April 1896.

48. Isaac Mayer Wise, *Pronaos to Holy Writ* (Cincinnati, 1891), 183–84.

49. The most informative biographies of Isaac Mayer Wise are by Jacob Rader Marcus, *The Americanization of Isaac Mayer Wise* (Cincinnati, 1931); Joseph H. Gumbiner, *Isaac Mayer Wise: Pioneer of American Judaism* (New York, 1959); James G. Heller, *Isaac Mayer Wise: His Life, Work and Thought* (New York, 1965); Sefton D. Temkin, *Isaac Mayer Wise: Shaping American Judaism* (New York, 1992). For his writings, see *The Essence of Judaism* (Cincinnati, 1868); *Judaism: Its Doctrines and Duties*, David Philipson and Louis Grossman, eds. (Cincinnati, 1872); *Selected Writings of Isaac Mayer Wise* (Cincinnati, 1900); *Reminiscences* (Cincinnati, 1901).

8. The Retrieval of Tradition

1. Chester Gillis, *Roman Catholicism in America* (New York, 1999), 29.

2. Pentecostals are those Christians focused on the Holy Ghost (spirit) as the means of grace and salvation. Some are Fundamentalists, Christians who affirm the inerrancy of the Bible, the virgin birth, and more generally the belief that Christianity is the exclusive means to salvation. Pentecostalism is spirit driven; Fundamentalism is text driven. *Fundamentalism Comprehended*, Martin E. Marty et al., eds. (Chicago, 1995).

3. As we noted in chapter 3, "classical" Reform Jewish worship services differed little from "High Church" Protestant worship, as they were overwhelmingly in English, utilized an organ, choir, and universal hymns ("All the World Shall Come to Serve Thee"), eliminated most ceremonies, customs, and rituals characteristic of Jewish "tradition," and the rabbis' sermons were virtually identical to those of Protestant clergymen such as Harry Emerson Fosdick and Washington Gladden.

4. I actually counted during the lengthy "announcement" portion of the Sabbath eve services.

5. Peter Eisenstadt, *Affirming the Covenant: A History of Temple B'rith Kodesh, 1848–1898* (Rochester, 1999), 228.

6. For a thoughtful discussion of the change in "tone" as well as "content" of Reform Jewish practice, see Eugene B. Borowitz, *Reform Judaism Today, Book Three: How We Live* (New York, 1978), 15–75.

7. The second most common explanation provided by rabbis is the "counterculture" or "renewal" movements of the late 1960s and the number of rabbinic students who, as college students, engaged in more traditional ritual experimentations as a strong countercultural statement.

8. A sociologist who explores this idea is Benedict Anderson in *Imagined Communities: Reflections on the Origins and Spread of Nationalism* (New York, 1991).

9. Ronald N. Ashkenas and Todd D. Jick, *Coping with Change: The Reform Synagogue and Trends in Worship* (New York, 1984), 3, 10, and 12. It is doubtful, however, that many observers would have actually confused Reform and Orthodox "modes of worship" in the early 1980s, or even Reform and Conservative worship.

10. Ibid., 11.

11. *Unfinished Rabbi: Selected Writings of Arnold Jacob Wolf*, Jonathan S. Wolf, ed. (Chicago, 1998).

12. The interviews with Betsy Klein and Georgia Rosen (pseudonyms) are in Catherine Anne Wilkinson, "To Live and Die in Dixie: German Reform Jews in the Southern United States" (senior thesis, Princeton University, 1990), 14–16.

13. Ashkenas and Jick noted the "real sense of loss" many Reform Jews felt as classical Reform steadily receded, their "feeling that valuable and familiar practices were being destroyed," and their "passionate and highly emotional outbursts." See *Coping with Change*, 12–13. In this particular congregation the shift to a new prayerbook (*Gates of Prayer*) resulted in a "sense of mourning over the loss of the [classical Reform] *Union Prayer Book*," and the rabbis were forced to schedule a special, annual "classical Reform" service to "honor" the *Union Prayer Book*.

14. Most Reform rabbis summarize this essence of Reform Judaism in two words that have become virtually a mantra: *informed choice*.

15. The 1999 Statement of Principles may be found at http://www.ccarnet.org/platforms/principles/.

16. In contrast to this embrace of tradition in 1999, when the *Shabbat Manual* (*Tadrikh le-Shabbat*) was completed in the late 1960s, W. Gunther Plaut wanted to call it a *Shabbat Guide*, but his colleagues were not yet ready for the word *guide*. W. Gunther Plaut, *Unfinished Rabbi: An Autobiography* (n.p., 1981), 208–13.

17. Examples of such volumes include *Tanach: The Stone Edition*, Nosson Scherman, ed. (Brooklyn, 1996); *The Complete Artscroll Siddur*, Nosson Scherman and Meir Zlotowitz, eds. (Brooklyn, 1985); Paysach Krohn, *Bris Milah Circumcision* (Brooklyn, 1985, 1999); and the Schottenstein *Daf Yomi* editions of the Talmud (New York, 2002).

18. In the Orthodox community the word *Torah* is used in the widest sense, indicating not only the Pentateuch or even the Hebrew Bible but the entire range of postbiblical Hebrew texts.

19. David Bernstein, "Four Habits of Highly Effective Day Schools," *Jewish Action* 62.2 (Winter 2001): 24.

20. Tova Mirvis, *The Ladies Auxiliary* (New York, 1999), 137.

21. Oral interviews with Rabbi David J. Radinsky, Charleston, S.C., 4 June 2002, and Esther Rabhan, Savannah, Ga., 6 June 2002.

22. Like other "sins" in Judaism, repentance is possible. But it must include, according to this same rabbi, sincere regret, confession to God, a resolve not to repeat the offense, and seeking forgiveness from the person gossiped about.

23. Mirvis, *Ladies Auxiliary*, 20.

24. To see how this Orthodox emphasis on the sin of gossip has influenced nontraditional Jewish ethics, see Stephen M. Wylen, *Gossip: The Power of the Word* (Hoboken, N.J., 1994).

25. Correspondence with Rabbi Neil Scheindlin, 10 July 2001.

26. *Siddur Sim Shalom: For Shabbat and Festival* (New York, 1998), xviii.

GLOSSARY

Abraham The first of the biblical patriarchs described in Genesis who lived in the land of Canaan and became the father of the Hebrews or Israelites.

adjunta The board of trustees of the Spanish and Portuguese congregations of the seventeenth and eighteenth centuries.

Antiochus IV Known as Epiphanes ("god manifest"), he was the Seleucid (Greek) king against whom the Maccabees successfully revolted.

ark Repository of the *sefer Torah* (Torah scroll) in the front wall of the synagogue.

Amidah The second major portion of the Jewish worship service, containing prayers of praise, petition, and thanks. Also called *tefillah, shemoneh esray*, and the Eighteen Benedictions.

aravah The willow used in a *lulav* on Sukkot.

Ashkenazic *Ashkenaz*, a word found in Genesis 10:3, was the name Jews used in the Middle Ages for northern France and western Germany, and Ashkenazic Jews are generally those Jews from western, central, and eastern Europe.

Av A month (July-August) of the Jewish lunar-solar calendar.

avodah she'b'lev Literally, "service of the heart." The most elevated and sincere level of prayer.

bima Pulpit in the synagogue.

b'nai mitzvah The plural of bar mitzvah.

b'not mitzvah The plural of bat mitzvah.

brit The covenant or contractual relationship between God and Israel.

brit milah The "covenant of circumcision" that welcomes boys into the Judaic religion eight days after birth. Sometimes it is simply called *brit* or *bris*.

challah A braided loaf of white egg bread eaten in celebration of the Sabbath and holy days.

chametz Leavened bread, the opposite of matzot, which may not be eaten on Passover.

chanukiyah A Hanukkah candelabrum, with space for nine candles or oil lamps.

charoset The mixture of nuts, apples, and wine into which the bitter herbs are dipped during the Passover seder, or ritual meal.

dvar Torah brief Torah study or commentary

davening A Jewish worshipper who is investing each word and melody with all their emotional, physical, and spiritual energy.

David The king of his own biblical tribe, Judah, for seven years and the king of the rest of the tribes for thirty-three years, who united the tribes politically and religiously, defeated numerous enemies, and made Jerusalem his capital.

Days of Awe See *yamim nora'im.*

dreidel A four-sided top used for games of chance on Hanukkah.

Elijah A ninth–century B.C.E. biblical prophet who, according to I Kings in the Bible, performed numerous miracles and serves as the harbinger of the Messiah.

Elul A month (August-September) preceeding Tishri in the Jewish lunar-solar calendar and the time for preparing oneself for the Day of Atonement.

etrog A citron, an expensive kind of citrus fruit and one of the "four species" that are waved on Sukkot.

g'lilah Tying and dressing the Torah scroll. Following the Torah service, the *golel* (m.) or *golelet* (f.) rolls the scroll tightly, fastens it securely, covers it with a mantle, and adds the *yad* (pointer) and breastplate.

gorod A Jewish town in the Russian Pale of Settlement.

graggers The noisemakers used on Purim to "blot out" the name of Haman every time it is pronounced by the reader.

hadarim Literally "rooms." The term used for the site of after-school Hebrew lessons, especially in Jewish immigrant neighborhoods (sing., *heder*).

hadas The myrtle twig used in a *lulav* on Sukkot.

haftarah The reading from the prophetic books of the Hebrew Bible that follows the Torah reading in the synagogue on Sabbaths and holy days.

hagbah Lifting the Toral scroll. Following the Torah and *haftarah* reading, someone comes forward and lifts the open Torah scroll over their head for a few seconds so that two columns of words are visible to the congregation. As this is done, the congregation sings a formal liturgical response.

Haggadah The book that contains the liturgy for the Passover seder.

halachah The body of rabbinic law as well as a single Jewish law (adj., halachic).

hamantaschen The traditional Ashkenazic Purim food: a tricorn cookie or pasty dough, typically with a poppy seed, apricot, or prune filling, in the shape of "Haman's ears or hat" (sing., hamantasch)

Hanukkah The eight day festival of lights celebrating the victory of the Maccabees, observed in the month of Kislev around the time of the winter solstice.

Hasmonean The term used for the ruling dynasty (theocracy) after the revolt of Judah Maccabee.

havdalah Literally, "separation." The ritual that marks the conclusion of the Sabbath, Yom Kippur, and all other major holidays.

havurot An informal group of Jews who gather periodically, usually in homes, for celebration, study, and worship.

hazan A cantor who chants the liturgy in the synagogue and often leads the congregation in worship.

Hoshanah Rabbah The seventh day of Sukkot, or the "Great Hosanna," is a semifestival in which seven circuits are made around the synagogue with a *lulav*, and it is an extension of Yom Kippur, the day on which the gates of judgment finally close.

huppah The canopy under which the bride and groom stand at a Jewish wedding.

Joshua The biblical book of Joshua, the first of the prophetic books, describes the Israelite conquest of the land of Canaan forty years after the exodus from Egypt.

Judah Maccabee The Jew who led a revolt against the Hellenistic Syrians who occupied the land of Israel ca. 165 B.C.E. and whose victory is commemorated by Hanukkah.

junto See *adjunta*.

Kaddish A prayer sanctifying God's name recited in numerous places in the Jewish liturgy, especially by mourners in memory of the departed.

kashrut The laws concerning permitted and forbidden foods, found in their earliest form in the biblical book of Leviticus.

kavanah Intention; purposeful fulfillment of God's commandments.

kedushah Literally "holiness, sanctification." A prayer in the *Amidah* (Eighteen Benedictions).

ketubah A Jewish marriage contract that spells out the financial obligations of bride and groom and establishes the rights of the bride in the event of divorce or widowhood.

kiddush Literally "sanctification." The prayer recited over a cup of wine at home or in the synagogue to consecrate the Sabbath, a festival, or a joyous occasion.

kiddushin The term for the Jewish marriage ceremony, which includes both engagement (ring and legal obligations) and marriage (right to live together as husband and wife).

kippah A small hat worn to cover the head in worship or, by some traditional Jews, all the time, as a sign of respect in the presence of God.

Kislev A month (November-December) of the Jewish lunar-solar calendar.

kol bo A term used for a synagogue employee who was a "jack-of-all-trades."

Kol Nidre Literally, "all vows." The prayer that opens the Yom Kippur evening liturgy, especially associated with the melody by which it is sung.

lansmanschaften Synagogues or clubs in the United States made up of Jewish immigrants from the same European region or city.

Latkes Fried potato pancakes, eaten especially on Hanukkah.

lulav The branch or shoot of the palm tree, but more generally a combined branch of palm (*lulav*), myrtle twigs (*hadas*; pl. *hadasim*), and willow branches (*aravot*) waved on Sukkot.

ma'areev The "evening" or first of the three daily prayer liturgies.

maftir An additional (or repetitive) Torah reading added to the seven basic sections of the weekly reading; the person called up to recite the blessing over that portion.

Mahamad See *adjunta*.

mashgiach The man authorized by the rabbinate to supervise kashrut in butcher shops, food factories, hotels, restaurants, and supermarkets.

matzot Unleavened bread which is eaten on Passover in commemoration of the exodus from Egypt (sing., matzah).

mechitzah The "divider" (sometimes only an aisle) that separates the women's section from the men's section in a traditional synagogue sanctuary.

megillah A scroll of parchment containing the book of Esther from the Hebrew Bible and read on Purim.

melamed A teacher in a synagogue school.

mestechko A Jewish village in the Russian Pale of Settlement.

mincha The "afternoon" or last of the three daily prayer liturgies.

minhag A custom (such as wearing a *kippah* in the synagogue) that has, in some communities, the force of law.

minyan Literally "a number, a few," and the quorum of ten adult Jewish males (Orthodox) or males and females (Conservative) needed for public worship in some Jewish communities.

Mishnah Rabbi Judah's compendium of rabbinic law assembled ca. 200 and forming the basic text of the Oral Torah.

mishloach manot It is meritorious to give presents to at least two poor people on Purim and to "send presents" of at least two kinds of candies, cookies or fruit to at least one friend.

mitzvah One of the 613 commandments in the Torah (pl. mitzvot).

mohel A Jewish professional skilled in the ritual and medical aspects of circumcision (pl. *mohalim*).

Moses The prophet in the Torah to whom God revealed the Torah.

musaf The additional service that follows the morning (*shachreet*) service.

neilah The concluding service in the late afternoon of Yom Kippur.

nigunim Liturgical melodies without words.

Nisan A month (March-April) of the Jewish lunar-solar calendar.

nissuin See *kiddushin*.

Nusach Ha-ari The Ashkenazic rite dominated western Jewish liturgy until the eighteenth century and the rise of Hasidism when the "rite of Isaac Luria," much like the Sephardic rite, was accepted in these same communities.

omer The sheaf of grain that was brought to the Temple each of the fifty days from Passover to Shavuot. The fifty-day period is called the days of the counting of the *omer*.

oneg Literally, "joy," and used to refer to Sabbath joy and a social gathering with food following worship services.

Pentateuch A name for the Torah, five books of Moses, or the first five books of the Hebrew Bible.

Oral Torah Law supposedly orally transmitted from God to Moses and then through the centuries and that supplements the written biblical legislation. The verbal revelation (Torah) and Oral Torah together form Torah in the full rabbinic meaning.

parnassim The elected leaders of Spanish-Portuguese congregations (sing., *parnas*).

Prophets The second (and largest) part of the Hebrew Bible, or *TaNaKH*.

pur A "lot" cast by Haman to decide the day on which he would kill the Jews of Persia.

RIETS The Rabbi Isaac Elhanan Theological Seminary of Yeshiva University in New York City is the major center of centrist or "modern" Orthodoxy and the seminary that trains modern Orthodox rabbis.

ruchaneeyut The Hebrew word for "spirituality."

Sabbath The seventh day (Friday sundown to Saturday sundown), dedicated to prayer, study, and a cessation from work (Hebrew, *shabbat*; Yiddish, *shabbos*).

sechach The "covering" for the sukkah or dwelling in which Jews dwell during Sukkot and that must be made from a material that grows in the ground.

seder The liturgical meal observed at the family table on the first (and often second) night of Passover.

Sephardic The adjectival form of *Sephard*, a word found in Obadiah 1:20, and subsequently designating Jews who trace their ancestry to the Iberian peninsula.

shabbat hachodesh The fourth of four special Sabbaths, all of which occur in the spring, on which a special scriptural reading (Exodus 12:1–20) is added to the weekly reading from the Torah.

shabbat parah The third of four special Sabbaths, all of which occur in the spring, on which a special scriptural reading (Numbers 19:1–22) is added to the weekly reading from the Torah.

shabbat shekalim The first of four special Sabbaths, all of which occur in the spring, on which a special scriptural reading (Exodus 30:11–16) is added to the weekly reading from the Torah.

shabbat zachor The second of four special Sabbaths, all of which occur in the spring, on which a special scriptural reading (Deuteronomy 25:17–19) is added to the weekly reading from the Torah.

shammash The candle which is used to light the others in a *chanukiyah*.

Shema Deuteronomy 6:4 and an integral part of Jewish liturgy.

shemoneh esray See *Amidah*.

sheva berachot The "seven blessings" that constitute the *nissuin*, the Jewish wedding ceremony.

shiur The act of reading texts for the departed during the approximately eleven months in which their eternal fate is determined.

shochet A certified Jewish expert in the kosher slaughtering of animals for meat.

shofar The curved or bent horn of an animal, usually a ram, blown in the synagogue on Rosh Hashanah.

siddur A Jewish prayer book that contains the liturgical prayers for festivals, Sabbaths, and weekdays.

Sivan A month (May-June) of the Jewish lunar-solar calendar.

Sukkot The week-long fall harvest festival that comes two weeks after Rosh Hashanah (plural of sukkah).

tallith The prayer shawl in which, traditionally, Jewish males (and, increasingly, women) wrap themselves in morning worship.

Talmud Composed of the Mishnah and its commentary (Gemara), it forms the second basic text of the Oral Torah.

tefillah See *Amidah*.

teshuvah Literally "return," or repentance, a central theme of the Yom Kippur liturgy.

Tishri The first month of the year (September-October) in the Jewish lunar-solar calendar.

Torah A parchment scroll of the five books of Moses (or Pentateuch), handwritten in a centuries-old manner.

treyf Food that violates the dietary laws

Writings The third part of the Hebrew Bible (or *TaNaKH*).

yahrzeit The annual observance of the death of a parent, spouse, or child through the lighting of a candle and the recitation of the Kaddish prayer.

yamim nora'im "Days of Awe" or the period of the Jewish Holy Days in the fall, centering on Rosh Hashanah and Yom Kippur.

yarmulke See *kippah*.

yeshivot Jewish academies of higher education headed by scholars famed for their mastery of talmudic learning (sing. yeshiva).

Zohar The classic text of Jewish mysticism, written in medieval Spain but attributed to an ancient Palestinian rabbi, Shimon ben Yochai, who lived one thousand years earlier.

SELECTED FURTHER READING

Beliefs, Festivals, and Life-cycle Events

On beliefs, the starting place is *Judaism: The Key Spiritual Writings of the Jewish Tradition*, Arthur Hertzberg, ed., rev. ed. (New York, 1991), especially chapters 1 ("People"), 2 ("God"), 3 ("Torah"), 4 ("The Cycles of the Year"), and 5 ("Land"); and *Contemporary Jewish Religious Thought: Original Essays on Critical Concepts, Movements, and Beliefs*, Arthur A. Cohen and Paul Mendes-Flohr, eds. (New York, 1987), especially "Chosen People," 55–59, "Revelation," 815–25, "Spirituality," 903–7, "Torah," 995–1005, and "Woman," 1039–53. Continue with *Great Jewish Ideas*, Abraham Ezra Millgram, ed. ([Washington, D.C.], 1964), especially part 2 ("Torah, the Jewish Way of Life"), 61–146, and part 3 ("The Jewish Vision of God and Man"), 149–259; "Contemporary Jewish Theology" (part 3), in *Faith and Reason: Essays in Judaism*, Robert Gordis and Ruth B. Waxman, eds. (New York, 1973); *God in the Teachings of Conservative Judaism*, Seymour Siegel and Eliot Gertel, eds. (New York, 1985); David Novak, *The Election of Israel: The Idea of the Chosen People* (New York, 1995); "Symposium: The Condition of Reform Jewish Belief Today," in *CCAR Journal: A Reform Jewish Quarterly* (Summer, 1998): 3–62; *Duties of the Soul: The Role of Commandments in Liberal Judaism*, Niles E. Goldstein and Peter S. Knobel, eds. (New York, 1999); *Contemporary Jewish Theology: A Reader*, Elliott N. Dorff and Louis E. Newman, eds. (New York, 1999), especially 3 ("Contemporary Reflections on Traditional Themes" [God, Creation, Revelation, Covenant/Chosenness]), 95–277; and four neglected but important traditional works, Eliezer Berkovits, *God, Man, and History: A Jewish Interpretation* (New York, 1959 and 1965); Eliezer Berkovits, *Major Themes in Modern Philosophies of*

Judaism (New York, 1974), especially "Reconstructionist Theology: A Critical Evaluation," 149–91 and "Dr. A. J. Heschel's Theology of Pathos," 192–224; Michael Wyschograd, *The Body of Faith: Judaism as Corporeal Election* (Minneapolis, 1983); *With Perfect Faith: The Foundations of Jewish Belief*, J. David Bleich, ed. (New York, 1983).

On festivals, the starting place is the holiday anthologies edited by Philip Goodman, including *The Purim Anthology* (Philadelphia, 1949), *The Passover Anthology* (Philadelphia, 1961), *The Rosh Hashanah Anthology* (Philadelphia, 1970), *The Sukkot and Simchat Torah Anthology* (Philadelphia, 1973), *The Shavuot Anthology* (Philadelphia, 1974), *The Hanukkah Anthology* (Philadelphia, 1976), and *The Yom Kippur Anthology* (Philadelphia, 1992). Continue with three classics, Hayyim Schauss, *Guide to Jewish Holy Days* (New York, 1970; a reprint of his earlier *The Jewish Festivals from Their Beginnings to Our Own Day* [Cincinnati, 1938]); Abraham Joshua Heschel, *The Sabbath: Its Meaning for Modern Man* (New York, 1990 [1951]); Theodor H. Gaster, *Festivals of the Jewish Year* (New York, 1974 [1952]). Do not overlook S. Y. Agnon, *Days of Awe* (New York, 1965 [1948]); Abraham P. Bloch, *The Biblical and Historical Background of the Jewish Holy Days* (New York, 1978); *Gates of the Seasons: A Guide to the Jewish Year*, Peter S. Knobel, ed. (New York, 1983); Michael Strassfeld, *The Jewish Holidays: A Guide and Commentary* (New York, 1985); Daniel B. Syme, *The Jewish Holidays: A Guide for Jewish Living* (New York 1988); Pinchas H. Peli, *The Jewish Sabbath: A Renewed Encounter* (New York, 1991; a reprint of his earlier *Shabbat Shalom* [Washington, DC, 1988]); *Gates of Shabbat: A Guide for Observing Shabbat*, Mark Dov Shapiro, ed. (New York, 1991); *On the Doorposts of Your House: Prayers and Ceremonies for the Jewish Home*, Chaim Stern, ed. (New York, 1995); Ron Wolfson, *The Art of Jewish Living: The Passover Seder* (Woodstock, Vt., 1996); Ronald H. Isaacs, *Sacred Seasons: A Sourcebook for the Jewish Holidays* (Northvale, N.J., 1997); "Creative Liturgies," in *CCAR Journal: A Reform Jewish Quarterly* (Fall 1998): 3–43; Daniel Sperber, *Why Jews Do What They Do: The Handbook of Jewish Customs Throughout the Cycle of the Jewish Year* (Hoboken, N.J., 1999); *Oneg Shabbat*, Joseph F. Mendelsohn, ed. (New York, 1999); Simcha Kling, *Embracing Judaism*, Carl M. Perkins, ed., 2d rev. ed. (New York, 1999), especially chapter 9 ("Holy Days and Festivals"), 106–21; Dov Peretz Elkins, *New and Old Prayers and Readings: For the High Holy Days, Shabbat, and Festive Occasions* (Princeton, 2000); Ron Wolfson, *Hanukkah: The Family Guide to Spiritual Celebration* (Woodstock, Vt., 2001).

On life-cycle ceremonies in general, the starting place is Isaac Klein, *A Guide to Jewish Religious Practice* (New York, 1992 [1979]). Continue with (Conservative) Ronald H. Isaacs, *Becoming Jewish: Handbook for Conversion* (New York, 1993) and Simcha Kling, *Embracing Judaism*, especially chapter 10 ("The

Jewish Life Cycle"), 122–33; (Orthodox) Blu Greenberg, *How to Run a Tradi-tional Jewish Household* (New York, 1983); (Reform) *Gates of Mitzvah: A Guide to the Jewish Life Cycle*, Simeon J. Maslin, ed. (New York, 1979); (Reconstruc-tionism) *Songs, Blessings, and Rituals for the Home*, David A. Teutsch, ed. (Wyncote, Pa., 1991). On marriage there is the very popular Anita Diamant, *The New Jewish Wedding* (New York, 1985); and Maurice Lamm, *The Jewish Way in Love and Marriage* (Middle Village, N.Y., 1991). On death see Maurice Lamm, *The Jewish Way in Death and Mourning* (New York, 1969); Ron Wolf-son, *A Time to Mourn, a Time to Comfort* (Woodstock, Vt., 1996); Leon Wieselti-er, *Kaddish* (New York, 1998); Samuel C. Heilman, *The Ethnography of a Be-reaved Son* (Berkeley, 2001).

The Branches, Sectors, Streams, or Wings
The best way to study them is individually. But for an overview there are many choices, beginning with chapters 1–4 of Joseph L. Blau, *Modern Varieties of Ju-daism* (New York, 1964). Continue with Mordecai M. Kaplan, *The Greater Ju-daism in the Making: A Study of the Modern Evolution of Judaism* (New York, 1960); Bernard Martin, *A History of Judaism*, vol. 2, *Europe and the New World* (New York, 1974), especially chapter 7 ("American Judaism from Its Beginnings to the End of the Nineteenth Century"), 286–318, and chapter 15 ("Jewish Life and Religious Thought in America in the Twentieth Century"), 394–436; Arthur Hertzberg, *Being Jewish in America: The Modern Experience* (New York, 1979); Gilbert S. Rosenthal, *Contemporary Judaism: Patterns of Survival*, 2d ed. (New York, 1986); Gershon Cohen, "Conservative Judaism," 91–99, Em-manuel Rackman, "Orthodox Judaism," 679–84, and Michael Meyer, "Reform Judaism," 767–72, all in *Contemporary Jewish Religious Thought*, Cohen and Mendes-Flohr, eds.; Jack Wertheimer, *A People Divided: Judaism in Contempo-rary America* (New York, 1993).

For Conservative Judaism start with Pamela S. Nadell, *Conservative Judaism in America: A Biographical Dictionary and Sourcebook* (New York, 1988). It con-tains a fine historical introduction, essays on the Conservative movement's sem-inary, rabbinical association, and national congregational organization, extensive appendixes, an important bibliography, as well as more than 125 biographical es-says. Continue with *Tradition and Change: The Development of Conservative Ju-daism*, Mordecai Waxman, ed. (New York, 1958); Herbert Parzen, *Architects of Conservative Judaism* (New York, 1964); Abraham J. Karp, *History of the United Synagogue of America, 1913–1963* (New York, 1964); Moshe Davis, *The Emer-gence of Conservative Judaism: The Historical School in Nineteenth-Century Ameri-ca* (Philadelphia, 1965); Herman Rosenbaum, *Conservative Judaism: A Contempo-rary History* (New York, 1983); *Tradition Renewed: A History of the Jewish*

Theological Seminary, vol. 1, *The Making of an Institution of Jewish Higher Learning*, Jack Wertheimer, ed. (New York, 1997), vol. 2, *Beyond the Academy*, Jack Wertheimer, ed. (New York, 1997). The best sociological study is Marshall Sklare, *Conservative Judaism: An American Religious Movement* (Glencoe, Ill., 1955; New York, 1972). To follow the Conservative synagogue, see the quarterly *United Synagogue Review*, published by the national organization of Conservative synagogues, the United Synagogue of Conservative Judaism (volume 54 appeared in 2002), and for Conservative rabbinic thought, the quarterly *Conservative Judaism* (volume 53 appeared in 2002) and the annual *Proceedings of the Rabbinical Assembly* (volume 62 appeared in 2000).

For Orthodox Judaism start with *Judaism in America: A Biographical Dictionary and Sourcebook*, Moshe Sherman, ed. (Westport, Conn., 1996). In addition to a historical essay, as well as essays on Orthodox rabbinical organizations and Orthodox periodicals, there are 120 biographical essays on rabbis, educators, and philanthropists who have made contributions to American Orthodoxy, and an extensive bibliography. Continue with the most important collection of essays on the history of American Orthodoxy, *American Jewish Orthodoxy in Historical Perspective*, Jeffrey S. Gurock, ed. (Hoboken, N.J., 1996). An additional collection of valuable essays is in *Ramaz: School, Community, Scholarship, and Orthodoxy*, Jeffrey S. Gurock, ed. (Hoboken, N.J., 1989). An illuminating study of Orthodox rabbis, synagogues, women, and education in America of the 1920s and 1930s is Jenna Weissman Joselit, *New York's Jewish Jews: The Orthodox Community in the Interwar Years* (Bloomington, 1990). On the major Orthodox seminary, see Aaron Rakeffet-Rothkoff, *Bernard Revel: Builder of American Jewish Orthodoxy* (Philadelphia, 1972) and Jeffrey S. Gurock, *The Men and Women of Yeshiva: Higher Education, Orthodoxy, and American Judaism* (New York, 1988). On the national umbrella organization of Orthodox synagogues, see Saul Bernstein, *The Orthodox Union Story: A Centenary Portrayal* [1898–1988] (Northvale, N.J., 1997). On Orthodox education, see William B. Helmreich, *The World of the Yeshiva: An Intimate Portrait of Orthodox Jewry* (New York, 1982). On American Orthodoxy in the nineteenth century, see Lance J. Sussman, *Isaac Leeser and the Making of American Judaism* (Detroit, 1995); on the twentieth century see Charles S. Liebman, "Orthodoxy in American Jewish Life," in *Aspects of the Religious Behavior of American Jews* (New York, 1974), 111–88; and on the late twentieth-century revival of Orthodoxy, see Murray Herbert Danziger, *Returning to Tradition: The Contemporary Revival of Orthodox Judaism* (New Haven, 1989); *Cosmopolitans and Parochials: Modern Orthodox Jews in America*, Samuel C. Heilman and Steven M. Cohen, eds. (Chicago, 1989); and Samuel C. Heilman, "Orthodox Jews, the City, and the Suburb," in *Studies in Contemporary Jewry: An Annual* 15 (1999): 19–34. On the Lubavitcher Hasidism, the messianic claim of Rabbi Schneerson, and the relationship of this claim to Orthodox Judaism, see David Berger, *The Rebbe, the Messiah, and the Scandal of Orthodox Indifference* (New York, 2001). On the Orthodox synagogue see Samuel C. Heilman, *Synagogue Life: A Study in Symbolic Interaction* (Chicago, 1973). To follow developments in the Orthodox synagogue, see the quarterly *Jewish Action*, published by the national organization of synagogues, the Union of Orthodox Jewish Congregations in America and Canada (volume 62 appeared in 2002); and for Orthodox rabbinic thought, the quarterly *Tradition: A Journal of Orthodox Jewish Thought* (volume 35 appeared in 2002).

For Reconstructionist Judaism, start with Mordecai M. Kaplan, *Judaism as a Civilization: Towards a Reconstruction of American-Jewish Life* (New York, 1934; Philadelphia, 1994); and the essay by Charles S. Liebman, "Reconstructionism in American Jewish Life," in *Aspects of the Religious Behavior of American Jews*, 189–285. Continue with Ira Eisenstein, *Creative Judaism*, a digest of *Judaism as a Civilization* (New York, 1936); Ira Eisenstein, *Judaism Under Freedom* (New York, 1956); Mordecai M. Kaplan, *Questions Jews Ask: Reconstructionism Answers* (New York, 1966); Rebecca T. Alpert and Jacob J. Staub, *Exploring Judaism: A Reconstructionist Approach* (New York, 1985); *Imagining the Jewish Future: Essays and Responses*, David A. Teutsch, ed. (Albany, 1992); Kaplan's journals, 1913–34, Mordecai M. Kaplan, *Communings of the Spirit*, Mel Scult, ed. (Wyncote, Pa., 2001). For Reconstructionist lay and rabbinic thought, see the *Reconstructionist* (volume 66 appeared in 2002).

For Reform Judaism start with *Reform Judaism in America: A Biographical Dictionary and Sourcebook*, Kerry M. Olitzky, Lance J. Sussman, and Malcolm H. Stern, eds. (Westport, Conn., 1993). It contains a short historical introduction, essays on the Reform movement's national organization, seminary, and rabbinical organization, extensive appendixes, and 170 biographical essays, complete with primary and secondary sources. Continue with the histories by David Philipson, *The Reform Movement in Judaism* (New York, 1931 [1907]); *Hebrew Union College–Jewish Institute of Religion at One Hundred Years*, Samuel B. Karff, ed. (Cincinnati, 1976); Howard M. Greenstein, *Turning Point: Zionism and Reform Judaism* (Chico, 1981); Arnold M. Eisen, *The Chosen People in America: A Study in Jewish Religious Ideology* (Bloomington, 1983), especially chapter 3 ("Reform Judaism and the 'Mission unto the Nations,' "), 53–72; Michael A. Meyer, *Response to Modernity: A History of the Reform Movement in Judaism* (New York, 1988), especially chapter 6 ("America: The Reform Movement's Land of Promise"), 225–63, chapter 7 ("'Classical' Reform Judaism"), 264–95, chapter 8 ("Reorientation"), 296–334, and chapter 10 ("The New American Reform Judaism"), 353–84; Alan Silverstein, *Alternative to Assmiliation: The Response of Reform Judaism to American Culture, 1840–1930* (Hanover, N.H., 1994).

On Reform Jewish thought, see *Contemporary Reform Jewish Thought*, Bernard Martin, ed. (Chicago, 1968); Eugene B. Borowitz, *A New Jewish Theology in the Making* (Philadelphia, 1968); *American Reform Responsa: Collected Responsa of the Central Conference of American Rabbis, 1889–1993*, Walter Jacob, ed. (New York, 1983); Eugene B. Borowitz, *Liberal Judaism* (New York, 1984); *The Changing World of Reform Judaism: The Pittsburgh Platform in Retrospect*, Walter Jacob, ed. (Pittsburgh, 1985) and its companion volume, *Contemporary American Reform Responsa*, Walter Jacob, ed. (New York, 1987); Eugene B. Borowitz, *Judaism After Modernity: Papers from a Decade of Fruition* (Lanham, Md., 1999). On the Reform rabbinic organization, see *Tana Rabbanan: Our Rabbis Taught: Essays on the Occasion of the Centennial of the Central Conference of American Rabbis*, Joseph B. Glaser, ed. (New York, 1990) and the *Yearbook* of the same organization (volume 110 appeared in 2000). For two important collections of primary sources, see *The Growth of Reform Judaism: American and European Sources until 1948*, W. Gunther Plaut, ed. (New York, 1965) and *The Reform Judaism Reader: North American Documents*, Michael A. Meyer and W. Gunther Plaut, eds. (New York, 2000). The best anthropological study is Freida Furman, *Beyond Yiddishkeit: The Struggle for Jewish Identity in a Reform Synagogue* (Albany, 1987). To follow developments in the Reform synagogue, see the quarterly *Reform Judaism* (volume 30 appeared in 2002), published by the national Reform synagogue organization, the Union of American Hebrew Congregations, and for Reform rabbinic thought see the quarterly *Central Conference of American Rabbis Journal: A Reform Jewish Quarterly* (volume 49 appeared in 2002), published by the national rabbinic organization cited above.

Rabbis

On rabbis, the starting place is the collection of essays on the history of the Conservative, Orthodox, and Reform rabbinate in *The American Rabbinate: A Century of Continuity and Change, 1883–1993*, Jacob Rader Marcus and Abraham J. Peck, eds. (Hoboken, N.J., 1985). Supplement this with *The American Rabbi*, Gilbert S. Rosenthal, ed. (New York, 1977); *The Rabbinate in America: Reshaping an Ancient Calling* (New York, 1993); Pamela S. Nadell, *Women Who Would Be Rabbis: A History of Women's Ordination, 1889–1985* (Boston, 1998).

Scholarly biographies of rabbis include *The Life of Gustave Gottheil: Memoir of a Priest in Israel*, Richard J. H. Gottheil, ed. (Williamsport, Pa., 1936); Abraham J. Karp, "New York Chooses a Chief Rabbi," in *Publications of the American Jewish Historical Society* 44:3 (March, 1955): 129–98; Arthur A. Cohen's "Introduction" to Milton Steinberg, *Anatomy of Faith* (New York, 1960), 11–60; James G. Heller, *Isaac M. Wise: His Life, Work, and Thought* (New York, 1965);

Jacob J. Weinstein, *Solomon Goldman: A Rabbi's Rabbi* (New York, 1973); William W. Blood, *Apostle of Reason: A Biography of Joseph Krauskopf* (Philadelphia, 1973); *Exploring the Thought of Rabbi Joseph B. Soloveitchik*, Marc D. Angel, ed. (Hoboken, N.J., 1976, 1997); Simon Noveck, *Milton Steinberg: Portrait of a Rabbi* (New York, 1978); Fred Rosenbaum, *Architects of Reform: Congregational and Community Leadership—Emanuel-El of San Francisco, 1849–1980* (Berkeley, 1980); *Rabbi Jacob J. Weinstein: Advocate of the People*, Janice J. Feldstein, ed. (New York, 1980); Aaron Rakeffet-Rothkoff, *The Silver Era in American Jewish Orthodoxy: Rabbi Eliezer Silver and His Generation* (Jerusalem and New York, 1981); Melvin I. Urofsky, *A Voice that Spoke for Justice: The Life and Times of Stephen S. Wise* (Albany, 1982); Richard Libowitz, *Mordecai M. Kaplan and the Development of Reconstuctionism* (New York, 1983); Robert D. Shapiro, *A Reform Rabbi in the Progressive Era: The Early Career of Stephen S. Wise* (New York, 1988); I. Harold Sharfman, *The First Rabbi* [Abraham J. Rice]: *Origins of Conflict Between Orthodoxy and Reform: Jewish Polemic Warfare in pre–Civil War America: A Biographical History* (n.p., 1988); Marc Lee Raphael, *Abba Hillel Silver: A Profile in American Judaism* (New York, 1989); Marc Lee Raphael, "Rabbi Leo Jung and the Americanization of Orthodox Judaism: A Biographical Essay," in *Reverence, Righteousness, and Rahamanut: Essays in Memory of Rabbi Dr. Leo Jung*, Jacob J. Schacter, ed. (Northvale, N.J., 1992); Avi M. Schulman, *Like a Raging Fire: A Biography of Maurice N. Eisendrath* (New York, 1993); Mel Scult, *Judaism Faces the Twentieth Century: A Biography of Mordecai M. Kaplan* (Detroit, 1993); Paul Wilkes, *And They Shall Be My People: An American Rabbi and His Congregation* [Worcester, Mass.] (New York, 1994); Shaul Simon Deutsch, *Larger Than Life: The Life and Times of the Lubavitcher Rebbe Menachem Mendel Schneerson*, vol. 1 (New York, 1995); Bobbie Malone, *Rabbi Max Heller: Reformer, Zionist, Southerner, 1860–1929* (Tuscaloosa, Ala., 1997); Jeffrey S. Gurock and Jacob J. Schacter, *A Modern Heretic and a Traditional Community: Mordecai M. Kaplan, Orthodoxy, and American Judaism* (New York, 1997); Sefton D. Temkin, *Creating American Judaism: The Life and Times of Isaac Mayer Wise* (Portland, 1998); Hollace Ava Weiner, *Jewish Stars in Texas: Rabbis and Their Work* (College Station, Tex., 1999); Aaron Rakeffet-Rothkoff, *The Rav: The World of Rabbi Joseph B. Soloveitchik*, 2 vols. (Hoboken, N.J., 1999).

The most useful rabbinic autobiographies include Isaac Mayer Wise, *Reminiscences* (Cincinnati, 1901; 2d ed., New York, 1945); David Philipson, *My Life as an American Jew: An Autobiography* (Cincinnati, 1941); Bernard Drachman, *The Unfailing Light: Memoirs of an American Rabbi* (New York, 1948); Stephen

Wise, *Challenging Years: The Autobiography of Stephen Wise* (New York, 1949); Abraham L. Feinberg, *Storm the Gates of Jericho* (New York, 1964); *Amen: The Diary of Rabbi Martin Siegel*, Mel Ziegler, ed. (New York, 1970); Stanley R. Brav, *Dawn of Reckoning: Self-Portrait of a Liberal Rabbi* (Cincinnati, 1971); Morris Samuel Lazaron, *As I See Him* (Gerards Cross, UK, 1978); *The Path of a Pioneer: The Autobiography of Leo Jung* (London and New York, 1980); W. Gunther Plaut, *Unfinished Business* (n.p., 1981); Israel Goldstein, *My World as a Jew: The Memoirs of Israel Goldstein* (New York, 1984); Stuart E. Rosenberg, *The Real Jewish World: A Rabbi's Second Thoughts* (New York, 1984); Janice Rothschild Blumberg, *One Voice: Rabbi Jacob M. Rothschild and the Troubled South* ([Mercer, Ga.], 1985); Ira Eisenstein, *Reconstructing Judaism: An Autobiography* (New York, 1986); Roland B. Gittelsohn, *Here Am I: Harnessed to Hope* (New York, 1988); Ben Kamin, *Stones in the Soul: One Day in the Life of an American Rabbi* (New York, 1990); Tirzah Firestone, *With Roots in Heaven: One Woman's Passionate Journey into the Heart of Her Faith* (New York, 1998); Richard G. Hirsch, *From the Hill to the Mount* (Jerusalem and New York, 2000).

Scores of rabbis have published collections of essays and sermons on Judaism and Judaic thought. Among the most useful are Abraham J. Feldman, *Lights and Shadows: Eight Addresses* (Hartford, Conn., 1928); Israel Herbert Levinthal, *A New World is Born: Sermons and Addresses* (New York, 1943); *From the Sermons of Rabbi Milton Steinberg: High Holydays and Major Festivals*, Bernard Mandelbaum, ed. (New York, 1954); David Polish, *Eternal Dissent: A Search for Meaning in Jewish History* (New York, 1960); Abraham E. Halpern, *A Son of Faith: From the Sermons of Abraham E. Halpern, 1891–1962* (New York, 1962); Leon A. Jick, *In Search of a Way* (Mt.Vernon, N.Y., 1966); *Therefore Choose Life: Selected Sermons, Discourses, and Writings of Abba Hillel Silver*, Herbert Weiner, ed. (Cleveland, 1967); Joseph H. Lookstein, *Faith and Destiny of Man: Traditional Judaism in a New Light* (New York, 1967); Simon Greenberg, *Foundations of a Faith* (New York, 1967); Samuel Chiel, *Spectators or Participants* (New York, 1969); Saul I. Teplitz, *Life Is for Living: Sermons and Reflections* (New York, 1969); Sidney Greenberg, *Hidden Hungers: High Holiday Sermons on the Art of Living* (Bridgeport, Conn., 1972); Israel H. Levinthal, *The Message of Israel: Sermons, Addresses, Memoirs* (New York, 1973); Dov Peretz Elkins, *A Tradition Reborn: Sermons and Essays on Liberal Judaism* (South Brunswick, N.J., 1973); Max J. Routtenberg, *Decades of Decision* (New York, 1973); Solomon B. Freehof, *Preaching the Bible: Sermons for Sabbaths and High Holy Days* (New York, 1974); Joseph H. Lookstein, *Yesterday's Faith for Tomorrow* (New York,

1979); Israel Goldstein, *Jewish Perspectives: Selected Addresses, Sermons, Broadcasts, and Articles* (Jerusalem, 1985); David Polish, *Abraham's Gamble: Selected Sermons For Our Times* ([Evanston, Ill.], 1988); *Max Nussbaum: From Berlin to Hollywood—A Mid-Century Vision of Jewish Life*, Lewis M. Barth and Ruth Nussbaum, eds. (Malibu, 1994); "Engendering Change: Past, Present, and Future" [Women Rabbis], in *CCAR Journal: A Reform Jewish Quarterly* (Summer 1997): 1–83; *Unfinished Rabbi: Selected Writings of Arnold Jacob Wolf*, Jonathan S. Wolf, ed. (Chicago, 1998); Aryeh Solomon, *The Educational Teachings of Rabbi Menachem Mendel Schneeerson* (Northvale, N.J., 2000).

The Synagogue

On the synagogue the starting place is *The American Synagogue: A Historical Dictionary and Sourcebook*, Kerry A. Olitzky, ed. (Westport, Conn., 1996). It contains an extensive history (and bibliography) of this institution as well as histories of more than 250 Conservative, Orthodox, Reconstructionist, and Reform congregations. The best historical study is Leon Jick, *The Americanization of the Synagogue, 1820–1870* (Hanover, N.H., 1976), and the March 2002 issue of *American Jewish History* devoted to discussing the importance of Jick's study. Hundreds of synagogue histories exist; a good starting place for tracking them down is Alexandra S. Korros and Jonathan D. Sarna, *American Synagogue History: A Bibliography and State-of-the-Field Survey* (New York, 1988). The best collection of essays on the synagogue is *The American Synagogue: A Sanctuary Transformed*, Jack Wertheimer, ed. (Cambridge and New York, 1987). Among the best studies of Orthodox synagogues is Samuel Heilman, *Synagogue Life: A Study in Symbolic Interaction* (Chicago, 1976; New Brunswick, N.J., 1998). On the Conservative synagogue see *Jews in the Center: Conservative Congregations and Their Members*, Jack Wertheimer, ed. (New Brunswick, 2000). On homosexual synagogues see Moshe Shokeid, *A Gay Synagogue in New York* (New York, 1995). Additional studies of distinction include Riv-Ellen Prell, *Prayer and Community: The Havurah in American Judaism* (Detroit, 1989); *The Changing Face of Jewish and Christian Worship in North America*, vol. 2, Paul F. Bradshaw and Lawrence A. Hoffman, eds. (Notre Dame, 1992); Oscar Israelowitz, *Synagogues of the United States: A Photographic and Architectural Survey* (Brooklyn, 1992); David Kaufman, *Shul With a Pool: The "Synagogue-Center" in American Jewish History* (Hanover, N.H., 1998).

On Jewish education, see (Conservative) Michael Rosenak, *Commandments and Concerns: Jewish Religious Education in Secular Society* (Philadelphia, 1987),

Courtyard: A Journal of Research and Thought in Jewish Education (volume 1 appeared in 1999/2000), Carol Ingall, *Transmission and Transformation: A Jewish Perspective on Moral Education* (New York, 1999); (Reconstructionist) Michael Alper, *Reconstructionist Jewish Education* (New York, 1957), *Creative Jewish Education: A Reconstructionist Perspective*, Jeffrey L. Schein and Jacob J. Staub, eds. (Chappaqua, N.Y., 1985), *Windows on the Jewish Soul: Resources for Teaching the Values of Spiritual Peoplehood*, Jeffrey L. Schein and Joseph M. Blair, eds. (Wyncote, Pa., 1994), Joseph Reiner, *Succeeding at Jewish Education: How One Synagogue Made It Work* (Philadelphia, 1997); (Reform) "A CCAR and NATE Symposium: Cutting-Edge Issues in Reform Jewish Education" (six essays), in *CCAR Journal: A Reform Jewish Quarterly* (Winter 1998): 36–116. For a useful survey of the quarter-century or so after World War II, see Walter I. Ackerman, "Jewish Education," in *Movements and Issues in American Judaism: An Analysis and Sourcebook of Developments Since 1945*, Bernard Martin, ed. (Westport, Conn., 1978), 184–205.

On spirituality begin with an overlooked classic, David R. Blumenthal, *God at the Center: Meditations on Jewish Spirituality* (San Francisco, 1988); and the penetrating book by Neil Gillman, *Sacred Fragments: Recovering Theology for the Modern Jew* (Philadelphia, 1990). Continue with Joshua Loth Liebman, *Peace of Mind* (New York, 1946); Anson Laytner, *Arguing with God: A Jewish Tradition* (Northvale, N.J., 1990); *Moments of Transcendence: Inspirational Readings for Rosh Hashanah*, Dov Peretz Elkins, ed. (Northvale, N.J., 1992); *Moments of Transcendence: Inspirational Readings for Yom Kippur*, Dov Peretz Elkins, ed. (Northvale, N.J., 1992); Harold Kushner, *To Life!: A Celebration of Jewish Being and Thinking* (Boston, 1993); David R. Blumenthal, *Facing the Abusing God: A Theology of Protest* (Louisville, 1993); Lawrence Kushner, *Eyes Remade for Wonder: A Lawrence Kushner Reader* (Woodstock, Vt., 1998); *A Shabbat Reader: Universe of Cosmic Joy*, Dov Peretz Elkins, ed. (New York, 1998); *Day by Day: Reflections on the Themes of the Torah from Literature, Philosophy, and Religious Thought*, Chaim Stern, ed. (Boston, 1998); Marcia Falk, *The Book of Blessings: New Jewish Prayers for Daily Life, the Sabbath, and the New Moon Festival* (Boston, 1999); Sidney Schwartz, *Finding a Spiritual Home: How a New Generation of Jews Can Transform the American Synagogue* (San Francisco, 2000); Rifat Soncino, *Six Jewish Spiritual Paths: A Rationalist Looks at Spirituality* (Woodstock, Vt., 2000).

ELECTRONIC RESOURCES

All these sites have links to programs, philosophy, and affiliated organizations.

American Conference of Cantors (Reform)
   www.rj.org/acc
Cantors Assembly (Conservative)
   www.cantors.org
Central Conference of American Rabbis (Reform)
   www.ccarnet.org
Hebrew Union College–Jewish Institute of Religion (Reform)
   www.huc.edu
Jewish Educators Assembly (Conservative)
   www.usa.org/jea
Jewish Reconstructionist Federation
   www.jrf.org
Jewish Theological Seminary (Conservative)
   www.jtsa.org
National Association of Temple Administrators (Reform)
   www.rj.org/nata
National Association of Temple Educators (Reform)
   www.rj.org/nate
North American Association of Synagogue Executives (Conservative)
   www.naase.org
Rabbi Isaac Elhanan Theological Seminary (Orthodox)
   www.riets.org

Rabbinical Assembly (Conservative)
    www.rabasembly.org
Reconstructionist Rabbinical Association
    www.rra.org
Reconstructionist Rabbinical College
    www.rrc.org
Union of American Hebrew Congegations (Reform)
    www.uahc.org
Union of Orthodox Jewish Congregations of America
    www.ou.org
United Synagogue of Conservative Judaism
    www.uscj.org

INDEX